Legally Married

Legally Married

Love and Law in the UK and the US

Scot Peterson and Iain McLean

EDINBURGH
University Press

Edinburgh University Press Ltd
22 George Square, Edinburgh EH8 9LF
www.euppublishing.com

Typeset in 11.5/13.5 Minion Pro by
Servis Filmsetting Ltd, Stockport, Cheshire
and printed and bound in Great Britain by
CPI Group (UK) Ltd, Croydon CR0 4YY

A CIP record for this book is available from the British Library

ISBN 978 0 7486 8377 2 (hardback)
ISBN 978 0 7486 83789 (paperback)
ISBN 978 0 7486 83796 (webready PDF)
ISBN 978 0 7486 83819 (epub)

Contents

Preface		ix
Introduction: Changing Attitudes		1
1	Different Theories of Marriage	12
2	Marriage from the Reformation to the Rules of the Fleet	48
3	From Lord Hardwicke's Act to Civil Marriage and Divorce	79
4	Marriage across the Seas: Ireland, South Africa, Canada and the United States	116
5	Current Policy Questions: Fighting Fair about Same-sex Marriage	152
6	Legislatures Argue and the Supreme Court Decides	187
Bibliography		221
Index		234

To our spouses, Richard and Jo

At the [. . .] meeting there were present not only people of various [Islamic] sects but also unbelievers, Magians, materialists, atheists, Jews and Christians, in short unbelievers of all kinds. Each group had its own leader, whose task it was to defend its views [. . .] One of the unbelievers rose and said to the assembly: we are meeting here for a debate; its conditions are known to all. You, Muslims, are not allowed to argue from your books and prophetic traditions since we deny both. Everybody, therefore, has to limit himself to rational arguments [*hujaj al-'aql*]. The whole assembly applauded these words.

al-Humaydi (d. 1095)

Source: Ibrāhīm al-Ibyārī (ed.), *Jadhwat al-muqtabis fī tārīkh 'ulamā' al-Andalus* (Beirut: Dār al-Kitāb al-Lubnānī, 1983), vol. 1, pp. 175–6, translated by Carlos Fraenkel and originally quoted in Carlos Fraenkel, 'In Praise of the Clash of Cultures', *New York Times*, 2 September 2012, available online at http://opinionator.blogs.nytimes.com/2012/09/02/in-praise-of-the-clash-of-cultures/ (last accessed 6 May 2013). We are grateful to Professor Fraenkel for the original citation.

Preface

THIS BOOK IS addressed to voters, policymakers and those who would like to influence policymakers. We explain how and why states have defined and redefined marriage over the centuries. Despite claims by religious leaders to the contrary, since the Protestant Reformation of the sixteenth century the state has always led and the churches have followed in this area. The church has been the agent of the state and not vice versa (as might have been the case in Roman Catholic countries). We show how institutions have changed, and in the later chapters of the book we discuss the options available to non-absolutist policymakers. We reject absolutism – both the view that nobody may be allowed to conduct same-sex marriage, and the view that every celebrant must be forced to. If policymakers do likewise, as we hope they will, then they must continue to deal with the problems of recognition and of conscience that have existed for centuries. Those only interested in policy should skip straight to Chapter 5, but we hope that most readers won't. We think the history is fascinating, and we are certain that it is relevant to current policy options and dilemmas.

In the Introduction we examine the rapid pace at which marriage has become a relevant issue for policymakers. Although it seemed to be losing relevance during much of the twentieth century, it returned to the political agenda as legislators and judges considered whether to offer it to same-sex couples. Divisions have emerged along lines of age, religion and even geography, when some countries or devolved governments have begun to offer same-sex marriage but others have not.

We open Chapter 1 with a description of a recent same-sex wedding reported by the *New York Times*. We think that this shows that some age-old issues of marriage across different communities (in this case a Mennonite and a Jew) and all the other joys and anxieties of a wedding are no different for opposite-sex and same-sex couples. We then take a tour of the different philosophical and religious views of marriage that have circulated from the time of the Hebrew scriptures and the Athenian philosophers to the present day. As well as Roman Catholic and varieties of Protestant Christianity, we attempt to summarise Jewish, Muslim and Hindu approaches to marriage. Finally we comment on secularist approaches, including those which reject the concept of marriage altogether. In a multi-faith society such as all of those we discuss in later chapters, any legally persuasive argument must be couched in terms of what John Rawls called 'public reason'. That is, as the epigraph to this book suggests, such an argument cannot appeal to the revelations or divine commands of any particular religion as a grounding for public policy, although those commands and revelations must be sovereign in each religion's internal decision-making – into which the state intrudes at its peril.

Chapter 2 drills down in more detail to the marriage law of England and Scotland before 1753. Starting at the top, the marriages of both Henry VIII and Mary, Queen of Scots reveal policymakers grappling unsuccessfully with church and customary rules – with momentous consequences for both monarchies. In both countries the law of marriage was shaped by the Protestant Reformation. However, as Scots know but English readers may not, the Reformation took very different courses in the two countries, and although it went through a violent phase in the seventeenth century in both, the violence did not have the same effect. In the eighteenth century, regulating marriage was seen by politicians as being primarily about property and succession: not about religion, and not about the poor, who had no property and therefore needed no rules to say who got the property when its owner died.

By the mid-eighteenth century, when Chapter 3 opens, politicians and lawyers were very agitated by the problem of clandestine marriages, in which, typically, a social climber would secretly marry an heiress for her money. The result was the first general regulatory act, the Clandestine Marriage Act (Lord Hardwicke's Act) of 1753. We show that this was the first statute to require most weddings in England and Wales to be conducted in the established church. But there were three crucial loopholes. The first two excluded Quakers and Jews from the regulations. Both communities married only members of the same community. Both had rejected earlier attempts to force them to marry in the established church. Hardwicke and Parliament decided that including them in regulation was more trouble than it was worth. The third exclusion was Scotland. Hardwicke had a bill for Scotland drafted but failed to get it enacted. He was very well aware that the Gretna loophole existed, but failed to find a way to close it.

Lord Hardwicke's Act is of much more than antiquarian interest. First, it has shaped every subsequent regulatory statute up to the Marriage Act 1949 and the Marriage (Same Sex Couples) Bill 2012. The exemptions of Jews and Quakers from regulation persist, so that the current bill provides for Quaker and Jewish same-sex marriages in a different way to any others. Second, it shows that policymakers tried, but failed, to grapple with the question of multiple jurisdictions in one state. Bounders who wished to marry underage heiresses needed only to elope to Gretna Green in Scotland.

Chapter 4 expands the focus to include four more countries: Ireland, Canada, South Africa and the United States. By widening the lens, it becomes apparent that marriage has been driven by social, cultural and religious cleavages. In Ireland, the Roman Catholic– Protestant cleavage is most important, and today it is reflected in the constitutional recognition of the family as 'the natural primary and fundamental unit group of Society'. Canada is one of two federal states included in the study. Its federalism was driven in large part by the division between the largely Francophone, Roman Catholic region, now called Quebec, and the rest of the country, which is predominantly Anglophone and Protestant. It is also one of two countries in this book to have permitted same-sex marriage. We examine how that happened. South Africa divides on racial lines. In South Africa, participation of gay men and lesbians in the fight against apartheid and the recognition of sexual orientation as a protected class in the 1996 constitution underlie the adoption of equal marriage. The United States combines federalism and a racial divide. Marriage there has regularly discriminated against minority groups, including blacks and Chinese, and we also examine the historical case of Utah, where polygamy was practised in the mid-nineteenth century.

Chapter 5 is our policy chapter. There we address what we think are the best, and the worst, arguments about marriage. Arguments we discount include arguments about specific sexual practices of married couples, either inside or outside their own marriages. We believe that judges have other, better things to worry about than the interplay of sex organs belonging to consenting adults. We also discuss the new natural law theory (NNL), which drives much of the debate by opponents of same-sex marriage. Because NNL does not comply with Rawls's conception of public reason, we argue that those arguments are less important than some make them out to be. Finally, we discount the connection between polygamy and same-sex marriage. The fact that it has been practised, in nineteenth-century Utah and more recently in South Africa and elsewhere, means that it cannot be ruled out as a way of structuring marriage. However, we give good reasons why it is not, and should not be, a practical political option.

The two issues that we think are more important, both for voters and for policymakers, are religious freedom and differences in the way that couples are treated when they travel from one legal jurisdiction to another. We offer three possible models for protecting religious freedom, which range from less robust to more robust. We do not claim to provide an answer to which choice should be made, but we think that our approach clarifies the lines along which decisions must be taken. Courts and legislatures will also have to address questions of how to treat couples who might be married in one state but travel to another. This, too, is a question that can be handled in a variety of ways, and it is one that we raise without providing a definitive answer.

Chapter 6 discusses the outcomes of two US Supreme Court cases decided in 2013 and reviews the progress of UK legislation to that date.

This book is not about several things. First, it is not about the actual substance of what we refer to as the *status* of marriage. This changes a great deal over time, and it varies a great deal from one country to another. At oral argument in *U.S.* v. *Windsor*, which we will discuss at length in Chapter 6, the US Supreme Court acknowledged that more than 1,100 federal laws there affect the rights and responsibilities of married couples.[1] These include different tax arrangements for spouses, as well as different kinds of benefits which are oriented towards particular types of families, perhaps unfairly.[2] In the UK the recent Labour government began to phase out the married couple's allowance, so that it applies only to couples at least one of whom was born before 6 April 1935.[3] These benefits are important to the status of marriage, but because they differ so much across different cases in this study, we simply assume that they exist without examining their details in any one national marriage regime.

A second and related topic, which we do not examine here, is gender roles in marriage. When he was writing in 1765, William Blackstone used current terminology and referred to women and men as *feme-covert* and *covert-baron*, to signify that they were one person in law: women could not contract, and their property was held in common and controlled by their husband.[4] During the 1800s this attribute of marriage, coverture, slowly eroded and was abandoned, and eventually women were treated as legally independent persons even after they married. As with the attributes of marriage that the government grants through transfer payments and the like, these changes to women's roles relate to the *status* of marriage. They are independent of the choices that people can make about *whom* they marry, which relate more closely to the aspect of marriage as *contract*, which is Blackstone's focus in the epigraph to the Introduction which follows, and is our main focus in this book.

Finally, another important set of questions, which we do not discuss in detail, is the variability of gender, including transgender people. In 2009 the Texas Court of Appeals considered the case of Andrew Mireles and Jennifer Jack.[5] Following their divorce, Jack attacked the divorce decree, arguing that there had never been a marriage at all, because Mireles had been assigned female gender at birth. Both the trial court and the Court of Appeals agreed with Jack, declared the marriage void and set aside the decree. The fact that Jack attacked the decree and informed the court that Mireles was transgender strongly implies that she was unhappy with the judge's decision in the divorce, otherwise she would not have brought it up. And one may question, as we will in the following chapters, whether it should be possible to manipulate the law in the way that may have been done here. In Chapter 4 we will also see that trying to draw lines based on race becomes difficult: how near must an ancestor be before her descendant is of the same race? The same kind of problem is present when we try to draw lines based on gender. No one has ever claimed that people should be barred from marriage based upon their failure to meet stereotypical gender roles. The point here is that gender is not a clear-cut matter, and we acknowledge that fact and its importance to many people. Nevertheless, when we talk about same-sex couples we mean primarily those who are cisgender (that is, those whose perceived gender matches the gender they were assigned at birth). Our arguments apply *a fortiori* to transgender people when we refer to same-sex marriage. The question we are concerned with is about choosing whom to marry and whether the law recognises that choice. And that applies to all people.

About the authors

We are both expats: a Scot and an American brought together by a common fascination with issues of church and state and both working in England. Iain was trained as a historian and has always worked as a political scientist, while Scot was trained as a lawyer. We are both fascinated by political history.

We share an exasperation with English imperialism – intellectual imperialism in this case. Those who write about the constitution of the UK usually mean the constitution of England. Those who write about the origins of the US constitution of 1787 often locate them in English common law and politics, and rarely notice the Scottish influence on it.

Nowhere does the importance of understanding that Scotland is different matter more than in matters of church and state, therefore including matters of marriage. The preservation of the Presbyterian establishment was a precondition for the union of 1707: without it the union would not have been ratified by the Scottish Parliament. That is a sufficient reason to explain why Scottish marriage law, already different from that in England in 1707, has remained different. We have worked extensively on these matters, which inform our approach in this book.

We would like this book to act as a neutral explainer of the current issues in law, religion and marriage in the jurisdictions we discuss, but it is proper to declare where we stand (which readers can easily find out anyhow). Iain is a Quaker and has advised the central bodies of British Quakerism on the implementation of their 2009 decision to recognise same-sex marriage in Quaker meetings and to seek an appropriate change in the law. Scot is a member of the Church of England who, when in the United States, has advised Episcopalians about internal and external church matters and has represented groups as diverse as Orthodox Jews and Vietnamese Buddhists. He was also involved in drafting legislation in the City and County of Denver that began the process toward recognition of same-sex relationships there.

Acknowledgements

We have had a great deal of assistance from a number of people in the process of writing this book. Informal discussions which have influenced our thinking have taken place with Leslie Green, Diarmaid MacCulloch, Judith Maltby and Simon Sarmiento.

We received suggestions on specific topics from John Filling, Chris Brooke, Richard Finn OP, Sam Weinberg and Lyman Gamberton. Early versions of chapters were presented at the Seventeenth Law and Religion Symposium, Brigham Young University (2010), with particular thanks due to Cole Durham and Brett Scharffs, the New Forms of Public Religion Conference, St John's College, University of Cambridge (2012) and the University of Oxford Department of Politics Government Colloquium (2013). Useful insights came from a group from Balliol College during a reading week in Kintail, Scotland, particularly Will Jones, Mark Thakkar, Alex Teytelboym and Max Goplerud. Essential assistance with the manuscript and copy-editing was provided by Christie Slawson, Johanna Stephenson and our copy-editor for Edinburgh University Press, Jonathan Wadman.

Scot extends sincere thanks to Balliol College and the Oxford University Department of Politics and International Relations for funding the Bingham Research Fellowship in Constitutional Studies, which began during the final phases of this project.

Internet resources were essential for keeping up with rapid developments in this area. Aggregator services include the mailing list provided by the International Center for Law and Religion Studies, Brigham Young University (info@iclrs.org) and Howard Friedman's Religion Clause Blog (religionclause.blogspot.com). Substantive forums and mailing lists include SCOTUSblog (scotusblog.com), Law

& Religion UK (lawandreligionuk.com), Thinking Anglicans (thinkinganglicans.org.uk), the joint Oxford and Cambridge University blog Politics in Spires (politicsinspires.org), and Eugene Volokh's religion and law mailing list (religionlaw@lists.ucla.edu). We also received helpful suggestions from two anonymous reviewers for Edinburgh University Press. All errors and omissions are, of course, our own.

Notes

1. *U.S.* v. *Windsor* (US) Case No. 12-307, Transcript of Argument, pp. 59–60, available online at http://www.supremecourt.gov/oral_arguments/argu ment_transcripts/12-307.pdf (last accessed 6 May 2013).
2. Linda McClain, *The Place of Families: Fostering Capacity, Equality, and Responsibility* (Cambridge, MA: Harvard University Press, 2006), ch. 3.
3. 'Married Couple's Allowance', HM Revenue and Customs website, http://www.hmrc.gov.uk/incometax/married-allow.htm (last accessed 6 May 2013).
4. William Blackstone, *Commentaries on the Laws of England* (Chicago: University of Chicago Press, [1765] 1979), vol. 1, p. 430.
5. *Mireles* v. *Mireles* (TX App. 1st Dist. 2009), Memorandum Opinion, Case No. 01-08-00499-CV, 2009 WL 884815.

Introduction
Changing Attitudes

> Our law considers marriage in no other light than as a civil con-
> tract [. . .] And, taking it in this civil light, the law treats it as it does
> all other contracts; allowing it to be good and valid in all cases,
> where the parties at the time of making it were, in the first place
> willing to contract; secondly, able to contract; and lastly, actually
> did contract, in the proper forms and solemnities required by law.[1]
>
> William Blackstone, 1765

For much of the twentieth century marriage was in decline.
Across many countries, fewer people were getting married, more
people were getting divorced, the age at which people got married
for the first time was steadily rising. Many people, especially religious
people, found these trends upsetting. Many, whether religious or not,
lament the decline in stable two-parent families because they are generally regarded as the best environment in which to raise children.
But on this, as on many other aspects of marriage, data beyond the
headline statistics are hard to get. In general, sociologists seemed to
have lost interest in studying marriage and its effects.

Some basic statistics for Great Britain are given in Table I.1. It
shows, for instance, that while marriage is by far the most common
status, only half the adult British population are married. Cohabiting
is the next most common status (more detailed analysis published
by the Office for National Statistics shows that, for instance, more
Britons aged between twenty-five and thirty-four are cohabiting than
are married).

Weddings in England and Wales reached their peak, at about
416,000, in 1970. By 2009, the latest year available from the Office for
National Statistics, this number had almost halved to 232,000. There
has also been a radical change in the places people get married. In

Table I.1 Sex by marital status

All persons aged sixteen and over, Great Britain, 2011		
Marital status	*Men*	*Women*
Married	52%	49%
Civil partnership	1%	0%
Cohabiting	11%	11%
Single	27%	21%
Widowed	3%	9%
Divorced	4%	7%
Separated	2%	2%
Weighted base (000s) = 100%	23,819	24,942
Unweighted sample	7,100	7,800

Source: General Lifestyle Survey, UK Office for National Statistics.

1837, immediately after the introduction of civil marriage in England and Wales (see Chapter 3), only 0.7 per cent of weddings were civil weddings; now the proportion is 67 per cent. Of the remainder, most (24 per cent of all weddings) were conducted by the Church of England, which conducted 97 per cent of all English and Welsh weddings in 1837.[2]

In Scotland, weddings peaked at over 53,000 in 1940 and again had almost halved, to 29,000, by 2011. In 2010, just over half (51 per cent) of weddings in Scotland were civil. Of the rest, about 21 per cent were conducted by the Church of Scotland. The next largest belief category was humanism. Humanist celebrants have been allowed to conduct weddings in Scotland since 2005; in 2010 they conducted about 7 per cent of all Scottish weddings.[3]

As to the USA, the US Bureau of the Census estimates that just under 50 per cent of all adult Americans are married, and about 32 per cent have never been married.[4] Data on what proportion of weddings are religious are not collected by federal authorities, but an impressionistic survey by *USA Today* in 2003 found a civil marriage rate of 40 per cent in the eighteen states that kept state-level data.[5] This number, even if reliable in itself, cannot be reliably extrapolated to the nation.

However, interest in marriage as a policy matter revived rather suddenly at the start of the twenty-first century. This was entirely due

to the efforts of a very small group: same-sex couples who wanted to get married. Although the numbers are small, the issue is important in every jurisdiction, and it is the immediate reason for our decision to write this book. In 2012, the Scottish Government announced that it planned to introduce a law to permit same-sex marriage,[6] closely followed by the UK government, which is responsible for marriage law in England and Wales. The Northern Ireland government has no plans to introduce it there.

In the rest of the Anglophone world, Canada introduced same-sex marriage nationwide after a Supreme Court decision in 2004 and federal legislation in 2005. The same sequence occurred in South Africa: a Constitutional Court decision in 2005, followed by legislation in 2006. In New Zealand, a bill to permit it received a comfortable majority in principle early in 2013 and was approved by the parliament on 17 April 2013. In the USA, where marriage is con-stitutionally reserved to the states, there is a wide range of rules. As at July 2013, thirteen states and the District of Columbia permit same-sex marriage.[7] A further four permit same-sex unions that grant the same legal rights as marriage but withhold the title.[8] A few states have statutory bans on same-sex marriage, and currently twenty-nine have bans written into their state constitutions. Plans to introduce same-sex marriage are currently before the legislature of Illinois. California briefly introduced same-sex marriage by court order in 2008. This was overturned by a popular initiative, 'Proposition 8', in November 2008. Both Proposition 8 and a crucial section of the federal Defense of Marriage Act 1996 have been held to be unconstitutional in federal district and appeal courts. The US Supreme Court held hearings on their constitutionality in March 2013. At the time of writing this Introduction the result is unknown; Chapter 6 of this book explains what happens next.

The Republic of Ireland, the only majority-Catholic country that we consider in this book, legalised civil partnerships in 2010. To legalise same-sex marriage would probably require a constitutional amendment. A constitutional convention which is sitting in 2013 has invited responses on the issue.[9] There are no current bills to legalise same-sex marriage in India, Australia, Pakistan, or Bangladesh.

Outside the English-speaking world, there is a pending bill in Colombia, following a decision by the Constitutional Court there.

Elsewhere in Latin America, Uruguay and Argentina have both legalised same-sex marriage, while Mexico and Brazil allow local options and some jurisdictions have approved it. In Europe (as of May 2013) same-sex marriage has been introduced in Belgium, Denmark, France, Iceland, the Netherlands, Norway, Portugal, Spain and Sweden.

This all represents one of the most rapid changes in both legal and social attitudes in recorded history. As recently as 1972, the US Supreme Court summarily dismissed 'for want of a substantial federal question' an appeal by a same-sex couple against the refusal of Minnesota to grant them a wedding licence.[10] The first state supreme court to contemplate requiring same-sex marriage was that of Hawaii, in 1993. This resulted in the federal Defense of Marriage Act 1996 and a state constitutional amendment in 1998, both restricting marriage to opposite-sex couples. The first US jurisdiction to introduce same-sex civil unions was Vermont, in 2000; the first state supreme court to mandate same-sex marriage under a state constitution was that of Massachusetts, in 2003.[11]

In the UK, a same-sex couple married in Canada went to the English and Welsh family courts in 2006 requesting to have their marriage recognised in England and Wales. Their request was dismissed.[12] Both they and subsequent claimants attempted to call in aid the European Convention on Human Rights, which is domesticated in the UK by the Human Rights Act 1998. However, the European Court of Human Rights (ECtHR) has not been willing to accept that there is a right under the convention to same-sex marriage, and prefers to offer its member states a wide 'margin of appreciation' in the jargon which that court uses. The human rights law of the European Union now tracks that of the Council of Europe, whose court is the ECtHR. Currently, nine member states of the Council of Europe recognise same-sex marriage, of which seven are member states of the EU.

Legal change interacts with social change. For the purposes of this book, there is no need to ask which is the chicken and which is the egg. The best time series (that is, a reliable opinion poll asking the same question year after year) for the UK is *British Social Attitudes*, which has been asking the British people about their attitudes to same-sex relationships since 1983. Their question is 'Sexual relations

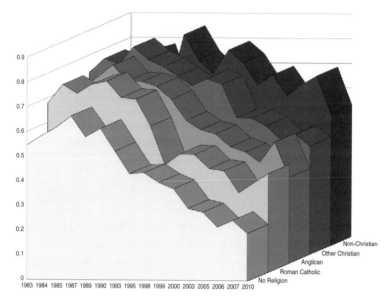

Figure I.1 Proportion agreeing that homosexuality is mostly or always wrong, by religious affiliation

Source: British Social Attitudes; our calculations.

between two adults of the same sex are always wrong/mostly wrong/ sometimes wrong/rarely wrong/not wrong at all'. The proportion of respondents replying 'mostly wrong' or 'always wrong' dropped from 75 per cent in 1987 to 36 per cent in 2007; the proportion saying 'not wrong at all' rose from 11 per cent to 39 per cent in the same period.

We can also break down the responses by the respondent's religion. Figure I.1 shows that the rate of decline in opposition is roughly the same for all religious groups. However, those with no religion are the most liberal and those with a non-Christian religion are the most conservative.

Opinion poll data for the USA show the same pattern. The Pew Research Center is a reputable polling organisation that, like *British Social Attitudes,* has been asking the same questions for a number of years. Figure I.2 shows the rapid change in US public opinion on the acceptability of same-sex marriage. Pew's numbers are replicated by

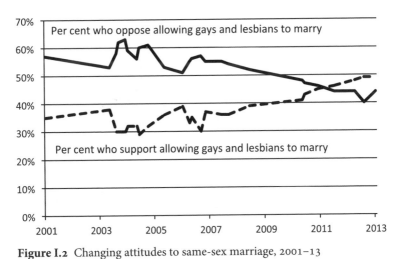

Figure I.2 Changing attitudes to same-sex marriage, 2001–13

Source: Pew Research Center for the People and the Press, 'Growing Support for Gay Marriage: Changing Minds and Changing Demographics (March 2013), http://www.people-press.org/files/legacy-pdf/3-20-13%20 Gay%20Marriage%20Release.pdf (last accessed 1 June 2013).

other polling organisations. The absolute level of reported support for same-sex marriage seems to be very sensitive to the precise question that is asked, but the trend is the same in all polls: from a substantial majority against at the turn of the millennium to equality in 2012.

These rapid changes are driven by two effects. One is generational replacement. Young voters coming of age are overwhelmingly in favour of same-sex marriage, in both the UK and the USA. But, surprisingly for a social issue, there is also a fairly substantial proportion of older voters who have changed their minds in the same direction – 14 per cent of Pew's sample for instance. When probed, respondents give as the commonest reason given for switching the fact that they now have friends or family who are gay.[13]

The statistician Nate Silver, who shot to fame for correctly predicting the result of the 2012 US presidential election, has recently used the wealth of data at state level, plus the knowledge that the change in attitudes to same-sex marriage is driven roughly half by generational replacement and half by people changing their minds, to produce a statistical model of the expected vote in each state of the USA for a

state-wide referendum on whether to permit same-sex marriage (see Table I.2). The model shows that, on Silver's projections, there will be a popular majority in favour of same-sex marriage in forty-four of the fifty states of the USA (as well as the District of Columbia) by 2020.

Social change as rapid as this has taken everybody by surprise, most of all those who hold to traditional religious views of marriage. Although the Jewish, Christian and Muslim sacred books all either describe founding fathers (such as Abraham and Solomon) as having multiple wives, or allow for polygamy (certain passages in the Qur'an), the view that marriage is the union for life of one man and one woman is most firmly held among religious believers. Only a small number of (themselves small) religious denominations had by 2013 announced their support for same-sex marriages according to the rites of the religion. Those denominations include Quakers, Unitarians, Liberal and Reform Judaism, and in the USA the Society of Friends (Quakers), the United Church of Christ, the Metropolitan Community Church and parts of the Episcopal Church. And this creates the central dilemma discussed in this book. How, if at all, can religious freedom and the freedom of lesbians, gay men and bisexuals to marry the partner of their choice be reconciled?

Accordingly, policymakers have to deal with a world where some jurisdictions permit same-sex marriage, others permit same-sex legal partnerships short of marriage, and others again permit neither. This is obviously a problem of international law. But it is also a domestic problem in any country where marriage law is devolved. That description applies at least to the USA, Canada and the UK. In Canada, there are thirteen jurisdictions (provinces and territories), although a uniform rule has been imposed on them by the federal judiciary and parliament. In the USA there are fifty-one (fifty states plus the District of Columbia); in the UK there are three (England & Wales; Scotland; Northern Ireland). In each of these cases, policymakers have had to deal with the fact that marriage law may vary from place to place within a single country. That means, necessarily, that there are some classes of people who are validly married in some parts of the country but not in others, and people married overseas who would not qualify to marry at home. There is nothing new about this situation. It predates the issue of same-sex marriage by centuries. But how states adapt to same-sex marriage must be shaped by

Table I.2 Projected support for same-sex marriage in ballot initiative (%)

State	2008	2012	2016	2020
Rhode Island	56.3	63.1	69.3	75.1
District of Columbia	57.1	63.1	68.7	74.0
Massachusetts	56.4	62.9	69.0	74.5
Hawaii	52.2	58.6	64.6	70.3
Connecticut	52.0	58.2	64.1	69.8
New York	51.9	58.1	64.0	69.7
Vermont	51.6	57.8	63.8	69.4
New Hampshire	50.6	57.1	63.2	69.1
New Jersey	50.6	57.0	63.1	69.0
Delaware	49.2	55.7	62.0	68.0
Washington	49.6	55.7	61.5	67.2
Maryland	48.6	55.0	61.2	67.2
California	48.6	54.6	60.4	66.1
Oregon	48.0	54.0	59.7	65.4
Nevada	46.7	53.0	59.2	65.2
Minnesota	46.3	52.3	58.2	64.0
Illinois	45.8	52.2	58.4	64.6
Pennsylvania	45.8	52.0	58.0	64.0
Colorado	45.8	52.0	58.0	63.8
Wisconsin	45.6	51.8	58.0	64.0
Maine	44.8	51.1	57.2	63.2
New Mexico	43.3	49.6	55.8	61.9
Michigan	42.7	48.9	55.0	61.2
Arizona	42.2	48.4	54.6	60.7
National	**42.2**	**48.3**	**54.4**	**60.5**
Montana	41.9	47.8	53.7	59.6
Alaska	41.5	47.6	53.7	59.9
Virginia	41.1	47.2	53.3	59.5
Florida	40.4	46.6	52.9	59.3
Ohio	40.4	46.6	52.8	59.1
Iowa	40.2	46.5	52.8	59.1
North Dakota	38.5	44.8	51.2	57.7
Nebraska	37.9	44.0	50.2	56.5
Indiana	37.8	43.7	49.8	55.9
Missouri	37.5	43.6	49.7	56.0
West Virginia	37.3	43.5	49.9	56.3
South Dakota	37.1	43.3	49.7	56.1
Kansas	36.8	42.8	48.9	55.1
Idaho	36.4	42.4	48.5	54.8

Table I.2 (*cont.*)

State	2008	2012	2016	2020
Utah	36.3	42.1	48.1	54.2
Kentucky	35.7	41.8	48.0	54.4
Wyoming	34.6	40.6	46.8	53.2
Tennessee	34.5	40.3	46.3	52.6
North Carolina	34.2	40.2	46.3	52.7
Texas	33.4	39.4	45.8	52.4
Oklahoma	32.5	38.4	44.7	51.2
South Carolina	31.6	37.3	43.3	49.7
Arkansas	31.1	36.8	42.8	49.1
Georgia	30.8	36.7	42.9	49.5
Louisiana	29.3	35.1	41.4	48.1
Alabama	24.4	29.9	35.9	42.5
Mississippi	20.9	25.9	31.5	37.8

Source: Nate Silver, 'How opinion on same-sex marriage is changing, and what it means', Five Thirty Eight, *New York Times*, 26 March 2013, http://fivethirtyeight.blogs.nytimes.com/2013/03/26/how-opinion-on-same-sex-marriage-is-changing-and-what-it-means, last accessed 7 May 2013.
© 2013 The New York Times

those centuries of experience. For example, it is well known that a tradition of English couples getting married in Gretna Green arose in the eighteenth century and has recently revived. In both 1999 and 2000, more than 17 per cent of all marriages in Scotland took place in Gretna, the first village in Scotland for people travelling up the West Coast Main Line or the M6/M74.[14] Later we will explain how Gretna marriages came into existence, and how this shaped marriage law in both parts of Great Britain.

There are absolutists on both sides. There are religious people who believe that nobody, whether religious or not, has the right to violate what they see as the sacred law of marriage. And there are secularists who believe that, once same-sex marriage is permitted, all celebrants must be required to officiate at same-sex weddings. Probably, few absolutists on either side have picked up this book. If they have, they are in for a disappointment. We do not believe that there are good arguments for either absolutist position. Both involve substantial violations of rights. But where the exact line is drawn on issues like these depends both on recognition of those rights and on political reality. In what follows, we acknowledge the importance of the first of these and offer information to those involved in, or who wish to influence, the decisions being made by courts and legislatures.

Notes

1. William Blackstone, *Commentaries on the Laws of England* (Chicago: University of Chicago Press, [1765] 1979), vol. 1, p. 421.
2. 'Marriages', Office for National Statistics, http://www.ons.gov.uk/ons/taxonomy/index.html?nscl=Marriages#tab-data-tables (last accessed 6 May 2013).
3. 'Marriages and Civil Partnerships', in *Scotland's Population 2010: The Registrar General's Annual Review of Demographic Trends*, 156th edition, General Register Office for Scotland, http://www.gro-scotland.gov.uk/files2/stats/annual-review-2010/j176746-08.htm; 'Marriages and Civil Partnerships: Background Information', General Register Office for Scotland, http://www.gro-scotland.gov.uk/statistics/theme/vital-events/marriages-and-civil-partnerships/bckgr-info.html (last accessed 6 May 2013).
4. 'Marital Status: 2008–2010 American Community Survey 3-year Estimates', American FactFinder, http://factfinder2.census.gov/faces/tableservices/jsf/pages/productview.xhtml?pid=ACS_10_3YR_S1201&prodType=table (last accessed 6 May 2013).
5. Cathy Lynn Grossman and In-Sung Yoo, 'Civil marriage on rise across USA', *USA Today*, 6 October 2003, http://usatoday30.usatoday.com/news/nation/2003-10-06-civilmarriage-usat_x.htm (last accessed 6 May 2013).
6. Source: 'Same Sex Marriage', news release, Scottish Government, 12 December 2012, http://www.scotland.gov.uk/News/Releases/2012/12/ssm12dec (last accessed 6 May 2013).
7. In addition to the District of Columbia, these are California, Connecticut, Delaware, Iowa, Maine, Maryland, Massachusetts, Minnesota, New Hampshire, New York, Rhode Island, Vermont and Washington.
8. Colorado, Hawaii, Illinois and New Jersey. Two more states come close: Oregon and Nevada.
9. 'Chairman Calls for Submissions on Same-sex Marriage', Convention on the Constitution, 1 March 2013, https://www.constitution.ie/NewsDetails.aspx?nid=4e7cf4a7-9082-e211-a5a0-005056a32ee4 (last accessed 6 May 2013).
10. *Baker* v. *Nelson* (1972) 409 US 810.

11. *Goodridge v. Dept. of Public Health* (MA 2003) 798 NE 2d 941.
12. *Wilkinson v. Kitzinger* [2006] EWHC 2022 (Fam).
13. 'Gay Marriage: Key Data Points from Pew Research', Pew Research Center, 21 March 2013, http://www.people-press.org/2013/03/20/growing-support-for-gay-marriage-changed-minds-and-changing-demographics (last accessed 1 June 2013).
14. G. W. Jackson, *Marriages at Gretna, 1975–2000* (Edinburgh: General Register Office for Scotland, 2001), http://www.gro-scotland.gov.uk/files/op4-gretna.pdf (last accessed 7 May 2013).

1

Different Theories of Marriage

It is revolting to have no better reason for a rule of law than that so it was laid down in the time of Henry IV. It is still more revolting if the grounds upon which it was laid down have vanished long since, and the rule simply persists from blind imitation of the past.

Oliver Wendell Holmes Jr, 1897[1]

This book is about policy, and this quote from Oliver Wendell Holmes Jr, with its emphasis on the 'grounds' for law, points in a direction that we want to go. Many competing conceptions of marriage have existed in history, and a variety of approaches coexist today. Some are religious; some are not. Many are quite inconsistent in what they encourage or allow. Much of what follows is simply a description of these policies, but they should be kept in mind in the chapters that follow. And they should be judged according to a more general theory that we also introduce in this chapter: John Rawls's conception of public reason. But we begin with a short story about a recent wedding that took place in New York.

A wedding in New York City

On 31 March 2012 Mark Kushner married Chris Barley at the Four Seasons restaurant in New York City. The ceremony was led by Rabbi Samuel H. Weintraub. The couple had met in 2007, when Barley, who is four years younger than Kushner, was an intern at Kushner's architecture firm. Kushner, raised in a Modern Orthodox Jewish family, had come out to his family as gay when he was in his fourth year at the University of Pennsylvania. His family had accepted his homosexuality, but they told him that the rules remained the same: he would have to keep a kosher home and his partner would have to be Jewish. Barley grew up as a Mennonite (a strict Christian denomination) in south-eastern Pennsylvania. The two dated in 2007, and Barley came out to his family by introducing them to Kushner. Nevertheless Kushner later broke the relationship off, worrying that Barley had not had enough time to adjust to being gay to be able to enter into a successful, long-term relationship; also, for Kushner, there was 'the Jewish issue'. After a few months dating other Jewish men, Kushner flew to Rotterdam, where Barley was interning with an architecture firm, and decided that he should try to work it out. When Barley returned to New York, they began taking classes so that Barley could convert to Judaism. During a Passover vacation with his family and Barley, Kushner proposed. Barley told the *New York Times*, 'I'd always liked the idea of marriage, but it wasn't something I really pictured for myself. But then, it became a possibility, and that was kind of amazing.' At the wedding, Barley broke the glass at the end of the ceremony, and the couple were married under a traditional Jewish wedding canopy that a friend was to make into an Amish quilt.[2]

Kushner had wanted a marriage like his parents had, but he told the *New York Times*, 'There are two versions of my parents. Growing up, me marrying a man would've been outside of the realm of possibilities. But by the time I proposed to Chris, they'd come around.' This history of the couple, taken from the Weddings and Celebrations section of the *New York Times*, shows that same-sex marriage, like opposite-sex marriage, can be about courtship, reconciling different stages of emotional and psychological development, family acceptance and religious accommodation. Yet many would find the ceremony Rabbi Weintraub conducted a travesty. Indeed, Kushner's own parents would have found it unacceptable a few years before. The state of New York passed a Marriage Equality Act in 2011 allowing weddings such as Kushner and Barley's to take place; it had recognised out-of-state same-sex marriages since 2008. This rapid change in law and social attitudes underlies the difficulty that many have with these marriages. Nevertheless, radically different religious and non-religious approaches to marriage have existed for centuries. This chapter outlines some of them and outlines the church–state relations that have developed alongside them. Those changes will be developed further in the later chapters of this book.

Can the definition of marriage be changed?

In June 2012, in response to a UK government consultation on civil marriage for same-sex partners, the Church of England submitted a statement of its position, authorised by the archbishops of Canterbury and York:

> The Church of England cannot support the proposal to enable 'all couples, regardless of their gender, to have a civil marriage ceremony'. Such a move would alter the intrinsic nature of marriage as the union of a man and a woman, as enshrined in human institutions throughout history. Marriage benefits society in many ways, not only by promoting mutuality and fidelity, but also by acknowledging an underlying biological complementarity which, for many, includes the possibility of procreation.[3]

We quote this statement right at the start of this book because it illustrates multiple confusions that we attempt to disentangle. First, the statement is not limited to marriage in the Church of England or even to Christian marriage; it was submitted in response to a consultation on same-sex civil marriage. Thus, it applies, or should apply, equally to a service like the one Rabbi Weintraub conducted and to civil marriage, which involves no religious element. Second, the statement declares that the 'intrinsic nature' of marriage is that it is between a man and a woman. This means that the essence of marriage involves it being between one man and one woman. Third, the claim argues that this 'intrinsic nature' has been 'enshrined in human institutions throughout history'. Thus, at a minimum, this one-man, one-woman aspect of marriage cannot have varied over time. Finally, while the claim acknowledges that marriage carries social benefits, such as mutuality and fidelity, which apply to same-sex, as well as opposite-sex, couples, it goes on to assert that marriage involves 'an underlying biological complementarity' which 'for many, includes the possibility of procreation'. This part of the claim, which is related, if not identical, to the essentialism of the second part, renames the one-man, one-woman aspect of marriage as biological complementarity (that is, that one partner has a penis and the other a vagina), so that procreation is possible. These claims are, we shall argue, essentially sectarian Christian ones, although the Church of England's submission attempts to use them to define the terms of marriage for all varieties of Christianity, for all other religions and for civil marriage as well.

We meet these claims in this book in a number of ways. First, marriage has changed over time, not only in its incidental aspects that have constrained or enlarged the scope of who may marry whom. Class, race, blood relationship and number of spouses: all of these seemingly essential characteristics that have defined who could marry whom have varied a great deal over time, as has the question of whether marriage is a lifetime commitment. For instance, only in 1967 did the US Supreme Court deem unconstitutional state laws that made it a crime for two people of different races to marry.[4] These variations have made it increasingly difficult to identify any essential qualities that marriage may have, although we will see that it does have some. These have to do with sexual exclusivity, an intention of lifetime commitment and the free choice of the parties. We do not believe that a satisfactory, non-sectarian claim that marriage is based upon biological complementarity can be sustained, particularly in light of the history of marriage, the importance of 'choice' and the fact that reproductive capacity has never been a necessary condition for a valid marriage. At the same time, we concede the importance of arguments like these *within* a particular tradition. Thus, religious freedom must be a counterweight to the diversity of models of marriage that we will examine.

Philosophers, political scientists, lawyers and sociologists have characterised marriage in a number of different ways, some of which are compatible and some incompatible with the Church of England's description. Before we begin our historical examination of what marriage has meant at different times, a central part of our project here, we should outline some of these more abstract interpretations of marriage.

Classical views of marriage

A radical view expressed by the ancient Greeks is that attributed to Aristophanes in Plato's *Symposium*.[5] Because Plato (c. 424 BC–c. 347 BC) always presented his philosophical arguments in the form of dialogues, we do not know, nor does it matter, whether the comedian Aristophanes actually held the view that Plato attributes to him. Although the *Symposium* is more light hearted than Plato's other dialogues, a serious philosophical argument lies beneath the surface.

According to Plato's Aristophanes, attraction between individuals arises from their origin in a single being, like 'being one of two sides of a filleted fish, one half of an original whole', which tries to reunite with its other half. Men and women who are sliced from an androgynous fish that has both sexes are attracted to those of the opposite sex. 'Aristophanes' continues:

> Women who are sliced from the wholly female sex are not at all interested in men but are attracted towards other women, and female homosexuals come from this original sex. Men who are sliced from the wholly male original sex seek out males, and being slices of the male, while they are still boys they feel affection for men and take pleasure in lying beside or entwined with them. In youth and young manhood this sort of male is best because he is by nature the most manly.

These are, for Plato/Aristophanes, entirely natural attractions. Indeed, women who originate in an androgynous fish are more likely to commit adultery than other women. And men who are attracted to men are the most manly. They fulfil the specific excellence of men best, at least in their youth and young manhood. The view that a certain sort of homoerotic love was the noblest is repeated elsewhere in Plato's work,[6] and was shared by some other Athenians.

Plato's pupil Aristotle (c. 384 BC–c. 322 BC) is more concerned with the institutional relationship of the family, as it relates to the political and social environment in which marriages exist. In the *Politics*, marriage is necessary because men and women cannot live without one another:

> There must necessarily be a union or pairing of those who cannot exist without one another. Male and female must unite for the reproduction of the species – not from deliberate intention, but from the natural impulse . . . to leave behind them something of the same nature as themselves . . . They share this impulse with

both plants and animals. Men and women are different in nature: the head of the household rules over both wife and children . . . as free members of the household . . . The relation of the male to the female is permanently that in which the statesman [temporarily] stands to his fellow-citizens.[7]

In the *Nicomachean Ethics*, Aristotle describes both the incentive that men and women have to marry and the specific goods that make marriages work as they do:

> Human beings live together not merely for procreation, but also to secure the needs of life. There is division of labour from the very beginning and different functions for man and wife. Thus they satisfy one another's needs by contributing each his own to the common store.[8]

Even in the classical world the character of male–female (and same-sex) attraction varied over time. Aristophanes's appraisal is concerned with a natural relationship that arises from a fictional pre-existing unity. Aristotle is concerned to explain marriage and the family as they relate to broader themes in politics. Since the sexes are different, they have different capacities for good and for contributing to the broader common good. But the relationship is hierarchical. While men should show a kind of justice to their wives and children, they are inherently suited to rule them, as an aristocrat or as a permanent kind of democratic ruler over fellow citizens. This essential, biological difference and the differing roles that go with it in the family are the basis for more recent claims about the complementarity of husbands and wives, reflected in the Church of England's position in the quote above.

Religious views of marriage

Christianity: Roman Catholicism

The Roman Catholic Church has also built upon the Aristotelian conception of complementarity. However, since at least the Council of Trent (1545–63), it has also considered marriage between Christians to be a *sacrament*, analogous to holy communion, baptism and the ordination of clergy.[9] For Roman Catholics, a sacrament is a sign of God's grace which has the power to make holy those who desire to receive it.

> In [Roman Catholic] Christian marriage, two baptized persons are assigned by Christ the role of visible symbol and reminder of his permanent and fruitful union with His Church, are consecrated in their union by a permanent Sacrament, and are granted a specific sacramental grace.[10]

Normally, Roman Catholic sacraments are conferred by ordained clergy, who represent Christ as head of the church; however, marriage is unique, because in marriage, 'Christ acts through the priesthood of the laity' and the spouses confer the sacrament on one another. Nevertheless, the underlying sacramental theology is that marriage effects a permanent bond between the couple, upon which they adopt a vocation (an alternative vocation is celibacy, adopted by clergy and members of religious orders, such as monks and nuns). In this vocation the married couple are 'devoted to the service of the new life in Christ, which involves the specific spiritual perfection of the spouses as a way of life'. A priest or deacon must witness the exchange of vows, and that person blesses the couple during the ceremony, as a representative both of the congregation and of Christ.

The practical consequences of this view of marriage are considerable. Because an enduring change has occurred through the sacrament, the couple cannot revert to their old status, except through the death of one spouse. This is why divorce is incompatible with the Roman Catholic theology of marriage. Moreover, because the procreation and education of children is integral to the purpose of the union, which arises in part from the 'fruitful' union between Christ and his church, it is essential, as the Anglican archbishops argue above, that the potential for procreation be part of the relationship. Even if the individual couple cannot have children (because of age or infertility), the substance of the procreative act (sexual intercourse) remains the same: 'the only difference lies in the deficiency in the natural order, in the work of nature, not in the free human act', and that difference is accidental, in Aristotelian terms, and not of the essence of the sexual act.

Once one accepts this position, and some Roman Catholics do not, it is a strong argument against same-sex marriage. If the sacrament of marriage was indeed introduced by Christ and his followers, and the Roman Catholics believe that it was, then it cannot conceivably include same-sex couples within its purview. Same-sex couples cannot, through any sexual act, conceive children. And they cannot conform to the strictures imposed by St Paul, which are important to the definition of this sacrament:

Wives, be subject to your husbands as you are to the Lord. For the husband is the head of the wife just as Christ is the head of the church, the body of which He is the Saviour. Just as the church is subject to Christ, so also wives ought to be, in everything, to their husbands.[11]

Paul here is expressing the same view as Aristotle in the *Politics* (above). Since with same-sex couples there is no wife (or there are two), the entire model breaks down.

Roman Catholic theology may not be as fixed on points like this as some like to claim, however. In his book *A Church That Can and Cannot Change*, John T. Noonan Jr, a Roman Catholic judge on the Ninth Circuit Court of Appeals in the US, shows that the Catholic Church has changed its position on questions ranging from slavery to lending money at interest.[12] While Catholics, including church fathers, once owned slaves, in *Veritatis splendor* (1993) Pope John Paul II included slavery as an institution that was intrinsically evil: always and forever, without any exception. Noonan examines the circumstances when these changes take place. He does not draw any analogy with the church's position on same-sex marriage, but many Roman Catholics disagree with that position, as they do with its position on contraception and in other matters.[13]

Christianity: The Reformation

Of course not all Christians are Roman Catholics. And most Protestant Christians do not believe that marriage is a sacrament at all.

Martin Luther (1483–1546), one of the first 'reformers' of the

Christian church, who gave their name to what is now called the (Protestant) Reformation, wrote: 'No one indeed can deny that marriage is an external worldly thing, like clothes and food, house and home, subject to worldly authority, as shown by so many imperial laws governing it.'[14] Luther begins with the positive fact that laws govern marriage, to infer that marriage is subject to worldly authority. Because marriage, along with the family, was part of the natural creation, which was regulated by the state, it was not a part of the spiritual order of redemption.[15] Marriage, for Luther, had social functions, which were designed by God and should be protected and regulated by the state, but only in accordance with what the Bible dictated, not according to broader rules of Catholic canon law, which had imposed excessive restrictions on supposedly incestuous marriage, such as with one's godparents' children. He believed in divorce in cases of adultery.[16]

Jean Calvin (1509–64), another founding theologian of the European Reformation, wrote:

> Marriage is a good and holy ordinance of God; and farming, building, cobbling, and barbering are lawful ordinances of God, and yet are not sacraments. For it is required that a sacrament be not only a work of God but an outward ceremony appointed by God to confirm a promise. Even children can discern that there is no such thing in matrimony.[17]

For Calvinists, including the founders of the national, presbyterian Church of Scotland, sacraments are limited to two: baptism and holy communion. Both are ceremonies that Christ himself participated in. Although he went to a marriage at least once, at Cana (where he performed the miracle of turning water into wine)[18] and he talked about them (mostly condemning divorce and infidelity),[19] no biblical evidence shows that he either himself married or participated actively in a marriage ceremony.

For Calvin and other Reformation theologians, marriage is a way to avoid sin, but it was not, as it was for Augustine of Hippo and other early church writers, itself tainted with original sin. Calvin's most lengthy discussion of the purpose for marriage, in *Institutes of the Christian Religion* (1536), is based upon the Seventh Commandment,

'Thou shalt not commit adultery'.[20] There he says that at the time of creation God created Eve as a helpmate for Adam. Marriage is the solution to this problem, which is blessed by God, and any other form of cohabitation is inconsistent with Calvin's Protestant theology, just as it is with Roman Catholic theology.

Heinrich Bullinger (1504–75), another founder of the Reformation who was influential in England, emphasised the character of marriage as a covenanted relationship, with reciprocal (although different) rights and duties on the part of both parties.[21] He believed that marriage existed before the Fall (the expulsion of Adam and Eve from the Garden of Eden)[22] and that while fornication (sex by an unmarried person) was a breach of the covenant with God, adultery (sex with someone other than one's husband or wife) was a breach of both the covenant with God and the covenant of marriage. Of course, drawing a continuous line from the Garden of Eden to modern marriage requires either a studious disregard for the Old Testament figures who had plural wives, including Abraham and Jacob,[23] or a lot of explaining.

The reformers' argument with the Roman Catholics focused in part on the Catholic insistence on celibacy for clergy and members of religious orders. Because it had led to inconsistency between the rules they were supposed to follow and their (perceived) actual behaviour and because the reformers found no biblical foundation for it, they condemned the church's treatment of celibacy as superior to marriage and its condemnation of clerical marriage as 'uncleanness and pollution of the flesh':

> Christ deigns so to honour marriage as to make it an image of his sacred union with the Church. What greater eulogy could be pronounced on the dignity of marriage? How, then, dare they have the effrontery to give the name of unclean and polluted to that which furnishes a bright representation of the spiritual grace of Christ?[24]

Thus Calvin accuses the Roman Catholics of undermining the institution of marriage by not promoting it among the clergy.

The philosopher Thomas Hobbes (1588–1679) went so far as to see the Roman Catholic rules on sacramental marriage and priestly celibacy as part of a power-grab:

Fiftly, the teaching that Matrimony is a Sacrament, giveth to the Clergy the Judging of the Lawfulnesse of Marriages; and thereby, of what Children are Legitimate; and consequently, of the Right of Succession to hæreditary Kingdomes.
Sixtly, the Deniall of Marriage to Priests, serveth to assure this Power of the Pope over Kings. For if a King be a Priest, he cannot Marry, and transmit his Kingdome to his Posterity; If he be not a Priest then the Pope pretendeth this Authority Ecclesiasticall over him, and over his people.[25]

Finally, because marriage for the reformers was not a sacrament that effected a permanent bond between the couple, divorce became possible. Huldrych Zwingli drafted an ordinance on how marriage would be conducted in the city of Zurich in 1525:

Since, now, marriage was instituted by God to avoid unchastity, and since it often occurs that some, by nature or other shortcomings, are not fitted for the partners they have chosen, they shall nevertheless live together as friends for a year, to see if matters may not better themselves by the prayers of themselves and other honest people. If it does not grow better in that time, they shall be separated and allowed to marry elsewhere.[26]

Not all reform theologians were so liberal. Bullinger, for example, refrained from defining all the circumstances that could serve as a basis for divorce (aside from adultery, which to him was clear). Instead, he believed that divorce should be a matter for the civil magistrate (in other words, the state).[27] In a Roman Catholic marriage, however, not even adultery could serve as a basis for dissolving what was considered a life-long bond. Reformation theology departed from this principle and allowed that the government could determine when it was proper for a couple to end their marriage.

Between the Catholics and the reformed churches of Luther and Calvin several important distinctions crop up. First, banning clerical marriage, or calling it unclean or sinful, is an insult to the institution and undermines it, according to the Protestants. If marriage is a human institution, then it is one that all humans should participate in, particularly clergy. Second, if marriage is not a sacrament or a vocation, then it ceases to be a life-long commitment. Conduct inconsistent with the marriage bond can justify its dissolution. John Milton (1608–74) wrote:

> For although God in the first ordaining of marriage, taught us to what end he did it, in words expresly implying the apt and cheer-full conversation of man with woman, to comfort and refresh him of the evill and solitary life, not mentioning the purpose of generation till afterwards, as being but a secondary end in dignity, though not in necessity; yet now, if any two be but once handed in the Church, and have tasted in any sort the nuptiall bed, let them find themselves never so mistak'n in their dispositions through any error, concealment or misadventure, that through their different tempers, thoughts and constitutions, they can neither be to one another a remedy against lonelines, nor live in any union or contentment all their dayes, yet they shall, so they be but found suitably weapon'd to the least possibility of sensuall injoyment [i.e. equipped for sex], be made, spight of antipathy to fadge [tolerate each other] together and combine as they may to their unspeakable wearisomnes and despaire of all sociable delight in the ordinance which God establisht to that very end.[28]

Milton takes a radical position here, arguing that the marital bond is primarily for apt and cheerful conversation and not for having children, and that when that purpose is not satisfied, the marriage should be dissolved. These differences arise from fundamentally different understandings of what marriage involves.

Judaism

Traditional Jewish law echoes the Aristophanic–Platonic concept of a single soul being reunited after having been split into two parts.[29] This reflects the Biblical story in Genesis, where Adam was divided into two. Having been split, the marriage reunites the two back into a single soul, which was destined to be one. This has implications for those who are single, as they are seen as in some sense incomplete. Nevertheless, divorce is allowed, and sometimes even mandatory, under Jewish law.

The marriage ceremony has two parts, a betrothal (*erusin*), which changes the couple's status with respect to the rest of the world, and the nuptials (*nissu'in* or *chuppah*), which bring about the mutual legal obligations of the marriage.[30] Both have been part of the same public ceremony since the Middle Ages, although in the past they could take place up to a year apart. After the betrothal, the laws of adultery apply, but the couple may not live together. They may only live together after the marriage. The betrothal part of the marriage ceremony involves the groom giving something to the bride and the couple tasting wine. The betrothal must take place in the presence of witnesses, and witnesses must sign the marriage contract, which is read at the wedding. While the presence of a rabbi is not essential to a Jewish marriage, the presence of witnesses is.[31] Originally, the nuptials took place in a tent or a special room that the groom set up for the bride. Now that custom is echoed in the canopy at a wedding ceremony, which is called a *chuppah*.

At the wedding ceremony a contract (*ketubbah*) is read out, in which the husband promises to take care of the wife and guarantees her a certain amount upon his death or if he divorces her. All of his property is collateral for the payment of this amount. It is signed by the two witnesses. Modern contracts also specify the wife's duties to the husband, and they grant the wife the power to divorce the husband.

One of the reasons for the marriage contract was to protect the wife, since the husband initially had unilateral power to divorce her. Indeed, if a woman commits adultery, divorce is mandatory.[32] Divorce is accomplished by the man giving the wife a divorce document or *get*. A Jewish religious court (*bet din*) oversees divorces and ensures that they are valid under religious law. Originally, men were allowed to divorce women unilaterally for any reason whatever; however, the medieval Talmudist Rabbeinu Gershom deprived husbands of this power.[33] Maimonides allowed a woman to divorce a man based upon an entirely subjective belief that he had become 'loathsome'.

Islam

The Islamic view of marriage is different in certain respects from that in any of the Christian denominations discussed above. Men and women are, according to Muslim belief, created from a single soul or *nafs*, and they enjoy mutual rights and responsibilities akin to the complementarity found in Aristotle and the Catholic doctrines discussed above.[34] Islam emphasises the necessity of consent on the part of both parties to the marriage, but it also permits parents and other members of the family to be involved in the choice of a spouse, offering advice and assistance in making a suitable match.[35] Liberal Islamic scholars point out that these rules may be a product of cultural influences on Islam rather than of religious law. The Prophet Mohammed's first wife, they argue, was a successful businesswoman and decided to marry him rather than the reverse. Generally, however, Islam does not sanction pre-marital courtship or dating.

Four requirements are necessary for a Muslim marriage contract (*nikah*): (a) the consent of the bride and groom (signified by the two pillars of offer and acceptance), (b) the consent of the bride's guardian,[36] (c) the presence of two Muslim witnesses and (d) agreement on the *mahr* or dowry to be received by the bride.[37] As Islam has no clergy as such, any knowledgeable Muslim male can preside over the ceremony. The *mahr*, according to the Qur'an, must be a free gift,[38] but in the event of a divorce by the wife, it must be returned under certain circumstances.

Islam permits polygamy, two verses in the Qur'an authorising the practice.[39] Polygamy technically means one person (of either gender) with multiple spouses. When a man has multiple wives, it is polygyny; when a woman has multiple husbands, she practices polyandry. While scholars agree that monogamy has become the norm in the Islamic world, and liberals argue that it is nearly impossible to meet the Qur'anic requirements for plural wives, more conservative scholars argue that plural wives are justified when the number of women is greater than the number of men, for example after a war, or when men might be tempted to sin:

The sexual urge is not uniform in all human beings, nor is their capacity to control themselves. For a number of reasons, a man may be exposed to a situation where the choice before him could be between a second marriage or a drift towards sin. In such situations, polygamy is permitted.[40]

Indeed, the majority of scholars regard polygamy as a spiritually beneficial act, and practical considerations may lead to plural marriage, including a desire to select a spouse in addition to one selected by one's parents and a desire to have biological children when the first wife cannot.[41]

Divorce is also permitted, although not encouraged: if spouses 'are not able to live in kindness, they should part amicably'.[42] The position of men and women in a divorce is not symmetrical. In some Islamic traditions, women cannot leave a marriage except through the fault of the husband, and may not receive custody of adolescent children or more than limited financial support.[43] They also face different procedural hurdles, for example a higher filing fee in religious courts in the UK (£250, as opposed to £100), based upon the requirement, applicable under all Islamic law, that women's allegations must be substantiated, while those of men need not.[44]

The connections between Islamic religious and civil marriage in non-Muslim countries are complex. It appears that many Muslims in the UK have religious but not civil marriages.[45] As of 2009, only 152 of 785 English mosques were registered, as English law requires, to perform marriages on the premises.[46] In one recent study, only half of those who approached the Sharia Council of the Birmingham Central Mosque wanting to divorce under Islamic law had been married under civil, as well as religious, law.[47] A large number of Muslims seem to believe, mistakenly, that their *nikah* is a valid civil marriage. In the United States, the number of Muslims is extremely difficult to determine, making demographic studies about marriage in Islam extremely challenging.[48] Further complicating matters is the divide between immigrant Muslims and African-American converts, including those who belong to the Nation of Islam. A recent book on families published in the United States fails to discuss legal recognition of Islamic marriage and does not even mention polygamy.[49]

Under Muslim religious law, homosexual conduct is forbidden. The rule is based upon the Prophet Mohammed's statement to the people of Lut: 'Do you commit lewdness such as no people in creation (ever) committed before you? For you practise your lusts on men in preference to women; you are indeed a people transgressing beyond bounds.'[50] Acceptance of this principle is universal among

Islamic scholars, and one conservative Muslim leader has written: 'Same-sex relationships are damaging to the divine institution of marriage and to society as a whole.'[51] Nevertheless, progressive scholars have argued that it is possible to justify same-sex marriage based upon Islamic texts, using independent, legal reasoning.[52]

Hinduism

There is no one source of religious or legal authority in the Hindu scriptures. Hindu marriage practice therefore varies widely but always involves the couple walking around a sacred fire several times. When the British ruled India, they attempted to codify Hindu law, but the first codification by a democratically elected Indian government is the Hindu Marriage Act 1955.[53] It controls marriage in India between not only Hindus but also Buddhists, Jains and Sikhs,[54] whose religions the drafters of the Act regarded as variants of Hinduism. As with UK statute law, it lays down the degrees of affinity within which a couple may not be married, and provides for divorce.

In the UK, the state does not intervene in Hindu weddings beyond providing for Hindu temples to be registered for civil marriages, if so requested. The diffuse nature of the Hindu scriptures means that it is harder than with Christianity, Judaism or Islam to define the essential religious content of a Hindu wedding.

Non-religious views of marriage

The Enlightenment view

During the eighteenth-century Enlightenment, philosophers were engaged in the project of trying to build moral and social principles without resort to religious premises. Enlightenment thinkers wanted to provide explanations for why different societies operated in different ways. One of the leaders of the Enlightenment was Adam Smith (1723–90), who believed that the form that social institutions take depends upon the material conditions that underlie them. Smith (along with the French social theorist Montesquieu and Smith's fellow Scot James Wilson) believed that the institution of marriage had evolved through history. Smith argues that the fundamental reason for monogamous marriage is the fact that human children, unlike cattle or even birds, require so much work to feed and take so long to develop.[55] And because a second, third and fourth child can be born while their elder siblings are still unable to care for themselves, human couples stay together and remain sexually attracted to one another for longer than other animals do.

Early on, according to Smith, families were authoritarian and hierarchical, and the father had the power to punish children and slaves, even with death, as well as to unilaterally divorce his wife. Once nations became wealthier, however, property had to be allocated, and women found ways of retaining it, even when they were married, thus giving husbands a disincentive to divorce. In Rome, Smith says, it became possible for a couple to live together and for the wife to retain her own property, provided that she 'separate[d] herself from her husband for 3 or four nights every year'.[56] And while originally men had more control over whether to end the marriage, once Christianity intervened the rules (ironically made by unmarried priests) became fairer. Initially, women were allowed to make decisions on the same basis as men, and eventually divorce was not permitted at all. Smith doubts whether the true reason for punishing women's adultery more harshly than men's was the possibility of spurious offspring. Instead, it was jealousy. Since men enjoy superior power in contracts of marriage, the injury to their honour from adultery is greater, and besides, 'men . . . make the laws with respect to this; they generally will be inclined to curb the women as much as possible and to give themselves the more indulgence.'

Marriage and divorce are initially and most fundamentally based on instinct and interest. Smith admires the 'British colonies in North America', where population increases because high wages make children assets rather than liabilities:

> A young widow with four or five young children, who, among the middling or inferior ranks of people in Europe, would have so little chance for a second husband is there frequently courted as a sort of fortune. The value of children is the greatest of all encouragements to marriage. We cannot, therefore, wonder that the people in North America should generally marry very young.[57]

Smith, along other Enlightenment authors, describes marriage in positive, empirical terms rather than in normative ones. The institution exists in order to formalise property relationships among people, to provide for children and to give them proper training, and to allow people to mate with a minimum of social conflict. It is also a product of social circumstances and of power relationships, for example, between the genders. And it arises from class interests. In Book V of *The Wealth of Nations*, Smith describes two systems of morality, which have always coexisted, which he calls the 'liberal, or . . . the loose system' and the 'strict or austere' system.[58] In the first, loose system, 'the breach of chastity, at least in one of the two sexes' is permitted. In the strict system, 'those excesses are regarded with the utmost abhorrence and detestation'. The reason for this distinction? 'The vices of levity are always ruinous to the common people, and a single week's thoughtlessness and dissipation is often sufficient to undo a poor workman for ever.' Strict rules about marriage protect those in the lower classes from wasting money on drinking, gambling and illicit sex.

In modern, commercial society, the woman's role in marriage also changes. Once production increases sufficiently to allow for leisure, women can become equals alongside men.[59] Another Enlightenment figure, Smith's close friend David Hume (1711–76), wrote: 'Sovereignty of the male is a real usurpation, and destroys that nearness of rank, not to say equality, which nature has established between the sexes.'[60] This 'equality' puts marriage in a different light, where women serve on the one hand to promote civilised manners in men, and on the other to provide them with friendship and even intellectual companionship. These aspects of male–female relationships are not exclusive to married couples, but they put marriage on a different footing from the purely hierarchical and procreative ones that had existed up to this point.

Hume also wrote:

It is mere superstition, to imagine that marriage can be entirely uniform, and will admit of only one mode or form . . . Nature, having endowed man with reason, has not so exactly regulated every article of his marriage contract, but has left him to adjust them, by his own prudence, according to his particular circumstances and situation. Municipal laws are a supply to the wisdom of each individual; and, at the same time, by restraining the natural liberty of men, make private interests submit to the interests of the public. All regulations, therefore, on this head are equally lawful, and equally conformable to the principles of nature; though they are not equally convenient or useful to society.[61]

Hume argues in this essay against both polygamy and divorce. But the basis for his argument, set out in this paragraph, is that nature does not dictate the form that marriage should take. Rather, reason allows humans to determine what is best for the individual, which should be judged based upon what is 'convenient or useful'. Arguments against polygamy include (1) the jealousy that arises in men who have fewer wives when they see that others have more, (2) the need to segregate women, which arises from this jealousy, and (3) inadequate education for children. Arguments against divorce include (1) the effect of divorce on the children, (2) the need to ensure that relationships are not transitory but survive attraction to other people and difficulties between the couple, and (3) the need to maintain common interests between the couple.

Smith and Hume differ from the religious views of marriage described above, because they see marriage as a function of something else: cultural development, class and economic structure and individual interests. Accordingly, while Hume, at least, argues against divorce and polygamy, his arguments depend upon their effect on society, not on any essential characteristic of marriage, which in turn depends upon *a priori* principles. Moreover, the arguments are empirical and can be tested with evidence. The same is not true of the religious views of marriage described above.

The rationalist view

No one can know what Bertrand Russell (1872–1970) would have thought of same-sex marriage – he was in the generation of Mark Kushner's and Chris Barley's great-grandparents, at least. Given his radical views on nearly everything else, he probably would have supported it.[62] But he would have done so on very unusual grounds, which actually are consistent with some conservative views of marriage. In Russell's most extended treatment of marriage, *Marriage and Morals* (1929), he argued that the sole purpose of marriage was to provide a stable environment for rearing children. He believed in pre-marital sex, provided there were no children; in companionate marriage (between younger, college-age people who did not intend to have children until they were permanently married and who could terminate the relationship by mutual agreement); and in sex outside marriage (his second wife was involved in an affair that produced two children when he wrote the book). He did not believe that married couples with children should divorce, except under the unusual circumstance when the couple was so unhappy that their relationship stopped providing a stable environment for their children. He divorced his second wife, with whom he had two children, in 1935.

Russell's argument is entirely rationalist and depends upon a number of circumstances being present. Children should receive good sex education at an early age and should be taught that sex is natural. Contraceptives should be widely available and people should use them to avoid having children until they are ready to form a stable family. And individuals should be tolerant of one another: even of a spouse's infidelity.

Russell says that a good marriage combines four elements:

> There must be a feeling of complete equality on both sides; there must be no interference with mutual freedom; there must be the most complete physical and mental intimacy; and there must be a certain similarity in regard to standards of values. (It is fatal, for example, if one values only money while the other values only good work.)[63]

He emphasises the rational independence of the two spouses, who freely choose to engage in physical and emotional intimacy. He emphasises the importance of real compatibility, but overarching all of these values is the responsibility that the two partners have to their children. Russell's is an interesting answer for those who focus on the procreative aspect of marriage, as he does just that; indeed, he is even unsympathetic with adultery as a basis for divorce when there are children.

Russell's argument seems entirely consistent with acceptance of same-sex marriage. His argument in *Marriage and Morals* depends a great deal on what was then a relatively new technology: reliable contraception. In the present day, the growth in the number of same-sex couples adopting or having children through assisted reproductive technology and surrogacy makes it possible for them to rear children just like opposite-sex ones. Since the sole purpose of the family and marriage for Russell was to provide a stable environment to rear children, his logic would seem to lead inexorably to the conclusion that same-sex couples should be able to marry.

No marriage at all?

In *The Autonomy Myth*, Martha Fineman, an American legal scholar, argues that marriage, as a legal category, should be abolished.[64] It carries too many incidents based in history, which lead to patriarchy and oppression, and even the 'private sphere' of the family is actually a way of giving legal sanction to domestic violence and perverse incentives. Instead, the law should adopt a caretaker-dependent category as the core of 'family', which protects relationships other than those of opposite-sex (or same-sex) couples, providing them with the legal recognition, subsidies and privileges now offered to married couples. Marriage might persist purely as a social, religious or cultural construct, but it would no longer be recognised in law.

The gay rights campaigner Peter Tatchell has argued more polemically along the same lines:

> The first Gay Priders saw the family as 'a patriarchal prison that enslaves women, gays and children'. Three decades later, the theme of this year's celebration is 'We are family: partnership and parenting rights – now!' The focus on safe, cuddly issues like gay marriage and adoption indicates how gay people are increasingly reluctant to rock the boat and more than happy to embrace traditional heterosexual aspirations.[65]

Michael Warner of Yale University has developed this argument further, as has Elizabeth Brake.[66] We will return to their arguments in Chapter 5.

These two descriptions simplify complicated arguments. But their essence is that participating in the institution of marriage will level gay and lesbian relationships down rather than improving them. Some theorists argue that because same-sex couples have had to create their own relationships, they have used more creativity than they would have otherwise done, and that that creativity will be squelched by forcing their relationships into what is seen as a conformist, patriarchal institution.

Thus, rather than dumbing down gay relationships and making them conform to straight stereotypes, it is argued, legal relationships should be pluralistic. Tatchell, for example, argues: 'Why can't we campaign for a more democratic, egalitarian alternative, where people can nominate as their next-of-kin and beneficiary any "significant other", such as a lover, cousin or life-long best friend?' Oddly, this argument is consistent with the position of Baroness O'Cathain, a conservative opponent of civil partnerships in the House of Lords. In 2004 she promoted an amendment to the government's civil partnership bill which would have eliminated the prohibition on blood relatives, such as parents and children or siblings, entering into these relationships.[67] Opponents called this a wrecking amendment because it would have made the bill unworkable. Tatchell praised her amendment the day after it was accepted,[68] although O'Cathain had previously admitted in committee that her objective was not only to expand the rights but to prevent same-sex couples from having them.[69]

Of course O'Cathain's position is entirely strategic. But we must assume that the others' are more sincere. A credible position opposing marriage altogether can still acknowledge the fact that the government should support some intimate relationships with financial and other assistance. The question is whether marriage (either between any sex or only between opposite sexes) should be the factor that determines which relationships are entitled to that support.

Liberal feminism

A more moderate, liberal feminist position on these questions is that of Linda McClain, whose book *The Place of Families* advocates same-sex marriage but also thinks that alternative care-giving roles ought to be recognised without abandoning marriage entirely.[70] McClain's argument rests on fundamental liberal principles including fostering the capacity of individuals to make moral choices about how they will lead their lives. In addition, she argues forcefully for equality in and among families. Neither same-sex nor opposite-sex couples should be encouraged, much less coerced, into adopting the existing breadwinner–homemaker model, where one individual earns and the other contributes uncompensated child-care and domestic service. Equality among families requires the government to provide support so that even economically disadvantaged families, including those with one parent, can rear children. Finally, same-sex couples are capable of providing exactly the same goods for society as opposite-sex couples: they form committed, intimate relationships and function as responsible and loving parents, even in the absence of marriage. According to McClain, the state should recognise that they do so by offering same-sex couples all of the support that it does to opposite-sex couples.

Like Martha Fineman's, McClain's project is a big one. She seeks to show that government has a greater responsibility for fostering capacity than it has undertaken hitherto. Government should make additional provision for single women who raise children. Although single fathers should undoubtedly receive these benefits as well, McClain's focus is on women, who assume a greater share of responsibility for raising children. Unequal social roles for men should be eliminated, along with the premises that they rely upon, like the fact that women 'civilise' men, as Hume argued above. But a central part of her argument is that recognition of same-sex marriage would strengthen marriage for everyone by explicitly saying that all intimate relationships that are capable of providing mutual support and caring for children are worthy of social appreciation.

Different views of marriage: conclusions

There are a variety of theoretical underpinnings for marriage. Religious understandings of marriage range from those that understand it as a life-long commitment to those that allow for divorce and even those that permit plural wives. Definitions that concentrate on procreation, the Catholic one and Russell's, begin with fundamentally different premises: the Catholic with biological complementarity and Russell's with absolute equality between the partners. Enlightenment and rationalist justifications focus on the circumstances that either give rise to different kinds of marital relationships or on the social goods that come from them. These conceptions are competing ones that do not have a common essence; however, they do share some features. In the rest of this book we will test these theories against both the legal arrangements that underpin marriage and against the arguments that were made when marriage was changing from one form to another.

Freedom of, and from, religion in the UK and the US

A central division between these views of marriage is the place of religion in society. Three overlapping models of religious freedom can be identified in the United States and the United Kingdom.[71]

From the time of the Wars of the Three Kingdoms (1639–51), which included the English Civil War, religious conflict in the nations that now make up the United Kingdom has been understood as potentially dangerous to civil peace. In 1706/07, when the parliaments of Scotland and England & Wales were united into a single legislature for Great Britain, one of the requirements imposed by the Scots was that the presbyterian system of church government, with its acceptance of divorce, would be preserved in an established church there. To this end the Treaty of Union incorporated the Act of Security, which had been passed by the Scottish Parliament before the union:

> The . . . true Protestant religion contained in the [Westminster] Confession of Faith, with the form and purity of worship presently in use within this church, and its presbyterian church government and discipline, that is to say the government of the church by kirk sessions, presbyteries, provincial synods and general assemblies . . . shall remain and continue unalterable, and that the said presbyterian government shall be the only government of the church within the kingdom of Scotland.[72]

When home rule was proposed for Ireland in the nineteenth century, legislators feared that Roman Catholic voters, who were in the majority there, might impose their religion upon Protestants. From 1886, legislation proposed in Westminster included a provision protecting religious liberty, whose wording derived from the first amendment of the US constitution (to be discussed shortly): 'The Irish Parliament shall not make a law so as to either directly or indirectly establish or endow any religion, or prohibit or restrict the free exercise thereof . . .'[73]

Neither of these efforts to depoliticise religion was entirely successful. In 1711 the British parliament adopted the Church Patronage (Scotland) Act, which restored the power of appointing clergy to lay patrons, arguably in violation of the Act of Security. And in 1833–43 a series of judicial decisions reinforcing that power led to the Disruption of the Church of Scotland, in which one-third of the clergy and between one-third and one-half of its members seceded and formed the non-established Free Church of Scotland.[74] The Church Patronage (Scotland) Act 1874 finally restored to congregations the power to choose their own clergy, although the resentment created by the Disruption remained until Parliament enacted the Church of Scotland Act 1921, which immunised the church against judicial interference in its doctrine, worship, government or discipline. The constitution adopted in 1937 in Ireland expressly referred to the people of Ireland as Trinitarian Christians.[75] Overall, however, the state in the UK has gradually withdrawn from religion, allowing civil rights to Roman Catholics from 1829 and disestablishing the Church of Ireland in 1871 and the Church in Wales in 1920.[76]

A more radical, explicit separation between church and state was adopted at the time of the ratification of the codified constitution of the United States of America. The first amendment, which was a precondition for some states' adoption of the constitution, provides that 'Congress shall make no law respecting an establishment of religion, or prohibiting the free exercise thereof'. Since the 1940s these prohibitions have applied to the states', as well as to the federal, government.[77] Thus, in the United States it is a violation of the constitution to have prayer in schools or a Christmas display in a courthouse, as those are violations of the non-establishment clause.[78] Similarly, it is a violation of constitutionally protected religious freedom to refuse government benefits to a person who loses her job because she cannot work on the Sabbath or to target the religious practices of those of a particular faith, such as Santeria (a religion of west Africa and the Caribbean, whose members practise animal sacrifice), unless there is a good reason for doing so.[79]

In the following chapters, we will argue that the law of marriage has evolved as separation between church and state has increased. As a population adopts increasingly diverse denominations of one religion, such as Christianity, or diverse religions, including Judaism, Hinduism and Islam, and members of those denominations and religions become integrated into civil society, marriage laws must change to accommodate those differences. In 1606 Richard Hooker could write of England: 'There is not any man of the Church of England but the same man is also a member of the commonwealth; nor any man a member of the commonwealth, which is not also of the Church of England.'[80] In the 2011 census, fewer than 60 per cent of the English and Welsh were Christian, and fully one-quarter had no religion at all.[81] In order to accommodate this change, marriage has had to adapt, so that it can comprehend different religious and non-religious understandings of the institution.

Public reason

The United States' separation of church and state and the UK's increasing separation both promote what John Rawls referred to as 'public reason'.[82] Public reason is not distinct from, nor does it deny the value of, private reason or religious reason.[83] Rather, it sets a limit on the ability of some people (particularly politicians, judges and voters taking a political position) to introduce what Rawls calls reasonable comprehensive doctrines (which can be religious or philosophical) into political debate. Reasonable comprehensive doctrines meet minimum standards of rationality, so that even those who do not accept them can understand that other reasonable people might do so. They are comprehensive in so far as they include conceptions of what is of value in human life, and ideals of personal character, friendship, and familial and associational relationship, among other things.[84] A plurality of conflicting reasonable comprehensive doctrines is a product of a free, democratic state with a culture of free institutions.[85]

Individuals may, while engaged in political debate, explain their reasonable comprehensive doctrines in a declaration, which explains one's position but by which one does not demand agreement from others.[86] However, according to Rawls in due course a person engaged in political debate must 'give properly public reasons to support the principles and policies [the] comprehensive doctrine is said to support'.[87] The fundamental principles underlying the requirement of public reason lie in Rawls's basic requirements:

> Each person has an equal claim to a fully adequate scheme of equal basic rights and liberties, which scheme is compatible with the same scheme for all; and in this scheme the equal political liberties, and only those liberties, are to be guaranteed their fair value.[88]

From this, it follows that coercive political power must be exercised only 'in accordance with a constitution the essentials of which all citizens may reasonably be expected to endorse'.[89] The ideal of citizenship imposes a moral duty of civility: that citizens be able to explain to one another how the principles and policies they advocate can be supported by the political values of public reason. Those political values may be a product of what Rawls calls an overlapping consensus, which is based on part but not all of a number of comprehensive doctrines. However, the reason that the consensus overlaps is that it can be expressed independently of those doctrines and in accordance with public reason.

James Madison (1751–1836) anticipated Rawls's next set of arguments in his *Memorial and Remonstrance against Religious Assessments* (1785) and his *Vices of the Political System of the United States* (1787).[90] The first of these was written during Madison's campaign with Thomas Jefferson to oppose a tax supporting religious teachers in Virginia. Madison points out there that 'Religion . . . must be left to the conviction and conscience of every man' and that it is 'an inalienable right'. He continues: 'No other rule exists, by which any question which may divide a Society, can be ultimately determined, but the will of the majority; but it is also true that the majority may trespass on the rights of the minority.' These are arguments in favour of religious freedom and against tyranny of the majority. Madison goes on to oppose religious establishment. He writes: 'During almost fifteen centuries has the legal establishment of

Christianity been on trial. What have been its fruits? More or less in all places, pride and indolence in the clergy, ignorance and servility in the laity, in both, superstition, bigotry and persecution.' In *Vices*, a memorandum he wrote in advance of the constitutional convention in Philadelphia, he singled out 'members of different religious sects' as a kind of faction. There and in *The Federalist*, a collection of essays promoting the ratification of the constitution, he argues that the size of a country like the United States can prevent factions from forming a tyrannous majority.

Rawls's reasons for separating church from state are akin to those offered by Madison, for they include, first, protection of the church from the state; second, protection of the state from the church; third, protection of citizens from their own churches; and fourth, protection of citizens from one another.[91] The church is protected from undue interference from the state, which could undermine important comprehensive doctrines held by its members. It protects the state from being taken over by a single, comprehensive doctrine, with which many of the citizens might disagree. Since, according to Rawls, people must be allowed to change their faith (heresy and apostasy cannot be legitimate crimes), citizens are protected even from their own churches. Finally, by maintaining neutrality, citizens are not allowed to infringe on one another's religious comprehensive doctrines, by force, by vote or otherwise.

These arguments apply with equal force to discussions of civil and religious marriage. Efforts to import religious arguments into the debate about same-sex marriage undermine important liberal values. Proponents of such arguments may seek to impose religious views on those who do not hold or agree with them, and at worst they may cause a dangerous move backwards toward intermingling religion and government.

Appeals to history, complementarity and procreation, like those made in the Church of England's statement quoted at the start of this chapter, are all efforts to translate religious ideals into public reason. However, they fall foul of many of the Madisonian/Rawlsian problems identified above. They lose their religious character by attempting to translate religious arguments into public reason, for example, by changing procreative arguments that make sense in religious terms into civic requirements that do not. Thus, they harm religion by watering it down. This is also true, as we will see, of the historical arguments offered by those who claim that marriage has not changed in the past. While this may be true of some kinds of religious marriage, it is not true of the law of marriage. Moreover, the arguments are also an attempt to enforce religious values on those who may not agree with them. Complementarity may make sense to a Catholic or to an Aristotelian, but it makes little sense to one who, like Russell or McClain, believes in the absolute equality of men and women. And all of this holds even if a majority of voters are Christians. A minority, no matter how small, must be respected, and its religious beliefs, even if they are quite strange to the majority (such as Quakerism or even animal sacrifice), should be allowed provided that they do not do real harm to other people.

The diversity of understandings of marriage makes it necessary for law to mediate among groups who hold quite different views of marriage, and a Rawlsian approach to discussions of marriage makes it possible to decide what choices people should be allowed to make about the spouse that they take and the kind of obligations that spouses have to one another. In the following chapters we will examine a number of changes that have taken place in the law of marriage in the UK and the US, showing that those changes have served largely political purposes, sometimes protecting the status quo for those who were in power, at other times accommodating changes in society, as the population grew larger and more culturally and religiously diverse. But the continuous trend we can observe is one that accommodates more and more people with increasingly diverse conceptions of how to construct marriages and families. And a Rawlsian explanation of how these changes have taken place must respect that diversity but at the same time identify commonalities that make good public policy possible.

Conclusion

In the middle of the last century, the Christian apologist C. S. Lewis wrote:

> I should like to distinguish two things which are very often confused. The Christian conception of marriage is one: the other is the

quite different question – how far Christians, if they are voters or Members of Parliament, ought to try to force their views of marriage on the rest of the community . . . My own view is that the Churches should frankly recognise that the majority of the British people are not Christians and, therefore, cannot be expected to live Christian lives. There ought to be two distinct kinds of marriage: one governed by the State with the rules enforced on all citizens, the other governed by the Church with rules enforced by her on her own members.[92]

After writing this, Lewis entered into a marriage of convenience, which was not intended for other than legal purposes, with Joy Davidman Gresham, an American writer, so that she could continue to live in the UK.[93] He subsequently married her in a religious ceremony. Lewis's broad point here is that religions, including Christianity, may in their marriage rites impose obligations on their members that are different from civil marriage. Thus, Roman Catholics may legitimately refuse to recognise divorce and refuse to remarry or even give communion to divorcees. Moreover, Lewis also makes the Rawlsian point that those who believe in Christian marriage should not force their view on others. Instead, civil marriage should include only minimally agreeable rights and obligations, which are consistent with many different views of marriage. Civil marriage should do what is necessary to make marriage a civil status, without integrating entire reasonable comprehensive doctrines (like the ones described in this chapter) into the legal system at the expense of other viable reasonable, comprehensive doctrines.

All this implies that there really are different kinds of marriage. Marriage has been very different at different times, and it is different today in different places, as well. That is what this book is about. Marriage has served multiple purposes, including providing a stable place for children to grow, giving people a secure way of transmitting property and limiting the number of sexual partners people can have. But because none of these really reflects an 'essence' of marriage, the modern, democratic state has the power to change what it recognises as marriage, provided that a majority of people or their representatives support the change. Changes should not exclude reasonable comprehensive doctrines, but they should acknowledge that a diversity of those doctrines are what make for a vibrant, liberal democracy. The first points, about the history of marriage and its diversity, are positive ones that are empirically testable, and our principal task here is to test them. The second, normative point, about what the state ought to do, is more debatable. We will argue that it is important and that all people, whatever their individual religious or political position, ought to be informed about it. That way they can advance arguments that others can understand and agree to on their own terms, without having to accept an entire reasonable comprehensive doctrine.

Notes

1. Oliver Wendell Holmes Jr, 'The Path of the Law', *Harvard Law Review* 10(8) (1897), p. 469.
2. Anna Jane Grossman, 'Vows: Chris Barley and Marc Kushner', *New York Times*, 13 April 2012, http://www.nytimes.com/2012/04/15/fashion/weddings/chris-barley-and-marc-kushner-vows.html (last accessed 7 May 2013).
3. 'A Response to the Government Equalities Office Consultation "Equal Civil Marriage" from the Church of England', http://www.churchofeng land.org/media/1475149/s-s%20marriage.pdf (last accessed 7 May 2013). The statement is unsigned, but at the General Synod of the Church of England which met in July 2012 the archbishops accepted responsibility for the document, which was drafted by their staff. 'Report of Proceedings 2012', *General Synod July Group of Sessions* 43(2), http://www.churchofengland.org/media/1527142/july%202012%20(2).pdf (last accessed 7 May 2013).
4. *Loving* v. *Virginia* (1967) 388 US 1.
5. Plato, *Symposium*, tr. M. C. Howatson (Cambridge: Cambridge University Press, 2008), 191d–192a.
6. E.g. Plato, *Phaedrus*, 237b–241a.
7. Aristotle, *Politics*, tr. Ernest Barker (Oxford: Oxford University Press, 1977), 1252a, 1259a–b; 'temporarily' is interpolated by Barker.
8. Aristotle, *Nicomachean Ethics*, tr. Martin Ostwald (Indianapolis: Liberal Arts Press, 1962), 1162a.
9. Catholic University of America, 'Sacraments (Theology of)', in *New Catholic Encyclopedia* (New York: McGraw-Hill, 1967). For one authoritative view of the Roman Catholic theology of marriage see Herbert McCabe OP, *The New Creation* (London: Continuum, 2010), ch. 8.

10. Catholic University of America, 'Marriage (Theology of)', in *New Catholic Encyclopedia* (New York: McGraw-Hill, 1967).
11. Ephesians 5:22–4. (All biblical quotations are from the New Revised Standard Version.)
12. John T. Noonan Jr, *A Church That Can and Cannot Change: The Development of Catholic Moral Teaching* (Notre Dame, IN: University of Notre Dame Press, 2005).
13. John Bingham, 'Gay marriage: church leaders at odds with opinion in the pews, study suggests', *Daily Telegraph*, 17 April 2013 (44 per cent of Roman Catholics support same-sex marriage; 41 per cent oppose it).
14. Martin Luther, 'On Marriage Matters', in Helmut T. Lehmann (ed.), *Luther's Works* (Philadelphia: Fortress Press, 1967), vol. 46, p. 265.
15. John Witte Jr, *From Sacrament to Contract: Marriage, Religion, and Law in the Western Tradition* (Louisville, KY: Westminster John Knox Press, 1997), p. 51.
16. Martin Luther, 'The Estate of Marriage', in Helmut T. Lehmann (ed.), *Luther's Works* (Philadelphia: Fortress Press, 1967), vol. 45, pp. 30–5.
17. Jean Calvin, *Institutes of the Christian Religion*, in *Works and Correspondence*, ed. J. T. McNeill (London: SCM Press, 1960), book IV, ch. 19, § 34, p. 1481.
18. John 2:1–11.
19. See Matthew 5:32.
20. Calvin, *Institutes of the Christian Religion*, book II, ch. 8, § 41.
21. Carrie Euler, 'Heinrich Bullinger, Marriage, and the English Reformation: *The Christen state of Matrimonye* in England, 1540–53', *Sixteenth Century Journal* 34(2) (2003), pp. 367–93; Witte, *From Sacrament to Contract*, p. 146.
22. Genesis 3:14–15.
23. For Abraham see Genesis 16:3, 21:1–13; for Jacob see Genesis 29:28, 31:48–54.
24. Calvin, *Institutes of the Christian Religion*, book IV, ch. 12, § 24.
25. Thomas Hobbes, *Leviathan*, ed. C. B. Macpherson (Harmondsworth: Penguin, [1651] 1968), ch. 47, 'Of the BENEFIT that proceedeth from such Darknesse, and to whom it accreweth'.
26. Huldrych Zwingli, *Selected Works*, ed. Samuel Macauley Jackson (Philadelphia: University of Pennsylvania, 1901), p. 122.
27. Euler, 'Heinrich Bullinger, Marriage, and the English Reformation', p. 377.
28. John Milton, *The Doctrine & Discipline of Divorce* (London, c. 1643), preface, available online at http://www.dartmouth.edu/~milton/reading_room/ddd/book_1/index.shtml.
29. Genesis 2:21.

30. 'Marriage', in Barbara Ball et al. (eds), *The Encyclopedia of Jewish Life and Thought* (Jerusalem: Carta, c. 1996).
31. Kopel Kahana, *The Theory of Marriage in Jewish Law* (Leiden: E. J. Brill, 1966), p. 38.
32. Sotah 6:1.
33. Menachem Elon et al., *Jewish Law: Cases and Principles* (New York: Matthew Bender, 1999), p. 25.
34. Azizah Y. al-Hibri and Raja' M. El Habti, 'Islam', in Don S. Browning, M. Christian Green and John Witte Jr (eds), *Sex, Marriage, and Family in World Religions* (New York: Columbia University Press, 2006), p. 157.
35. Ibid., p. 168.
36. As with family involvement in the negotiation of the contract, this requirement is a subject of dispute. Imam Abu Hanifa says that a woman may contract the marriage on her own. Raffia Arshad, *Islamic Family Law* (London: Sweet & Maxwell, 2010), § 3.4.2.
37. These four requirements are listed in Muhammad Abdul Bari, *Marriage and Family Building in Islam* (London: Ta-Ha, 2007), pp. 16–17. They are developed in more detail in Jamal J. Nasir, *The Islamic Law of Personal Status*, 3rd ed. (The Hague: Kluwer Law International, 2002).
38. Qur'an 4:4.
39. The term 'polygamy' includes plural spouses of either gender; technically, Islam permits polygyny (plural wives only). See Qur'an 4:3 ('If you fear that you shall not be able to deal justly with the orphans, marry women of your choice, two or three or four; but if you fear that you shall not be able to deal justly (with them), then only one . . .') and 4:129 ('You are never able to be fair and just as between women, even if it is your ardent desire. But turn not away (from a woman) altogether, so as to leave her (as it were) hanging (in the air). If you come to a friendly understanding, and practice self-restraint, God is Oft-forgiving, Most Merciful'); al-Hibri and El Habti, 'Islam', p. 186.
40. Khurshid Ahmad, *Family Life in Islam* (Leicester: Islamic Foundation, 1974), p. 24.
41. Arshad, *Islamic Family Law*, § 3.7.
42. Al-Hibri and El Habti, 'Islam', p. 200.
43. Robin Fretwell Wilson, 'The Perils of Privatized Marriage', in Joel A. Nichols (ed.), *Marriage and Divorce in a Multicultural Context: Multitiered Marriage and the Boundaries of Civil Law and Religion* (New York: Cambridge University Press, 2012), p. 265.
44. Ibid., p. 266.
45. Arshad, *Islamic Family Law*, § 3.11.
46. P. M. Bromley and Hugh K. Bevan (eds), *Butterworth's Family Law Service* (London: Butterworths, 1983), para. 505.
47. Gillian Douglas, Norman Doe, Sophie Gilliat-Ray, Russell Sandberg

and Asma Khan, *Social Cohesion and Religious Law: Marriage, Divorce and Religious Courts* (Cardiff: Cardiff Law School, 2011) p. 39, http://www.law.cf.ac.uk/clr/research/cohesion (last accessed 8 May 2013).

48. Bahira Sherif-Trask, 'Muslim Families in the United States', in Marilyn Coleman and Lawrence H. Ganong (eds), *Handbook of Contemporary Families: Considering the Past, Contemplating the Future* (Thousand Oaks, CA: Sage, 2004), pp. 394–407.
49. Ibid.
50. Qur'an 7:80–1, Al-Hibri and El Habti, 'Islam', p. 209.
51. Bari, *Marriage and Family Building in Islam*, p. 23.
52. Hassan El Menyawi, 'Same-sex Marriage in Islamic law', *Wake Forest Journal of Law & Policy* 2(2) (2012), pp. 375–530.
53. Republic of India, Act No. 25 of 1955, http://www.indiankanoon.org/doc/590166 (last accessed 8 May 2013).
54. Hindu Marriage Act 1955, § 2(1)(b).
55. Adam Smith, *Lectures on Jurisprudence* (Oxford: Clarendon Press, 1978), p. 141.
56. Ibid., p. 144
57. Adam Smith, *An Inquiry into the Nature and Causes of the Wealth of Nations* (Indianapolis: Liberty Classics, [1776] 1981), vol. I, p. 88.
58. Ibid., vol. II, p. 794.
59. Rosemarie Zagarri, 'Morals, Manners, and the Republican Mother', *American Quarterly* 44(2) (1992), pp. 192–215.
60. David Hume, 'Of Polygamy and Divorces', in *Essays, Moral, Political and Literary*, ed. Eugene F. Miller (Indianapolis: Liberty Fund, [1777] 1985), p. 184.
61. Ibid., pp. 181–2.
62. One good reason for this supposition is his support for the decriminalisation of male homosexual acts: 'Homosexual acts: call to reform law', letter, *The Times*, 7 March 1958, p. 11.
63. Bertrand Russell, *Marriage and Morals* (London: Routledge, [1929] 2009), p. 88.
64. Martha Albertson Fineman, *The Autonomy Myth: A Theory of Dependency* (New York: New Press, 2004).
65. 'Gay Pride is now respectable, and the worse for it', Peter Tatchell website, July 2002, http://www.petertatchell.net/lgbt_rights/queer_theory/gaypride.htm (last accessed 8 May 2013).
66. Michael Warner, *The Trouble with Normal: Sex, Politics, and the Ethics of Queer Life*, new ed. (Cambridge, MA: Harvard University Press, 2000); Elizabeth Brake, *Minimizing Marriage: Marriage, Morality, and the Law* (New York: Oxford University Press, 2012).
67. Hansard, HL Deb, 24 June 2004, vol. 662, col. 1362.
68. Michael White and Sarah Hall, 'Gay marriage bill "wrecked" in Lords',

The Guardian, 25 June 2004, http://www.guardian.co.uk/politics/2004/jun/25/lords.gayrights (last accessed 8 May 2013).

69. Hansard, HL Deb, 10 May 2004, vol. 661, cols 23GC *ff*.
70. Linda C. McClain, *The Place of Families: Fostering Capacity, Equality, and Responsibility* (Cambridge, MA: Harvard University Press, 2006).
71. Iain McLean and Scot Peterson, 'Secularity and Secularism in the United Kingdom: On the Way to the First Amendment', *Brigham Young University Law Review* 2011(3) (2011), pp. 637–56.
72. Act for Securing of the Protestant Religion and Presbyterian Church Government, The Records of the Parliaments of Scotland to 1707 website (hereinafter RPS) 1706/10/251, http://www.rps.ac.uk/mss/1706/10/251 (last accessed 8 May 2013).
73. Government of Ireland Act 1914, § 3; see also Government of Ireland Bill 1886, Bill 181, cl. 4(1). The provision was modelled on the First Amendment of the United States Constitution. Hansard, HC Deb, 13 February 1893, vol. 8, col. 1253 (speech by W. E. Gladstone). The Northern Ireland Constitution Act 1973 prohibited discrimination by the Northern Ireland Assembly based upon religious belief (§ 17, repealed by the Northern Ireland Act 1998, Schedule 15). Article 8 of the constitution of the Irish Free State (1922) prohibited religious discrimination; the 1937 constitution recognised the Roman Catholic Church (along with other churches), but that provision was repealed in 1973.
74. Stewart J. Brown, *The National Churches of England, Ireland, and Scotland, 1801–46* (Oxford: Oxford University Press, 2001), p. 358; G. I. T. Machin, *Politics and the Churches in Great Britain, 1832 to 1868* (Oxford: Clarendon Press, 1977), p. 142. For a description of the events leading to the Disruption, see Lord Rodger of Earlsferry, *The Courts, the Church and the Constitution: Aspects of the Disruption of 1843* (Edinburgh: Edinburgh University Press, 2008).
75. See Chapter 4, below.
76. Roman Catholic Relief Act 1829, Irish Church Act 1869, Welsh Church Act 1914, Welsh Church (Temporalities) Act 1919.
77. *Cantwell* v. *Connecticut* (1940) 310 US 296; *Everson* v. *Bd of Education* (1947) 330 US 1.
78. *Engel* v. *Vitale* (1962) 370 US 421; *County of Allegheny* v. *American Civil Liberties Union* (1989) 492 US 573.
79. *Sherbert* v. *Verner* (1963) 374 US 398; *Church of Lukumi Babalu Aye* v. *City of Hialeah* (1993) 508 US 520. We will address the 'good reason' part of this statement in Chapter 5.
80. Richard Hooker, *Of the Laws of Ecclesiastical Polity*, ed. John Keble (Indianapolis: Liberty Fund, [1594–7] 1888), Book VIII, ch. i.2.
81. Office of National Statistics, 'Religion in England and Wales 2011',

11 December 2012, http://www.ons.gov.uk/ons/dcp171776_290510.pdf (last accessed 9 May 2013).

82. John Rawls, *Political Liberalism* (New York: Columbia University Press, 1993); John Rawls, 'The Idea of Public Reason Revisited', *University of Chicago Law Review* 64(3) (1997), pp. 765–807.

83. Rawls, *Political Liberalism*, VI:3(1).

84. Ibid., I:2(2).

85. Rawls, 'The Idea of Public Reason Revisited', pp. 765–6.

86. Ibid., p. 786.

87. Ibid., p. 776.

88. Rawls, *Political Liberalism*, I:1(1)a.

89. Ibid., VI:2(1).

90. Iain McLean and Scot Peterson, 'Adam Smith at the Constitutional Convention', *Loyola Law Review* 56(1) (2010), pp. 95–133; James Madison, 'Memorial and Remonstrance against Religious Assessments', in *Writings*, ed. Jack N. Rakove (New York: Library of America, 1999), pp. 29–36; James Madison, 'Vices of the Political System of the United States', in *Writings*, ed. Jack N. Rakove (New York: Library of America, 1999), pp. 69–80.

91. Rawls, 'The Idea of Public Reason Revisited', p. 795.

92. C. S. Lewis, *Mere Christianity*, rev. ed. (London: HarperCollins, 2001), p. 112.

93. A. N. Wilson, *C. S. Lewis: A Biography* (London: Collins, 1990), pp. 257–61.

2

Marriage from the Reformation to the Rules of the Fleet

> I am accustomed to set my face against clandestine proceedings of all kinds . . . But there are exceptions to the strictest rules . . . I am not against hasty marriages, where a mutual flame is fanned by an adequate income.[1]
>
> Wilkie Collins

Royal marriages

We begin this chapter by reviewing a set of events that led to the Reformation in England and Scotland, and may have led Thomas Hobbes to make his caustic remarks about the secular power of the papacy (Chapter 1).

On 14 November 1501 Arthur, Prince of Wales married Katherine of Aragon, the daughter of Ferdinand of Aragon and Isabella of Castile.[2] Unfortunately, the fifteen-year-old prince died of tuberculosis shortly after his marriage. His younger brother Henry, the new heir to the English throne, married his brother's widow in 1509. He was crowned Henry VIII on Sunday, 24 June of that year. However, Katherine bore him no sons that survived: his first born, Henry, survived only a matter of days, and the only other child to survive was Princess Mary, born in 1516. In 1527, Henry began his efforts to dissolve his marriage of nearly eighteen years. Divorce was not possible according to Roman Catholic canon law (Chapter 1). But what was possible was a declaration that the marriage had been void from the beginning. In this case, because Katherine had been married to Arthur, Henry's brother, her marriage to Henry was arguably prohibited under canon law – the so-called impediment of the first-degree collateral – because they had been brother- and sister-in-law.

Henry had obtained a papal dispensation before the marriage, but he and his advisors now claimed that the pope who had issued it had exceeded his authority and that Katherine's inability to produce an heir arose from the sinful nature of their relationship. However, Katherine's nephew, the Holy Roman Emperor Charles V, had just captured the French king, Francis I, at the battle of Pavia in 1525, and Charles had designs on Italy. Moreover, if Henry's marriage were not annulled, England might fall into Charles's realms on Henry's death.

The pope, Clement VII, could not afford to alienate Charles by granting the annulment. A trial concerning the divorce at Blackfriars, a London priory, collapsed, and repeated negotiations with the Vatican were unsuccessful. In June 1529 Clement's unwillingness to grant the annulment became clear. King Francis, the Holy Roman Emperor and Pope Clement were in the process of resolving their differences, which would have entirely blocked any potential annulment. Henry's only alternative, if he wished to remarry, was to block the authority of the pope in England, which he did in February 1533. In 1532 Henry had begun sleeping with Anne Boleyn, probably following an exchange of vows before witnesses, and in January 1533 the two were married by a priest.[3] On 23 May of that year, the Archbishop of Canterbury, Thomas Cranmer, pronounced Henry's marriage to Katherine void and their daughter Mary illegitimate. Because the act passed in February barred ecclesiastical appeals to Rome, no appeal to the pope was possible.[4] The Church of England became independent of the Roman ecclesiastical hierarchy, and Henry became 'Supreme Head on earth of the Church of England'.[5] This was the beginning of the English Reformation.

Scotland's Reformation, unlike England's, came through the nobility, who adhered to continental Protestantism.[6] It began with acts of the Scottish Parliament in August 1560, ratifying a Protestant confession of faith and abolishing papal jurisdiction.[7] The regent at the time, Mary of Guise, had a single living daughter by her deceased husband, James V.[8] The daughter, also named Mary and known to us as Mary, Queen of Scots, had been sent to live at the French court in 1548 at the age of six. In 1558 she married Francis, the heir to the French throne, who succeeded his father and became king the following year. However, Francis died eighteen months later. Mary returned to Scotland, where she married Henry Stewart, Lord Darnley, who shared her maternal grandmother, Margaret Tudor, and therefore her claim to the English throne. The claims, which might have been competing ones, were reconciled by the marriage.

The *Oxford Dictionary of National Biography* describes Darnley as 'vain, foolish, idle and violent, with a rare talent for offending people, including his wife'.[9] Despite the earlier action of the Scottish parliament, Mary and Darnley still recognised the authority of the papacy. Because he and Mary were cousins, a papal dispensation was necessary for their marriage, just as one had been for Henry and Katherine. It was issued 25 September 1565 but backdated to May; the wedding actually took place in July, and Darnley became king. On 19 June 1566 Mary gave birth to Darnley's son, who later became James VI of Scotland and James I of England, an ancestor of all UK monarchs. (It is to be hoped that Darnley's character was not in his genes.) From November 1566, following Darnley's involvement in the murder of one of her advisors earlier in the year, Mary was peripherally involved in a plan to kill her husband. In February 1567, Darnley's house at Kirk o' Field exploded, and his body was found outside.

That April, James Hepburn, 4th Earl of Bothwell, met with a number of nobles, who agreed to support him in an effort to marry the queen. On the twenty-fourth, he abducted and raped her. According to the customs of the period, she had no alternative but to marry a third time. When the Earl of Morton, the Duke of Argyll and the Earl of Mar (Prince James's keeper) assembled military forces to avenge Darnley's murder, in which Mary was implicated, Mary surrendered, and they imprisoned her. However, she escaped to England, where Elizabeth I held her captive and agreed to her execution twenty years later. Bothwell died insane, held captive in exile by Frederick II, king of Denmark.

Theoretically, royal marriages like these preserved dynastic rule and made succession predictable. At the time, they were vital to the continuity of the state. In neither of these cases, however, was the succession as clear as the monarchs had hoped. Their spouses' existing relationship, either by blood or by marriage, threatened the legality of the marriage. Henry was able simply to ignore his marriage to Katherine, based upon her previous marriage to Arthur, once the pope had been eliminated from the decision process; this was the cause of the English Reformation. Mary had to obtain a dispensation in order to marry her cousin, Lord Darnley, because he was too closely related, although it was backdated by a more sympathetic pope. Henry's second marriage, to Anne, initially was not a formal affair. It was merely a pledge before witnesses that made it lawful to sleep with her and legitimated any children they might have. And Mary's third marriage, to Bothwell, was a product of abduction and rape. As these royal marriages show, rules and even religious laws can be manipulated to permit practical outcomes based upon political realities and the desire for power. And marriage – even royal marriage – was quite a different thing in the sixteenth century from what it is today.

Marriage at the Reformation and beyond

England and Scotland thus had different Reformations. In England, Henry's divorce from Katherine of Aragon required separation from Rome. In Scotland, the Reformation was a more gradual process, which went further than in England, culminating in Andrew Melvill's tugging at the sleeve of James VI/I and calling him 'God's sillie vassal':

> Thair is twa Kings and twa Kingdomes in Scotland. Thair is Chryst Jesus the King, and his kingdome the Kirk, whase subject King James the Saxt is, and of whase kingdome nocht [not] a king, nor a lord, nor a heid, bot a member![10]

In England, the monarch is the supreme governor of the established church. In Scotland, the church is non-hierarchical in numerous ways, including its lack of bishops, its historic inclusion of non-clerical members in its governing bodies and its lack of any institutional link with the state analogous to the bishops in the House of Lords.

From the time of the Reformation, the organisational differences between the Scottish and English churches have reinforced differences in the law of marriage in the two countries. In the eighteenth century, Scotland was a weak state with a weak church.[11] Although both nations retained the law of marriage as it had existed before the Council of Trent, marriage in Scotland retained a greater variety of forms for longer than it did in England. In this chapter, we describe the different forms marriage took in both countries and the effect that they had on marriage practice in the British colonies in North America. We go on to discuss the problem of clandestine marriage that led to the passage of Lord Hardwicke's Act in 1753, which will be discussed in the next chapter.

Law of marriage

From the sixteenth until the mid-eighteenth century marriage in England involved (1) a written contract between the parents specifying the financial arrangements, (2) a formal exchange of oral promises (spousals, hand-fasting or betrothal), (3) publicly proclaiming the couple's intent to marry in church on three successive Sundays (banns), (4) a church wedding and (5) sexual consummation.[12] For those without property, step 1 was less important, and the betrothal ceremony may have been treated as a binding union without the need for steps 3 or 4, particularly in remoter areas, such as the Scottish border country, Wales and the extreme south-west of England (Cornwall). As we have seen, in 1532/33 Henry VIII treated his exchange of promises, step 2, with Anne Boleyn as binding and proceeded directly to step 5 (sexual consummation); the formal wedding ceremony (step 4) came later.

Step 3, calling banns, is a way of ensuring maximum public notice of the pending wedding, so that objections can be raised based on, for example, too close a relationship between the bride and groom by blood or marriage (consanguinity or affinity) or an existing marriage by one of them to a living spouse (bigamy). The purpose of the wedding in church is to give notice of the fact of the marriage, so that in the future it is easy to prove that the couple has been married and that all of the legal rights and duties of marriage apply to them (including their and their relatives' inability to wed people when it would be bigamous or incestuous). The government has a legitimate interest, as does the social community, in making sure these two steps are followed, but they have not always been.

In addition to calling the banns, the marriage ceremony in the Church of England and other Christian denominations offers a final opportunity for objections to be made: 'If any man can shew any just cause, why [the couple] may not lawfully be joined together, let him now speak, or else hereafter for ever hold his peace.'[13] This kind of opportunity is present in most wedding ceremonies used to the present day. It provides suspenseful moments in fiction, as in Charlotte Brontë's *Jane Eyre*, when Rochester and Jane are about to marry:

> When is the pause after that sentence ever broken by reply? Not, perhaps, once in a hundred years. And the clergyman, who had not lifted his eyes from his book, and had held his breath but for a moment, was proceeding: his hand was already stretched towards Mr Rochester, as his lips unclosed to ask, 'Wilt thou have this woman for thy wedded wife?'—when a distinct and near voice said—
>
> 'The marriage cannot go on: I declare the existence of an impediment.'[14]

Rochester was about to commit bigamy, as he had a wife, who was still living.

Spousals and hand-fasting (step 2) were historically as important as, if not more important than, the wedding ceremony that followed. Popular belief in the indissolubility of betrothal was practically universal and unshakeable in the sixteenth century.[15] However, different forms of words imposed different requirements on the couple. A promise to marry *per verba de praesenti* (in English, 'in words of the present tense', such as 'I John take thee Joan') was binding on the parties; a promise *per verba de futuro* ('in words of the future tense', such as 'I John will take thee Joan') was not binding and could be superseded by another promise in the present tense, unless and until the couple had had sex (step 5), which made the promise binding, even if there had been no church wedding. It was not until 1563 that the Council of Trent declared that 'spouses shall not cohabit in the same house before they have received the nuptial blessing from the priest in church'.[16] Since Scotland and England had broken with Rome by this time, both countries retained marriage law from before the Council of Trent.

Henry VIII introduced a wrinkle into this system in 1540.[17] In that year he dissolved his marriage with Anne of Cleves, who may have been so ugly that Henry was impotent with her. Parliament passed an act that made marriages solemnised in church *and consummated* good against precontracts (promises *per verba de praesenti*) unless they themselves had been consummated. This meant that an uncon-summated marriage in church, like Henry's marriage with Anne, was voidable based upon a precontract that had been consummated.

Henry and Anne's case involved Anne's precontract with the Duke of Lorraine, which was probably not consummated, but Henry claimed that it had been, because Anne was too heavy to be a virgin.[18] Henry's innovation made consummation essential to marriage under English law, but even a consummated marriage (just in case anyone suspected Henry and Anne had had sex) was vulnerable to a consum-mated precontract.[19] The statute was repealed during Henry's son Edward's reign, because couples had seemingly conspired, claiming that their marriages had not been consummated and thereby obtain-ing an annulment.[20] Consummation was not a legally workable criterion for determining whether a couple was married. Even in the Roman Catholic tradition, consummation is not necessary in marriage.[21]

The legal rules concerning Church of England weddings (step 4) were set out in the Church of England's canons of 1603.[22] Canon 99 prohibited marriage within the degrees of consanguinity or affinity defined in the book of Leviticus, Canon 100 prohibited marriage without parental consent under the age of twenty-one. Canons 101 to 103 imposed conditions for common licences, which permitted marriage without banns. Only bishops and those acting on their behalf were permitted to issue licences; and they could only be issued if requirements concerning consanguinity and affinity had been met, parental consent had been obtained, and no lawsuit concerning a previous precontract or marriage was pending in the ecclesiastical courts. Even under the terms of a licence, the wedding was supposed to take place in the parish of one of the parties and between eight o'clock in the morning and mid-day.

The Puritans, a growing faction in the Church of England, some of whom emigrated to New England starting in 1620, objected to these rules later in the century. Among their other complaints about church government in England in the Root and Branch Petition of 1640, they pointed to the church's 'prohibiting marriages without their license, at certain times almost half the year, and licens-ing of marriages without banns asking'.[23] The basis for their first complaint was a prohibition on reading banns during the church seasons of Lent (forty days before Easter), Advent (four weeks before Christmas) and Rogationtide (a four-day period in late spring). The Puritans were exaggerating in the petition, since this only adds up to seventy-two days. But the prohibition made it necessary to be married with a licence rather than by banns during these periods, and licences were more expensive for the couple and produced fees for those who issued them. Clergy had a financial incentive, which the Puritans recognised, to make licences the only available option during extended periods.

The Commonwealth parliaments reformed marriage law twice. The first reform, the Directory of Worship, adopted during the Long Parliament (1640–8), required that marriages be 'solemnized by a lawfull Minister of the Word'.[24] The act made no provision for marriage by licence, retaining the concept of banns, and required that the wedding take place in a place of public worship, before a competent number of witnesses and at 'some convenient hour of the day'. The second reform, during Barebone's Parliament (1653), was more radical. It provided for the reading of banns either in church or, if the parties desired, in the marketplace, following which the wedding was celebrated by a justice of the peace rather than a member of the clergy.[25] The act was therefore the precursor of state-organised civil marriage. It continued: 'And no other Marriage whatsoever within the Commonwealth of England after the 29th of September, in the year One thousand six hundred fifty three, shall be held or accompted a Marriage according to the Laws of England.' This second reform did not last. The Second Protectorate Parliament (1656–8) nullified the provision requiring that marriages be before a justice of the peace.[26] These statutes also introduce an early definition of marriage as being between 'one man and one woman only'.[27] This definition seems, however, intended to address the problem of bigamy, which was a serious one in the 1500s and 1600s.[28]

These reforms caused confusion. During the Second Protectorate Parliament, a number of acts, including the second reform, were extended only for limited periods – what we would today call a sunset clause.[29] During the debate on marriage, the Speaker of the House of Commons said that if Parliament continued the 1653 act, 'the inconvenience will be great to many families in England', because weddings conducted under the Directory of Worship and also under the Anglican prayer book, which had been banned in 1644, would be void.[30] Two members of that parliament, Colonel White and Mr Fowell, argued that its action could bastardise children. White was concerned with those wed under the 1653 act (who might be bastardised if it were repealed), and Fowell was concerned with those not wed under it, 'for it is not one in one hundred [weddings] that is made pursuant to this [the 1653] Act'. Following the Speaker's casting vote in an equally divided house, the provision quoted above making the 1653 procedure exclusive was removed from the act, but the act remained in force.[31] Thus, for the remainder of the Commonwealth three methods were used to wed: the outlawed Book of Common Prayer service, the Directory of Worship, and the procedure under the 1653 act.[32]

At the restoration of the Stuarts in 1660, Parliament quickly passed an Act for the Confirmation of Marriages, resolving these confusions and reinstating a wedding in the Church of England as the only legitimate option.[33] The act recited that certain weddings had been celebrated 'since the beginning of the late troubles . . . in some other manner then hath formerly beene used and accustomed' and provided that civil weddings celebrated by justices of the peace would have the same effect as if they had been celebrated according to the rites of the Church of England. However, because of dislocations following the Civil War and the Great Fire of London in 1666, many still could not marry in their own parishes, and normal procedures could not regularly be followed.[34]

Changes in how one can be married (or to whom) can lead to serious problems.[35] Both Edward VI's repeal of Henry's statute and Charles II's regularisation of Commonwealth marriages normalised practice during a limited period. The modern analogy to this shifting ground in sixteenth- and seventeenth-century England is California in 2004–8. For a month in 2004, before he was stopped by the California state courts, Mayor Gavin Newsom of San Francisco directed city officials to issue marriage licences for same-sex couples. In August of that year, the state courts decided that Newsom had improperly ignored state law and declared those marriages void. In a new case in 2008, which challenged the law applied in the first case,[36] the California Supreme Court said that that law was unconstitutional under California's constitution. The court decided the second case on 15 May 2008, but it was reversed by California's voters on 4 November, when they amended the constitution to say that marriage could only take place between a man and a woman. The amendment, known as Proposition 8, was challenged in a subsequent lawsuit in federal court. The latest lawsuit claims that Proposition 8 is unconstitutional under the *United States* constitution and has recently been addressed by the US Supreme Court. That case will be discussed in detail in our final chapter. Between 17 June (when the California decision came into operation) and 4 November 2008 about 18,000 same-sex couples were married in California.[37] The California courts decided that those marriages, unlike the ones from San Francisco in 2004, were valid.[38] In 2008 the California courts followed the example of Edward VI and Charles II; in 2004, they had not done so.

Beginning in 1694 and prompted by the war with France, the English parliament began to tax marriage.[39] Initially, the tax was a stamp duty on licences and on certificates of marriage.[40] In the next session, the government raised a loan of £650,000 on the security of an act that imposed a duty on weddings of at least 2s. 6d., increasing with the social rank of the couple up to dukes, who had to pay an additional £50.[41] However, the government found itself unable to collect the duties, and therefore to pay the debt, bringing pressure from international creditors.[42] The problem of tax evasion is evident from the statute passed to punish those who performed weddings without banns or licence and those who assisted them.[43] The preamble to the later statute recites that the earlier one is being evaded

> by several Parsons, Vicars, and Curates, who ... substitute and employ ... divers other Ministers to marry great Numbers of Persons in their respective Churches and Chapels, without Publication of Banns, or Licences of Marriage first had and obtained; many of which Ministers so substituted, employed, permitted, and suffered to marry as aforesaid, have no Benefices or settled Habitations, and are poor and indigent, and cannot easily be discovered and convicted.

The fine imposed, initially on the clergy and later on those who assisted them, was £100 for each offence. Many argue that this system of taxes and fines aggravated the increase in the number of clandestine weddings, which became the subject of legislation in 1753, so-called Fleet marriages.[44]

These taxes applied to groups whose marriages the state did not recognise, including Quakers and Jews.[45] The origins of the Quaker faith, known formally as the Friends (and now the Society of Friends), lie in the English Civil War. Quakers believe in individual revelation (an 'inner light'), and early on engaged in disruption of worship, particularly in the established church, and refused to acknowledge social hierarchy by doffing their hats: they were firmly countercultural, also believing that it was appropriate for women to preach.[46] To this day, they believe in neither sacraments nor clergy. Accordingly, Quaker marriages, according to one of their founders, George Fox, are simply a religious commitment between the two people:

> For the right joining in marriage is the work of the Lord only, and not the priests or magistrates; for it is God's ordinance and not man's and therefore Friends cannot consent that they should join them together: for we marry none; it is the Lord's work, and we are but witnesses.[47]

Fox's statement was written in opposition to the requirement of civil marriages during the English Commonwealth (the 1653 Act described above), but Quakers regard their marriage declaration as having its origins in the presbyterian usage of the service in the Directory of Worship.[48]

The Church of England refused to recognise Quaker weddings, which were referred to in the Bishop of Salisbury's returns in the 1600s as 'pretended marriages', even though they were recorded in Quaker registers of births, marriages and deaths.[49] From the 1660s, however, the civil courts began to recognise Quaker marriages at least for some purposes.[50] The most notable case is that of Anne Theaker and her daughter Mary Ashwell, whose ownership of property depended upon the validity of Anne's first marriage to William Ashwell at a Friends' meeting in Lincoln. John, William's brother, claimed the property based upon the fact that Anne and William's marriage had not been legal. Before the trial in 1661, Martin Mason, a Friend, wrote to the judges: 'Shall the want of a mere punctilio in the formality of the law [of marriage] deprive so many thousand innocent people of protection by the law when the body or substance of the law is so clearly answered?' The Quakers and their council relied upon witnesses to the marriage, both non-Quaker and Quaker, the Quaker marriage certificate to prove that Anne had been conceived in wedlock, and an opinion by Sir Edward Coke that a marriage could not be legally challenged when one of the spouses was dead. The court decided in favour of Anne and Mary.

After the 1694 act taxed Quaker marriages without allowing for their legitimacy, the Quakers' central lobbying body, the Meeting for Sufferings, consistently sought exemptions from any regulations that the government might impose on marriage.[51] They were eventually successful in 1753, obtaining a complete exemption (and arguably full recognition of their marriages) when Parliament passed Lord Hardwicke's Act.

Consequences of marriage: England

Rebecca Probert has argued forcefully that in the eighteenth century the promise *per verba de praesenti*, made in the context of the betrothal and in place of the wedding, was not a full alternative to marriage, despite common claims to the contrary.[52] Ecclesiastical law recognised such a promise only as a bar to a future marriage or as a defence against a charge of fornication. Moreover, on occasion those courts would order the parties to have a religious wedding. However, the civil law, which dealt with property rights, recognised only marriage preceded by a wedding performed in the established church. Thus, property rights after a spouse's death (dower and curtesy)[53] could not be based upon mutual promises in the absence of a wedding, and a spouse's relief under the poor laws also had to be based upon a church wedding ceremony rather than a betrothal. Some marriages, such as those between people younger than twenty-one without the consent of their parents, were illegal but still binding on the parties, thereby barring any future marriage.

These legal rules were complex and deeply rooted in the formal legal requirements concerning different courts' jurisdiction and the rules of pleading (how people's legal claims were presented). Prior to 1753 ecclesiastical courts had jurisdiction over the fact of the marriage, that is whether marriage had taken place at all.[54] If different courts took different positions on what proof was necessary for a marriage, results could vary, and a couple might be married for some purposes but not for others. When the term 'jurisdiction' is extended to include the geographical area within which courts act, the couple can end up being married in some places but not in others.

According to Probert, 'a contract [*per verba de praesenti*] was both binding *and* incomplete, requiring the final formalities to be observed. Only when a couple married before an Anglican minister were full legal rights and responsibilities conferred upon them.'[55] The position that a promise *per verba de praesenti* was binding in England until Lord Hardwicke's Act began with the House of Lords' decision in *Dalrymple* v. *Dalrymple* in 1811.[56] Only then did courts read backwards to eliminate the practical and legal disadvantages that attended a failure to have a proper church wedding. Nevertheless, it remains true both that a promise *de praesenti* that could be proved and had not been released by the ecclesiastical courts was a bar to future marriages by the parties and that subsequent marriage could be void once a promise had been proven.

Others have emphasised the prevalence of informal marriage, particularly if other facts were present. Lawrence Stone writes:

> There is some uncertainty as to whether large numbers of persons living together as husband and wife at this time were in fact legally married. Neighbours and communities were on the whole prepared to regard stable cohabitation, the exchange in conversation of words such as 'husband' or 'wife', the use of the same surname, and the baptism of children as creating a socially acceptable presumption of marriage.[57]

The same thing occurs today in England, where many Muslims are married in their mosque, which is not necessarily a registered premises (Chapter 1). Within communities like these, religious marriage is given precedence over civil marriage, and religious divorce may have priority over civil divorce if the state allows that to happen.[58] However, Stone also argues that the ecclesiastical courts increasingly ignored evidence of precontract in the seventeenth and eighteenth centuries, making appeals for enforcement of such promises futile.[59] Without treating the present promise to marry as equivalent to marriage itself, however, common lawyers slowly encroached on the territory of their ecclesiastical colleagues, who operated in a different, parallel court system. The common lawyers developed the tort of 'breach of promise to marry', which permitted a person who had been betrothed to sue for money damages (but not an injunction requiring a church wedding) if their intended spouse broke the contract.[60] The new tort clarified the line between a promise to wed and the wedding itself by offering a new legal remedy for breach of the promise.

None of this can be conclusive as to what was happening between those who did not or could not, because of the cost, pursue legal remedies. In the debate on the bill that became Lord Hardwicke's Act in 1753, one of the opponents' main arguments against the act was that its requirements would make it too difficult for the poor to marry. Robert Nugent, who led the opposition to the bill, argued: 'Among the poor, Sir, there are many marriages made, and even such as prove very happy, that never would have been made, if so much as one proclamation of banns had been necessary.'[61] Lord Barrington, a supporter of the bill, admitted: 'As to the lower class of people, I shall grant that they generally chuse to be married in an irregular, rather than a regular manner, and many of them, I believe, would chuse to cohabit together, if it were not scandalous, without any marriage at all . . .'[62] Thus, contemporary evidence from both sides of this debate supports an inference that informal marriages of some kind, which did not include all five steps above, were common among the poor, who had little need for the formalities that governed the succession of titles and property.

The post-Reformation history of marriage in England reflects a legislative and governmental intention to gain control over this social institution. Increasingly the betrothal was overshadowed by a more formal, public wedding, which reduced the uncertainty involved in proving that a couple was married. At the same time, religious disagreements about who had the authority to perform weddings led to confusion, particularly in the time of the Civil War and following. When there was little property involved, it seems fair to conclude that people could marry informally provided that the community did not object to their relationship, although Probert has shown that most people did marry in church. As long as legislators, lawyers and judges were concerned both with righting wrongs (such as breaches of the promise to marry) and with regulating behaviour (such as bigamy and incest), the legal and civil treatment of marriage was bound to be a complicated matter.

Consequences of marriage: Scotland

Marriage in Scotland was defined much earlier by statute law than it was in England and Wales. In addition, Scottish marriage law is bound up with the changes in religious establishment in that country.

Well before the Reformation, Scottish law had granted remedies to those in irregular marriages. In 1503 Parliament passed the Terce Act,[63] which protected a widow's share of her husband's estate, even if she had not been lawfully married, provided that no one had challenged the marriage during the life of the husband and so long as the woman was of good standing and held as his lawful wife during the marriage.[64] This statute is the basis of the Scottish law of marriage by 'habit and repute'.[65] Marriage of this kind is analogous to what is sometimes called common-law marriage, in which people are considered married (provided they meet other requirements concerning consanguinity, affinity, capacity and consent), so long as they hold themselves out to the community as being married (sometimes for a specified period of time – here, until the husband's death). Although many people in England believe that this kind of marriage exists in their country, that is not true.[66]

In addition to 'regular' marriage, by a minister of the Church of Scotland, and marriage by habit and repute, two other irregular forms of marriage were legally recognised in Scotland, which have already been described: marriage by promise *de praesenti* and marriage by promise *de futuro cum copula*. However, as in England, the legal status of these two forms of marriage before the eighteenth century is the subject of dispute. The standard work on Scottish legal history argues that John Dalrymple, Viscount Stair, in his seventeenth-century work on Scottish marriage law is 'incorrect' when he states that a promise *de verba praesenti* followed by sex is a valid marriage.[67] However, by the 1700s John Erskine of Carnock considered the *copula* of sexual intercourse as binding on a couple who had committed themselves to a future marriage, and neither of the two could withdraw from the promise following the act.[68] The effect of this legal principle was to make it unnecessary to have a wedding ceremony at all, perhaps under a court order if one party baulked; rather, the wedding took place through the promise and the sexual act, and the court could simply issue an order stating that the couple was married based upon sufficient evidence that the two events had occurred.[69]

Another legal dodge developed on the basis of two statutes adopted in 1661 and 1698 which were supposed to regularise marriages.[70] Both imposed penalties on those who married outside of the Church of Scotland, including fines and imprisonment, as well as banishing those who performed the ceremonies, upon pain of death if they returned. Principally, these laws were directed against Roman Catholics (the former act specifies 'Jesuits') and others who had been 'excluded' from their churches during the frequent changes in church governance during the period. The first would have applied to presbyterians; the second, to non-jurors and episcopalians following the abdication of James VII. However, according to later sources, the practice under these statutes was for the couple to appear before the magistrate of the burgh, who imposed a nominal fine and reserved the question whether they should be imprisoned. An extract from the court's records, confirming that they had been found guilty and sentenced, served as their marriage certificate.[71] This had the effect of introducing civil marriage by the back door.

This complicated state of affairs, in which so many different procedures might lead to marriage, was even further complicated by the religious conflicts of the seventeenth and eighteenth centuries. At various points during the sixteenth and seventeenth centuries, episcopacy, the government of the church by bishops, was abolished and reinstated in Scotland. The *Second Book of Discipline* (1578) specifies: 'As to bishoppis, gif [if] the name επίσκοπος [*episkopos*] be properlie takin, thay ar all ane [one] with ministeris . . . for it is not the name of superioritie and lordschip, bot of office and watching.'[72] Early in the Reformation there was an extended debate about the role of bishops.[73] James VI and Charles I used them as ecclesiastical administrators, and they were removed and then reinstated during the Wars of the Three Kingdoms and at the Restoration.[74] These changes in what was viewed as legitimate church government also confused what counted as a wedding, and therefore a regular marriage: during times of episcopacy, episcopally ordained clergy could perform weddings; during times without it, only presbyterian clergy could.[75] As long as the definition of regular marriages remained both narrow and changeable, it was important to provide for a backup, in the form of an irregular wedding, which remained legally binding on the couple despite the rapid changes in what was considered legal church government.

The 1698 statute described above was supposed to firm up the monopoly of the Church of Scotland on performing wedding ceremonies. A decade later, as a part of the treaty and acts of union in 1706/07,[76] the Scots insisted on the incorporation of the Act of Security, ensuring that presbyterian government be 'the only Government of the Church within the Kingdom of Scotland' and that this 'Establishment' be 'held and observed in all time comeing as a fundamental and essential condition of any Treaty . . . without any alteration thereof or derogation thereto in any sort for ever'.[77] Following the union of the parliaments, the Church of Scotland's monopoly on marriage was supposed to have continued.

Two events undermined the assurances provided in the treaty and acts. In *Greenshields* v. *Provost and Magistrates of Edinburgh*, a minister who had been ordained by the Bishop of Ross was imprisoned by the city government in Edinburgh for conducting services there according to the prayer book, without having been admitted to preach by the city. The House of Lords ordered his release.[78] The following year Parliament passed the Scottish Episcopalians Act 1711, which authorised such services. Both of these events undermined the presbyterian exclusivity guaranteed by the treaty and acts, at least where Scottish episcopalians were concerned. Although the judgments in *Greenshields* did not claim that the minister had performed weddings, the Scottish Episcopalians Act provided that episcopal clergy were also allowed to marry people, provided that they published banns as ministers in the Church of Scotland did.

This act, and its companion the Church Patronage (Scotland) Act 1711, incited a series of schisms in the Church of Scotland, in which first Ebenezer Erskine formed the Associate Presbytery (later the Associate Synod) in 1737 and Thomas Gillespie founded the Relief Presbytery in 1761.[79] The Associate Synod divided numerous times, first when its Antiburgher faction seceded because of objections to the Burgess Oath imposed following the 1745 rising. Thus, although legislation concerning Scotland in the seventeenth and eighteenth centuries attempted to establish a marriage monopoly for the established church, this monopoly quickly broke down, and wedding ceremonies could be performed by clergy of other, non-established denominations.[80] Although most people wanted to have a minister present at their wedding, by the mid-eighteenth century, those ministers could legally be from any of five denominations (the Scottish Episcopal Church, the Church of Scotland, the Associate Synod (Burghers), the Associate Synod (Antiburghers) and the Relief Church). And of course there were still other denominations, including Roman Catholics and Quakers, whose marriages remained *prima facie* illegal under the civil law but whose members could still enter into irregular marriages through an exchange of mutual promises.[81]

As with the practice of the average person in England, who had no reason to engage in legal action or lacked the resources to do so, it is difficult to tell how frequently people married outside the church(es). However, once again contemporary records are relevant. In 1730 the kirk session of North Leith minuted:

> The session considering that all the marriages which have happened in this parish since the current Year commenced are Clandestine, and that none have been duely proclaimed in the Church, were of the opinion that the best way to put a stop to such abounding Irregularities will be, by making application to thee Baillies of the Canongate or Justices of the Peace, for executing the law against such delinquents . . .[82]

These practices were bound to be more common in communities like North Leith, which was a port town with a constantly seafaring population and a garrison which quartered troops in private houses. Nevertheless, the frustration expressed in the kirk session's minute shows that the established church had lost control over marriage and sought help from the civil authority in enforcing its claim to legal dominance.

In addition to this wide variety of ways to marry, Scottish law and practice also included another important difference from that of England: legal divorce. The Westminster Confession of Faith

(1647), drafted by Puritan divines who intended it to apply in Scotland, England & Wales and Ireland, allows for divorce in cases of adultery and for remarriage by the innocent spouse, 'as if the offending party were dead'.[83] The confession goes on to say that in addition to adultery, divorce is warranted by 'such wilful desertion as can no way be remedied, by the Church or Civil Magistrate'.[84] Although the Westminster Confession was never adopted by the Church of England, it remains a standard of the Church of Scotland to the present day and sets out key elements of religious doctrine and church discipline.

Even before the Reformation was complete, the kirk session of St Andrews (and possibly others) had recognised divorce based upon adultery.[85] In 1573, the Scottish parliament passed an act 'concerning those that divert from others, being joined of before in lawful marriage', which authorised excommunication and divorce when one spouse had deserted the other for four years.[86] According to D. M. Walker, the complex procedure that led to divorce could actually be initiated after only one year, provided that the final decree entered no sooner than four years after the desertion. At the same time, those who were deterred by the complexity of the act's procedures probably separated without divorce, with consequent adulteries and invalid, bigamous marriages.[87] In 1600, James VI's parliament passed a law 'regarding the marriage of adulterous persons', which made all marriages void between people who had been guilty of adultery and whose adultery had been the grounds for divorce from a previous spouse.[88]

The existence of divorce in Scotland but not in England led to one of the problems with geographical jurisdiction mentioned above. If a divorce was recognised in Scotland but not in England, was any subsequent marriage bigamous under English but not Scottish law? In *R. v. Lolley* (1812), the court held that it was.[89] Lolley had travelled from his home in Liverpool to Scotland with his wife. There he committed adultery and his wife sued for divorce, which the Scottish court granted. He returned to England where he married Helen Hunter. The English court found that 'no sentence or Act of any foreign country or state could dissolve an English marriage ... for ground on which it was not liable to be dissolved ... in England'. Lolley's lawyer was Henry Brougham, a Scot who later became Lord

Chancellor. He had had twenty-three years to think about the bad result when he was confronted with *Warrender* v. *Warrender*, which he decided the other way.[90] Sir George Warrender, a Scottish baronet, married Anne Boscawen, the daughter of the 3rd Viscount Falmouth, in London in 1810. In 1819 they separated, and in 1834 he sued for divorce in Scotland. Warrender claimed adultery on the basis that she had formed an improper relationship with Luigi Rabitti, an Italian music master. She defended on a number of grounds, but the most important for our purposes was that the Scottish courts did not have power to dissolve an English marriage. Brougham criticised the earlier decision, but without directly overruling it he found that the Scottish courts had the power to dissolve a marriage contracted in England between Scottish domiciliaries, those whose normal place of residence was Scotland.[91] The cases can be distinguished based upon the residence of the parties; Lolley was English, and Warrender was Scottish. But the latter case involves a reasoning process that goes beyond that question.

Brougham takes it as a given that Christian marriage is different from other kinds of religious marriage: 'This cannot be put upon any rational ground, except our holding the infidel marriage to be something different from the Christian, and our also holding Christian marriage to be the same everywhere.'[92] But Lady Warrender had gone on to argue that indissolubility, as an essential component of the marriage, was determined by the law of the place where the marriage was celebrated (the *lex loci celebrationis*). In response, Brougham points out that such a rule would make it possible to divorce in England, if one had married in Scotland. In fact, Brougham concludes, it is the place of the parties' residence that determines their marital rights. Similar problems arise in federal systems like the United States, and they are dealt with in similar ways: we will return to these problems in Chapter 4.

The different Reformation that took place in Scotland led to differences in its marriage laws from those in England, most obviously in relation to divorce. At the same time, however, the divisiveness in church–state relations and the fragmentations inherent in Scottish Presbyterianism made it more difficult there than it was in England for the government to intervene and regulate, or even to standardise, marriage. When laws did apply, such as the efforts to re-establish the power of the state church between 1690 and 1707, they quickly became subject to abuse and led to unintended consequences. The weak state and the weak church in seventeenth- and eighteenth-century Scotland made it more difficult to achieve uniformity in the law of marriage there than in England.

Marriage in the North American colonies

The American historian David Hackett Fischer has traced four distinct sets of folkways, which can be traced from distinct regions in Britain to regions in the United States where British migration took place.[93] In New England, and particularly Massachusetts, migration came predominantly from eastern and western England. Immigrants to Virginia came from areas centred on Bristol and London. The Delaware valley was populated largely from Yorkshire and northern England, and the so-called 'backcountry' of the Appalachian Mountains, from western Pennsylvania and West Virginia to North Carolina and Georgia, was populated with immigrants from Northern Ireland, the Scottish lowlands and northern England. Religious cleavages defined these groups, but they carried other customs (including architecture, politics and diet) with them. Marriage customs varied in quite definite ways as well.

The Great Migration from England to Massachusetts took place from 1629 to 1640, during the period when Charles I (and his Archbishop of Canterbury, William Laud) were imposing high-church Anglican principles on Puritans.[94] The Puritans of New England believed that marriage was a covenant, not a religious ceremony, on the same terms later adopted by the English Parliament during the Commonwealth. In Virginia, where the settler population increased from 8,000 to 40,000 during the period of Sir William Berkeley's governorship from 1641 to 1676, the traditional five-step process of the Church of England was the standard. The Delaware valley, populated particularly by Quakers, adopted a communally based conception of marriage, condemning intermarriage with non-Quakers and requiring consultation with parents, the women's meeting and the men's meeting, as well as a brief waiting period before the union could be approved by the men's meeting. In the backcountry practices came from the Scottish borders and northern

Ireland; brides were either voluntarily or involuntarily abducted by the groom, the latter cases reminiscent of the abduction of Mary, Queen of Scots by James Hepburn described in the opening section of this chapter.

Even though the southern colonies nominally followed the traditional practices of the Church of England, that church notoriously failed to provide clergy in numbers sufficient to serve the people, at least in the early years of settlement. For that reason, in the south proper ceremonies did not become at all frequent until after 1750.[95] In addition, those colonies had to deal with the problem of slavery. Because the essential element of marriage was consent, slaves were incapable of entering into marriage, because their owners retained power to sell them and separate the two spouses. Indeed, in some cases a slave owner's permission for a couple to marry amounted to manumission.[96] Overall, as government control over people's lives diminished in newly settled colonies in North America because of their distance from more built-up areas, the prevalence of regular marriage also decreased.

Andrew Jackson, whose parents had emigrated from County Antrim and who grew up on the border between North and South Carolina, married Rachel Donelson Robards in 1791, believing that she was divorced when she had not been.[97] Her husband later obtained the divorce based on Robards's adulterous relationship with Jackson. Even though members of the Tennessee community in which they lived knew about the situation, they accepted the couple as married, because they also knew that Robards's first husband had been abusive. Even though Jackson was accused of bigamy in the 1828 presidential campaign, he became the seventh President of the United States. Local community approval could be more important than legal technicalities in the newly settled regions of the colonies and the early United States.

Eighteenth-century breakdown

When the English government introduced a tax on marriage certificates, it assumed that the demand for marriage was inelastic: that is, those who wanted to wed would do so even if the cost increased. That proved not to be the case. Instead, people found ways around the formal wedding ceremony, and over time clandestine marriage became the norm. Its frequency grew most dramatically after 1695, and by the 1740s it had become recognised as a social problem that needed to be solved.

Early clandestine marriage mills operated in peculiars, churches that were outside the jurisdiction of a bishop, notably St James Duke's Place, Holy Trinity Minories and St James-on-the-Wall, all in London.[98] Lawrence Stone offers an educated guess, based upon surviving parish registers, that these churches together conducted between 2,500 and 3,000 weddings a year, a number, he says, approximately equal to the non-clandestine, official weddings by all of the other churches in London.[99] These operations ceased when the tax was imposed on licences and certificates.[100] Rural clergy also participated in this evasion of the law, celebrating weddings for those from outside their own parish. In 1730 the Rev. Amos Sweetapple, the incumbent of the small parish of Fledborough in Nottinghamshire, was made a surrogate, authorised to sell common licences to marry without calling banns.[101] In effect, this amounted to permission to wed all comers, and while between 1712 and 1730 only eleven couples had wed in the parish, from 1730 to 1754 he married 490 couples, all but fifteen of whom came from outside the village.

Clandestine marriages were binding in common and ecclesiastical law but failed to comply with their formal requirements including calling banns. The form most common in the mid-eighteenth century was the so-called Fleet wedding, where the couple was married in a tavern near the Fleet prison in London.[102] Fleet weddings took place in one of approximately twenty taverns, ale-houses and coffee shops, many of which retained a minister of doubtful credentials—frequently one who had been imprisoned in the Fleet prison for debt. The proprietors of these taverns employed touts who recruited couples, and they made a handsome profit from the marriage feasts that followed the ceremony, which was documented with a certificate on unstamped, and therefore untaxed, paper. Rebecca Probert argues that the number of these marriages has been overestimated in the past, but she concludes that 'they accounted for less than half of marriages celebrated in London': still a substantial number.[103]

Demand for these services came from a variety of circumstances.

Most obvious of these was a desire to hide an illicit marriage that did not conform to the canonical requirements of consanguinity: for example, marriage to a close relative, such as a cousin, or to a niece or nephew.[104] Bigamists who had deserted a spouse but wished to remarry also would have wanted as little notice as possible to attend their wedding.[105] Religious nonconformity and a dislike of marriage in the established church led non-adherents to the Church of England to marry outside the normal process.[106] The largest group, however, which attracted the most attention, consisted of underage brides and grooms who wished to evade the disapproval of their parents and others in the community who might disapprove and put pressure on the couple to discourage them from marriage.[107]

Stephen Parker characterises the increased concern with clandestine marriage that led to Lord Hardwicke's Act in 1753 as a 'moral panic'; David Lemmings describes the parliamentary debate on the act as 'hysteria'.[108] Although these estimations of the level of anxiety towards the question may be overstatements, it seems clear that there was widespread concern about the lack of social control over marriage in England during the period. As we shall see in the next chapter, that concern led to an unprecedented level of government intervention, but even that intervention was limited in scope, including only England and Wales and excepting certain religious minorities: Quakers and Jews.

Conclusion

Marriage law evolved very differently in England and Scotland before the union of 1707. The Reformation in Scotland was a more distinctively Protestant Reformation than the one in England, and the English notion of marriage as a sacramental act and the English prohibition of divorce gave it an entirely different character there. By the eighteenth century geographical differences in the law made it possible for a person's marital status to be clear in one place but less clear in another.

For most political agents, changes in marriage law had more to do with the protection of property and succession than they did with religion or romantic love. These were the people who already had wealth or power. Since poor people had less property or status to protect, the law of marriage mattered less to them. Nevertheless, people who were not part of the established marriage system could find other ways of making their relationships work, ways that were normally recognised by the courts and other state bodies. The courts were willing to recognise Quaker marriages in the context of property disputes.

Churches were mostly passive in this process, acting on behalf of the political elites in pursuing their aims. Churches conducted wedding ceremonies, but legal restrictions on who could marry were largely political ones. In the next two chapters we will examine how limitations on who and how one could marry were both controlled by the state more than they were by the church, first by restricting the scope of choice radically with Lord Hardwicke's Act, but also by extending it so that religious intermarriage, something that the established church resisted, became politically possible.

Notes

1. Wilkie Collins, *No Name* (Auckland: Floating Press, [1862] 2009), p. 719.
2. J. J. Scarisbrick, *Henry VIII* (New Haven, CT: Yale University Press, [1968] 1997), chapters 1, 7; E. W. Ives, 'Henry VIII (1491–1547)', *Oxford Dictionary of National Biography* (Oxford: Oxford University Press, 2004; online edition, May 2009), http://www.oxforddnb.com/view/article/12955, last accessed 8 May 2013.
3. Diarmaid MacCulloch, *Thomas Cranmer: A Life* (New Haven, CT: Yale University Press, 1996), Appendix II.
4. Ecclesiastical Appeals Act 1532.
5. Gerald Bray (ed.), *Documents of the English Reformation* (Cambridge: James Clarke, 1994), p. 114.
6. Jenny Wormald, *Court, Kirk and Community: Scotland, 1470–1625* (London: Edward Arnold, 1981), ch. 7.
7. The Confession of Faith, A1560/8/3–4, RPS, http://www.rps.ac.uk/trans/A1560/8/3 and http://www.rps.ac.uk/trans/A1560/8/4 (last accessed 8 May 2013).
8. John Guy, *Queen of Scots: The True Life of Mary Stuart* (Boston: Houghton Mifflin, 2004); Julian Goodare, 'Mary (1542–1587)', *Oxford Dictionary of National Biography* (Oxford: Oxford University Press, 2004; online edition, May 2007), http://www.oxforddnb.com/view/article/18248 (last accessed 8 May 2013).
9. Elaine Finnie Greig, 'Stewart, Henry, Duke of Albany [Lord Darnley]

(1545/6–1567)', *Oxford Dictionary of National Biography* (Oxford: Oxford University Press, 2004; online edition, January 2008), http://www.oxforddnb.com/view/article/26473 (last accessed 9 May 2013).

10. James Melvill, *The Autobiography and Diary of James Melvill, with a Continuation of the Diary*, ed. R. Pitcairn (Edinburgh: Wodrow Society, 1842), p. 296.

11. Iain McLean, *Adam Smith, Radical and Egalitarian: An Interpretation for the Twenty-first Century* (Edinburgh: Edinburgh University Press, 2006).

12. Lawrence Stone, *The Family, Sex and Marriage in England, 1500–1800* (London: Weidenfeld & Nicolson, 1977), p. 30.

13. *The Book of Common Prayer* (London: Everyman's Library, [1662] 1999), p. 300.

14. Charlotte Brontë, *Jane Eyre* (Auckland: Floating Press, [1847] 2008), p. 601.

15. Eric Josef Carlson, *Marriage and the English Reformation* (Oxford: Blackwell, 1994), p. 130.

16. John Bossy, 'The Counter-Reformation and the People of Catholic Europe', *Past & Present* 47(1) (1970), p. 57, n. 20.

17. Marriage Contracts and Consanguinity Act 1540. See Stanford E. Lehmberg, *The Later Parliaments of Henry VIII, 1536–1547* (Cambridge: Cambridge University Press, 1977), p. 101. We are grateful to Diarmaid MacCulloch for pointing us to this reference. See also MacCulloch, *Thomas Cranmer*, pp. 272–4.

18. Retha M. Warnicke, 'Anne [Anne of Cleves] (1515–1557)', *Oxford Dictionary of National Biography* (Oxford: Oxford University Press, 2004), http://www.oxforddnb.com/view/article/558 (last accessed 9 May 2013).

19. The statute leaves open the question of what happens when an unconsummated marriage has been preceded by an unconsummated precontract.

20. Marriages (Precontract) Act 1548; Carlson, *Marriage and the English Reformation*, p. 82.

21. John Witte Jr, *From Sacrament to Contract: Marriage, Religion, and Law in the Western Tradition* (Louisville, KY: Westminster John Knox Press, 1997), p. 40. Consummation was one aspect of a particular type of irregular marriage in Scotland: the promise *per verba de futuro cum copula* (also known as *subsequente copula*). That way of proving a marriage was rarely used and was of uncertain force until 1917; it was abolished in 1939. *Report of the Departmental Committee Appointed to Enquire into the Law of Scotland Relating to the Constitution of Marriage* (1937), Cmd 5354, p. 11; Marriage (Scotland) Act 1939, § 5.

22. *The Constitution and Canons Ecclesiastical* (London: Society for Promoting Christian Knowledge, [1603] n.d., c. 1900), available online at http://openlibrary.org/books/OL24429973M/The_constitutions_ and_canons_ecclesiastical (last accessed 29 May 2013).

23. 'The Root and Branch Petition', in Samuel Rawson Gardiner (ed.), *The Constitutional Documents of the Puritan Revolution, 1625–1660*, 3rd ed. (Oxford: Clarendon Press, 1979).

24. 'Act of 4 January 1644/45', in C. H. Firth and R. S. Rait (eds), *Acts and Ordinances of the Interregnum* (Abingdon: Professional, [1911] 1982), vol. I, p. 599.

25. 'Act of 24 August 1653', in Firth and Rait, *Acts and Ordinances of the Interregnum*, vol. II, p. 715.

26. 'Act of 26 June 1657', in Firth and Rait, *Acts and Ordinances of the Interregnum*, vol. II, p. 1131.

27. 'Act of 4 January 1644/45' in, Firth and Rait, *Acts and Ordinances of the Interregnum*, vol. I, p. 599.

28. Bernard Capp, 'Bigamous Marriage in Early Modern England', *Historical Journal* 52(3) (2009), pp. 537–56.

29. John Towill Rutt (ed.), *Diary of Thomas Burton, Esq.* (London: Henry Colburn, 1828), vol. II, p. 67.

30. Ibid., p. 69.

31. See also Firth and Rait, *Acts and Ordinances of the Interregnum*, vol. II, p. 1139.

32. Christopher Durston, *The Family in the English Revolution* (Oxford: Basil Blackwell, 1989), ch. 4.

33. Reprinted in J. Raithby (ed.), *Statutes of the Realm* (1819), vol. 5, available online at http://www.british-history.ac.uk/report.aspx?compid=47281 (last accessed 9 May 2013).

34. Rebecca Probert, *Marriage Law and Practice in the Long Eighteenth Century: A Reassessment* (Cambridge: Cambridge University Press, 2009), p. 172.

35. For this history see *In re Marriage Cases* (2008) 43 Cal. 4th 757, 183 P. 3d 384.

36. California Family Code, §§ 300(a), 308.5. The latter section was approved by California voters in a referendum in 2000, in which it was known as Proposition 22.

37. See e.g. Verta Taylor, Katrina Kimport, Nella Van Dyke and Ellen Ann Andersen, 'Culture and Mobilization: Tactical Repertoires, Same-sex Weddings, and the Impact on Gay Activism', *American Sociological Review* 74(6) (2009), p. 870.

38. *Strauss v. Horton* (CA 2009) 46 Cal. 4th 364, 470, 207 P. 3d 48, 119.

39. R. B. Outhwaite, *Clandestine Marriage in England, 1500–1850* (London: Hambledon Press, 1995), pp. 14–15.

40. Stamps Act 1694.
41. Duties on Marriages etc. Act 1694, § 9.
42. Outhwaite, *Clandestine Marriage in England*, p. 15.
43. Marriage without Banns etc. Act 1695.
44. See for example Probert, *Marriage Law and Practice in the Long Eighteenth Century*, pp. 175–6.
45. Duties on Marriage Act, § 63. ('Quakers, Papists and Jews Cohabiting, to Pay, but Not to Make Their Marriages Good in Law': 'All persons called Quakers, or reputed as such, and all Papists or reputed Papists . . . and all Jews . . . who shall cohabit and live together as Man and Wife, shall and are hereby made lyable the several and respective Duties . . .')
46. Diarmaid MacCulloch, *A History of Christianity: The First Three Thousand Years* (London: Allen Lane, 2009), pp. 653, 792–3.
47. George Fox, *A Collection of Select and Christian Epistles* (London: T. Sowle, 1698), p. 217.
48. Edward H. Milligan, *Quaker Marriage* (Kendal: Quaker Tapestry Booklets, 1994), p. 9.
49. Ibid., pp. 16–17.
50. Craig W. Horle, *The Quakers and the English Legal System, 1660–1688* (Philadelphia: University of Pennsylvania Press, 1988), pp. 234–6.
51. Probert, *Marriage Law and Practice in the Long Eighteenth Century*, p. 234.
52. Ibid., ch. 3.
53. 'Dower' is the right of the wife to one-third of the property of her husband on his death. 'Curtesy' is the right of the husband of a wife who has borne children to occupy her land during his lifetime. J. H. Baker, *An Introduction to English Legal History*, 2nd ed. (London: Butterworths, 1979), pp. 229–30.
54. Lawrence Stone, *Road to Divorce: England, 1530–1987*, new ed. (Oxford: Oxford University Press, 1992), p. 69.
55. Probert, *Marriage Law and Practice in the Long Eighteenth Century*, p. 46 (emphasis in original).
56. 2 Hag Con 54, 161 ER 665.
57. Stone, *Road to Divorce*, p. 52. Probert disputes this claim: Probert, *Marriage Law and Practice in the Long Eighteenth Century*, ch. 3.
58. Divorce (Religious Marriages) Act 2002; see Maleiha Malik, *Minority Legal Orders in the UK: Minorities, Pluralism and the Law* (London: British Academy, 2012), p. 7.
59. Malik, *Minority Legal Orders in the UK*, p. 76.
60. Ibid., p. 85.
61. William Cobbett (ed.), *Cobbett's Parliamentary History* (London: T. C. Hansard, 1813), vol. 15, col. 18, available online at http://www2.

odl.ox.ac.uk/gsdl/cgi-bin/library?e=d-000-00---omodhiso6--00-0-0-0 prompt-10---4------0-1l--1-en-50---20-about---00001-001-1-1isoZz-885 9Zz-1-0&a=d&c=modhiso6&cl=CL1&d=modhiso06-aao (last accessed 9 May 2013).

62. Ibid., col. 28.

63. APS ii, p. 252, col. 22 (RPS, A1504/3/122), http://www.rps.ac.uk/mss/ A1504/3/122 (last accessed 9 May 2013). Terce is the right of the widow to the liferent of one-third of her husband's heritable estate if no other provision has been made for her. 'Terce', in Mairi Robinson (ed. in chief), *Concise Scots Dictionary* (Edinburgh: Scottish National Dictionary Association, 1985).

64. The presumption of marriage was rebuttable, upon clear determination and sentence that the marriage was not lawful.

65. *Report of the Departmental Committee Appointed to Enquire into the Law of Scotland Relating to the Constitution of Marriage* (1937), Cmd 5354, p. 12.

66. Rebecca Probert, *The Changing Legal Regulation of Cohabitation: From Fornicators to Family, 1600–2010* (Cambridge: Cambridge University Press, 2012), pp. 214–17.

67. D. M. Walker, *A Legal History of Scotland, vol. IV: The Seventeenth Century* (Edinburgh: W. Green/T. & T. Clark, 2001), p. 658.

68. D. M. Walker, *A Legal History of Scotland, vol. V: The Eighteenth Century* (Edinburgh: W. Green/T. & T. Clark, 2001), p. 655.

69. See, for example, *Crawford* v. *Harvie* (1732) Comm. Ct Decrees III.

70. Act against Clandestine and Unlawful Marriages, APS vii, p. 231, col. 246 (RPS, 1661/1/302), http://www.rps.ac.uk/trans/1661/1/302 (last accessed 10 May 2013); Act against Clandestine and Irregular Marriages, APS x, p. 149, col. 6 (RPS 1698/7/113, http://www.rps.ac.uk/trans/1698/7/113 (last accessed 10 May 2013). See also Act against Irregular Baptisms and Marriages, APS ix, p. 387, col. 15 (RPS, 1695/5/118, http://www.rps. ac.uk/trans/1695/5/118 (last accessed 10 May 2013).

71. *Report of the Royal Commission on the Laws of Marriage*, 1868 (C. (1st series) 4059), pp. xxi–xxii; Walker, *A Legal History of Scotland, vol. V*, p. 660.

72. James Kirk (ed.), *The Second Book of Discipline* (Edinburgh: Saint Andrew Press, 1980), p. 222. Etymologically, the *Second Book* is correct. The Greek roots of 'episkopos' do indeed denote 'overseer', which is the word used by Quakers among others.

73. Wormald, *Court, Kirk and Community*, pp. 131–2.

74. Rosalind Mitchison, *Lordship to Patronage: Scotland, 1603–1745* (Edinburgh: Edinburgh University Press, [1983] 1990), pp. 17–18; MacCulloch, *A History of Christianity*, pp. 652–3.

75. D. M. Walker, *A Legal History of Scotland, vol. III: The Sixteenth*

Century (Edinburgh: W. Green/T. & T. Clark, 2001), pp. 671–2 ('During those periods the clergy of the Church out of favour at the time were unauthorised but continued to preach, administer the sacraments and to marry adherents, but such marriages were clandestine and inorderly.'); see also Walker, *A Legal History of Scotland, vol. IV*, p. 659.

76. Act Ratifying and Approving the Treaty of Union of the Two Kingdoms of Scotland and England, RPS, 1706/10/257, http://www.rps.ac.uk/trans/1706/10/257 (last accessed 10 May 2013); An Act for a Union of the Two Kingdoms of England and Scotland.

77. Act for Securing the Protestant Religion and Presbyterian Church Government, incorporated into the Act Ratifying and Approving the Treaty of Union, following Article XXV. See Iain McLean and Alistair McMillan, *State of the Union: Unionism and the Alternatives in the United Kingdom since 1707* (Oxford: Oxford University Press, 2005), pp. 51–3.

78. (1710) Colles 427, 1 ER 356.

79. J. H. S. Burleigh, *A Church History of Scotland* (London: Oxford University Press, 1960), part 4, ch. 1.

80. Actually performing the weddings remained illegal, however, until the Marriage (Scotland) Act 1834 came into force.

81. Nevertheless, following marriage by a Roman Catholic priest, a couple would have been guilty of fornication in the sixteenth century. Walker, *A Legal History of Scotland, vol. III*, p. 671.

82. North Leith Kirk session records, 12 May 1730 (Scottish Records Office, CH2/621/8), quoted in James Scott Marshall, 'Irregular Marriage in Scotland as Reflected in the Kirk Session Records', *Scottish Church History Records* 37 (1972), p. 17.

83. *The Humble Advice of the Assembly of Divines, Now by Authority of Parliament Sitting at Westminster, Concerning a Confession of Faith, with the Quotations and Texts of Scripture annexed* (London: Company of Stationers, 1647), ch. 24, para. 5, available online at http://www.churchofscotland.org.uk/__data/assets/pdf_file/0011/650/westminster_confession.pdf (last accessed 29 May 2013).

84. 'The Civil Magistrate' is Presbyterian terminology for the government.

85. Walker, *A Legal History of Scotland, vol. III*, p. 679.

86. Divorce for Desertion Act 1573, RPS, A1573/4/2, http://www.rps.ac.uk/trans/A1573/4/2 (last accessed 10 May 2013).

87. Walker, *A Legal History of Scotland, vol. V*, p. 663.

88. RPS, 1600/11/42, http://www.rps.ac.uk/trans/1600/11/42 (last accessed 10 May 2013).

89. 1 Russ & Ry 237, 168 ER 779

90. (1835) 2 Cl. & Fin. 488, 6 ER 1239.

91. Lady Anne, by marrying Sir George, acquired his domicile for all legal purposes. The parties in *Lolley* were all English.
92. 2 Cl. & Fin. at 532, 6 ER 1255.
93. David Hackett Fischer, *Albion's Seed: Four British Folkways in America* (New York: Oxford University Press, 1989).
94. Virginia DeJohn Anderson, 'Migrants and Motives: Religion and the Settlement of New England, 1630–1640', *New England Quarterly* 58(3) (1985), pp. 339–83.
95. Nancy F. Cott, *Public Vows: A History of Marriage and the Nation* (Cambridge, MA: Harvard University Press, 2000), p. 31.
96. Ibid. p. 33.
97. Ibid. p. 36.
98. Stone, *Road to Divorce*, p. 106.
99. Ibid. p. 107.
100. R. L. Brown, 'The Rise and Fall of the Fleet Marriages', in R. B. Outhwaite (ed.), *Marriage and Society: Studies in the Social History of Marriage* (London: Europa, 1981), p. 119.
101. Ibid. p. 105; Outhwaite, *Clandestine Marriage in England*, p. 35.
102. Brown, 'The Rise and Fall of the Fleet Marriages', p. 117.
103. Probert, *Marriage Law and Practice in the Long Eighteenth Century*, p. 190.
104. Stone, *Road to Divorce*, p. 99.
105. Capp, 'Bigamous Marriage in Early Modern England', p. 553.
106. See e.g. Stephen Parker, *Informal Marriage, Cohabitation and the Law, 1750–1989* (Basingstoke: Macmillan, 1990), p. 23; see also Outhwaite, *Clandestine Marriage in England*, p. 35; Probert, *Marriage Law and Practice in the Long Eighteenth Century*, ch. 4.
107. John R. Gillis, *For Better, for Worse: British Marriages, 1600 to the Present* (New York: Oxford University Press, 1985), p. 96; Parker, *Informal Marriage, Cohabitation and the Law*, pp. 20ff.
108. Parker, *Informal Marriage, Cohabitation and the Law*, p. 36; David Lemmings, 'Marriage and Law in the Eighteenth Century: Hardwicke's Marriage Act of 1753', *Historical Journal* 39(2) (1996), pp. 339–60.

3

From Lord Hardwicke's Act to
Civil Marriage and Divorce

QUEEN OF THE FAIRIES.
You shall sit, if he sees reason,
Through the grouse and salmon season;

PEERS.
No!

QUEEN.
He shall end the cherished rights
You enjoy on Friday nights:

PEERS.
No!

QUEEN.
He shall prick that annual blister,
Marriage with deceased wife's sister:

PEERS.
Mercy!

W. S. Gilbert, *Iolanthe* (1883), Act I

Contract, status and state control

In an article written in the 1970s, long before the debate on same-sex marriage had begun, the American legal theorist and judge John Noonan argued that the earliest Roman Catholic thinkers emphasised choice in marriage: 'If one wanted to marry enough one could choose one's own mate and the Church would vindicate one's choice

. . . No restrictions were based upon race, color, servitude, illegitimacy, caste, or hereditary status.'[1] This kind of thinking is relevant to our study, because the marriage law of the early Roman Catholic Church, before the Council of Trent, applied to both England and Scotland following the Reformation in many respects.

Noonan emphasises the importance of individuals freely exercising the option to marry, unconstrained by irrelevant criteria, such as race or class. The question we have to ask in this chapter is whether choice is a part of the minimal uniform standard for marriage, and we will argue that it is. One way of thinking about the exercise of this kind of choice is to compare it to entering into a contract. Kant, for example, thought of marriage as a reciprocal contract for the use of the spouses' sexual organs; Hegel disagreed, arguing that it was a contract not to have contracts at all.[2] Both recognised the connection between marriage and contract, which is also reflected in the famous quote from William Blackstone that forms the epigraph to the Introduction.

In this chapter we trace the debates that led to two acts of Parliament, in 1753 and 1836, along with the cleavages that brought them about. In the eighteenth century, it was a debate about class, supported by those who had wealth and status to preserve; opposed by those who hoped to gain them by marriage. In the 1830s, the debate was also about class, but the element of religion was stronger, and it became stronger still when divorce was introduced in England in 1857. The failure to regulate marriage uniformly in the United Kingdom led to conflicts between nations' laws, which the courts and the legislature then had to solve.

Our first focus in this chapter is on Lord Hardwicke's Act (1753), which limited the choice that could be exercised by those under twenty-one, focusing on the status of marriage and limiting the freedom of underage parties to enter into it. The act made the Church of England the guarantor of those limits on freedom, by making it the only denomination that could celebrate a legal marriage (with certain notable exceptions, to be discussed below). This protection of marriage became necessary when those from lower classes used marriage-as-contract to change their social status. When a poor young man married a wealthy heiress, their combined choice of a partner modified both their statuses: his for better, hers for worse (the same could be true in reverse, if a young heir absconded with a servant). The law made it easier for people in the upper social and economic classes to practice endogamy (marriage among themselves), thereby preserving social and economic hierarchies, for once parents had a veto over their children's choice of a spouse, they could stop them from marrying 'unwisely', outside their social and economic class.

In addition, as MPs argued during the debates on the bill, it concentrated political power. Clergy, who were dependent upon the patronage of the upper classes, could discourage unwise marriages even if the couple were of age. In Jane Austen's novel *Pride and Prejudice*, Mr Collins exemplifies this dependency, making his own marriage plans contingent upon the approval of his patron, Lady Catherine de Bourgh, and then interfering in both Elizabeth Bennet's and her sisters' plans for marriage to ensure that their marriages were consistent with Lady Catherine's ideas. Members of the House of Lords controlled whom their daughters married and therefore also potential claimants to their titles, land and other property (and membership of the upper house of the legislature). And since peers also controlled a large proportion of the membership of the House of Commons before 1832 through patronage, this concentrated political power in their hands, or so it was argued.

The Marriage Act 1836, which we will also discuss, changed the underpinnings of English and Welsh marriage law. It introduced civil marriage and increased the number of ways of entering into marriage by making it possible to celebrate a wedding in Nonconformist churches, outside the Church of England. One of the prominent questions at the time of the Reform Act 1832, which increased the representative character of the House of Commons, was religious inequality, and one important aspect of that was the monopoly imposed by Lord Hardwicke's Act. Following passage of the Reform Act, the pro-reform Whig party attempted to regularise marriage law and introduce an early form of what is now called marriage equality. But despite the efforts of the bill's sponsor, Lord John Russell, the Church of England retained its own procedures for marrying couples, including calling banns. Nonconformist churches, unlike the Church of England, had to register their places of worship if they wished to celebrate weddings, and they had to conduct them in the presence of a civil registrar, because their clergy, or at least some of them, were seen as transient and therefore unreliable for maintaining accurate records that could be relied upon in law, a necessary component to the status aspect of the relationship.

These controls were not, however, imposed uniformly. First, two religious groups were not included: Lord Hardwicke's Act exempted Quakers and Jews, and that exemption remained under the 1836 act. As we saw in Chapter 2, Quakers had long objected to state control over marriage. In 1753 their Meeting for Sufferings successfully lobbied Parliament for an exemption, based among other things on their internal regulation of marriage and their careful record-keeping practices.[3] Jews, too, were permitted to regulate themselves according to their own law. According to one theory prevalent at the time, Jews were not citizens, and their marriages could only be subject to their own laws, not to the laws of nations.[4] Like Quakers, they practiced endogamy.

In addition to Quakers and Jews, it was also necessary to differentiate between the nations of Great Britain and later the United Kingdom. When England and Scotland ratified the Treaty of Union in 1707, one of the essential conditions to union was protection of religion in Scotland. Imposing standard government rules about marriage and, as we have seen, divorce on the Scottish Church, where the rules were very different, would have been objectionable and could have had implications for the union.[5] From before the Reformation marriage in Scotland had slightly different rights and duties (for example upon the death of a spouse) from marriage in England. But having different rules about marriage in different geographic regions of the country introduced complicated questions about how Scottish marriages would be treated in England, particularly when a couple eloped to Gretna Green to wed. Besides imposing uniform rules on England, Parliament also considered imposing such rules on Scotland too. These barriers stood in the way and prevented it from doing so. The draft bill concerning Scotland is also discussed below.

Lord Hardwicke's Act (1753)

Lawrence Stone has pointed out that individuals, including Lord Hardwicke himself, are important to changes in the British law of marriage. 'As usual in political history, the action of powerful personalities played a critical role in each lurch forward in law reform.'[6] 'Like many of his contemporaries, Hardwicke had married a well-connected widow, which furthered his legal career, and Lord Waldegrave describes him as 'undoubtedly an excellent Chancellor, [who] might have been thought a great man, had he been less avaricious, less proud, less unlike a Gentleman, and not so great a politician'.

During the 1740s, when judges were becoming increasingly impatient with clandestine marriages in the Fleet (discussed in Chapter 2), Hardwicke is supposed to have torn up a register of those marriages in open court, refusing to admit it as evidence because of its unreliability.[7] Different explanations are available for why Hardwicke's bill to regulate clandestine marriages passed in 1753, after many unsuccessful attempts in previous decades, but we think the key is in the story about the register. Stone attributes the act's success to Hardwicke himself, who 'personally master-minded its passage ... in the face of some fierce opposition, by the use of rhetoric, logic, cajolery, and behind-the-scenes threats, deals, and lobbying'.[8] Rebecca Probert argues that it was a better bill than had been previously attempted and emphasises the priority that raising revenue and foreign policy normally took on the policy agenda, which would have kept MPs occupied on matters other than marriage.[9] In addition, however, it is important to remember that judges dislike uncertainty, and Fleet marriages and their records had made the jobs of the judges extremely difficult: they had to evaluate the credibility of increasingly unreliable evidence. The records were subject to forgery, backdating and all manner of manipulation, sometimes for a price, to legitimate marriages that were performed without banns or a proper church wedding.[10] As an 'excellent Chancellor', Hardwicke had an interest in making the law more predictable for the parties and for himself, as a matter both of efficiency and of professional pride.

Besides imposing strict limits on the age when one could wed, Hardwicke's Act made promises *per verba de praesenti* and *de futuro cum copula* (discussed in the Scotland section of Chapter 2) unenforceable in England. Weddings that did not meet the legal standards for age or parental consent and for public recognition were void: the couple's children were illegitimate and no property rights changed hands. Advocates of the act argued that it was necessary because the contractual aspect of marriage, most evident in promises of these kinds, had made it possible for unscrupulous suitors to change their social, political and economic status by marrying rich heirs and heiresses. The nightmare of every peer was that his eldest son would marry a laundry maid.[11]

Introducing the bill, the Attorney General, Sir Dudley Ryder, said:

> When a young gentleman or lady happens to be born to a good fortune, they are so beset with selfish designing people, and so many arts made use of for engaging their affection, that their innocence often becomes a prey to the lowest and vilest seducer. How often have we known the heir of a good family seduced, and engaged in a clandestine marriage, perhaps with a common strumpet?[12]

In a later passage, Ryder acknowledged that the bill was not intended to make weddings more difficult 'among the vulgar . . . If it were possible, I confess a distinction should be made between the marriages of people of rank or fortune, and those of the people we usually call the vulgar, but this it is impossible to do in this country.'[13] Nevertheless, the bill did contain loopholes, including a clause that made it impossible to challenge a marriage on the ground that banns had been read and the wedding celebrated where neither party lived. A couple could flee to a growing city like Birmingham, where no one would recognise them, and could be married in a matter of weeks. Since better-off couples were married by licence rather than by banns, this relaxed the requirements for poorer classes, provided that a priest was willing to marry them.

Proponents of the bill also argued that marriage was not necessarily a religious institution: the state could properly regulate it. Before the Reformation, they claimed, the church had steadily increased the difficulty of wedding by, for example, expanding the degrees of relationship that were incestuous. Ryder argued that they did so in order to increase the pope's revenue from granting dispensations, not to guard against any social evil.[14] He claimed that the doctrine 'that a marriage once solemnised by a clergyman in holy orders is so sacred a contract that it cannot be disannulled by any human law' was not a Christian doctrine; rather, it was a product of Rome.[15] Thus, he thought it 'inconsistent with common sense' to claim 'that the supreme legislature of a society cannot put contracts of marriage, as well as every other contract, under what regulations they think most conducive to the good of that society'.[16] Viewed in this light, the role of the Church of England in solemnising marriage was primarily a state function, not a religious one. It was acting as an agent of the government, exercising social control and promoting social policy.

The principal resistance to Lord Hardwicke's bill came from those who had benefited from or hoped to benefit from more relaxed rules for weddings. Robert Nugent, MP for St Mawes and a client of Lord Chesterfield, led this opposition. Nugent had been born to a Roman Catholic family in Ireland, where he seduced his cousin and then fled to London to avoid marrying her.[17] His illegitimate son from that union ended up in the Fleet prison. Nugent's first wife was the sister of the 5th Earl of Fingall, in whose house he served as tutor. That wife died in childbirth. His second wife was another wealthy heiress, Anne Craggs, whose son by a previous marriage attempted to prevent his mother's union with Nugent until she settled £50,000 on him.

Nugent said in his speech on the bill:

> The other house [of Lords] had some reason, and some sort of right, to agree to [the bill], because they represent themselves and those of their own body only, and because, should the Bill be passed into a law, they will thereby gain a very considerable and a very particular advantage; for they will in great measure secure all the rich heiresses in the kingdom to their own body . . . As to the national interest, I think it is allowed, that to prevent the accumulation of wealth, and to disperse it as much as possible through the whole body of the people, is a maxim religiously observed in every well-regulated society.[18]

It seems highly likely that Nugent intended, and his audience appreciated, the double entendre implicit in the word 'body'. The House of Lords represents a hereditary class: 'those of their own body'. And they wanted to secure the rich heiresses both to the upper house and to those same bodies. Nor could anyone have missed the fact that Nugent's reference to a 'maxim religiously observed' is to a decidedly non-religious maxim, that wealth should be spread through the population at large rather than retained in one small part of it.

Nugent mentions religion in another context, relying on it to defend the power of the clergy to wed couples without regard for civil rules and regulations. He hopes that Ryder will excuse him when he calls the marriage contract sacred:

> I must beg leave to say, that in my opinion, if there can be a religious and sacred engagement amongst mortals, the marriage contract is such; and it is for the interest of mankind that it should be thought to be so.[19]

Again, though, nuance is important: *if there can be* such an engagement (it may not be possible); and it is for the interest of mankind *that it should be thought to be so* (not that it actually was).

Nugent's speech seems cynical at best, particularly given his own behaviour with the opposite sex. But it is a defence of class mobility of the kind that he had benefited from. Free marriage makes it possible to avoid an unhealthy concentration of power and wealth. Moreover, both sides in this debate agree that religion is malleable – it can be modified to suit the social objectives of limiting or increasing social mobility. And the connection between status and contract is clear but complex, as well. Being able to freely contract marriage, a status that brings with it the inheritance of wealth and power, can undermine the existing social order.

Henry Fox, MP for Windsor, was a political adversary of Hardwicke and a deist. He had eloped with and married Lady Caroline Lennox in a clandestine marriage against the will of the bride's parents, the Duke and Duchess of Richmond.[20] In the debate on third reading, he extended Nugent's political economy argument to constitutional proportions:

> To accumulate the whole wealth of a society into a few families, is inconsistent with the happiness of every society, and to throw it all into the hands of our nobility is inconsistent with our constitution in particular . . . It is the increase of their elective power [we fear]

... for a factious majority of the other House, having by means of their elective power, got a majority in this, will soon force the crown to put the whole military power of the kingdom into their hands.[21]

He continues, speculating that if the House of Commons reasserted itself following such an usurpation, the House of Lords would return 'the compliment we once paid to them [during the Commonwealth], of voting this House useless and dangerous, and therefore to be abolished'. Like Nugent, Fox argues that bad marriage policy can adversely affect the entire nation, not only by undermining the economic foundations of the state but by concentrating power, potentially including military power, in a hereditary aristocracy. He goes on to argue that clandestine marriages, which have been respected out of regard for 'the laws of God and nature', have nevertheless been a way of avoiding an otherwise bad policy, restrictive regulations on weddings, which will reduce the number of poor people's marriages.

In his speech, Nugent had argued that marriages of the working class, whom he calls 'the most useful, I will not scruple to say, the best sort ... the healthy, the strong, the laborious and the brave', were vital to 'the quality', deriving their 'riches and their splendour'.[22] Their marriages, with or without banns and parental approval, benefited the nobility rather than undermining them and should be encouraged. Nugent ridiculed the need for wisdom and foresight where matters of marriage were concerned, at least among these people, for, he argued, 'God Almighty has endued all animals, and mankind among the rest, with an ungovernable and irresistible passion, which leads them to the procreation of their species';[23] this passion, combined with love, results in marriage.

It is to these two passions, and not to the dictates of wisdom, that most of the marriages among the poor are owing ... but by this Bill I am afraid, that you will force the poor to take so long time to consider of what they are about, that many of them will get the better of their passions, pursue the dictates of wisdom, and prevent their repenting after, by repenting before marriage.[24]

In other words, the bill would provide such a disincentive that labouring people would not marry at all.

Nugent goes on to argue that making marriage as difficult as the bill seeks to do, given the strength of the procreative passion, will lead to the abortion or infanticide of illegitimate children, the need to set up public brothels in each parish, and increased homosexuality.[25] All of this comes from another political economy argument: that marriage among the poor helped to increase the amount of available labour, which was vital to the productive capacity of the country.[26] After the law had been enacted, William Blackstone wrote: 'Restraints upon marriage, especially among the lower class, are evidently detrimental to the public, by hindering the encrease [*sic*] of people; and to religion and morality, by encouraging licentiousness and debauchery among the single of both sexes; and thereby destroying one end of society and government, which is, *concubito prohibere vago* [to prohibit random intercourse].'[27]

All of these are arguments about the social consequences of marriage. According to the advocates of the bill, clandestine marriages disrupt the social order and existing social status by allowing too much choice. Opponents object to the remedy based upon what marriage accomplishes in society. If some means of entering into marriage create social evils, they should be limited. But if the solution will concentrate power, reduce the number of marriages among the working class, lead to a decrease in population, or to an increase in abortion or homosexuality, it should not be adopted. These arguments have little or nothing to do with religion from either side, pro or con. Indeed, religion is treated, somewhat cynically, by the opponents of the bill as a way of convincing poor people and women that marriage is desirable. God creates the passions that have to be channelled through marriage, not the institution of marriage itself. The class-based arguments here are forerunners to Adam Smith's conception of marriage, discussed in Chapter 1, which differentiates between the 'liberal, or . . . the loose system' applicable to the upper classes and the 'strict or austere' system applicable to others. Marriage has different purposes for different economic classes: fostering the transmission of wealth in one and the production of workers in the other.

Rebecca Probert has argued that Lord Hardwicke's Act was a

success, showing that most people complied with the rules and married in church after 1753, as indeed she claims that they had largely done before.[28] Nevertheless, problems did arise, the most prominent of which was the potential to use technical non-compliance with the act, which could result in a void marriage, for divorce.[29] In one case from 1805, a wife annulled a marriage of eighteen years and in the process rendered six children illegitimate; she had deliberately overstated her age by several weeks when she married, as she had been under twenty-one. Accordingly, a series of acts in 1822 and 1823 removed the nullity provision, so that underage marriages were no longer void.[30]

Popular discontent with the act is reflected in efforts at repeal, which began as early as the 1760s: one such bill is included in Lord Hardwicke's own papers.[31] That bill repeals his act, while at the same time imposing strict prohibitions against prison marriages and retaining the existing registration requirements, both more focused solutions to the public policy problem that were proposed in the debates in 1753. The biggest problem created by Hardwicke's Act, however, arose from the legal and geographical division between England and Scotland.

Marriage regulation in Scotland

The Scottish Marriage Bill

In Scotland, as in England, marriage was strongly connected to the maintenance of distinctions based on class, namely economic and political power.[32]

At the same time that Parliament was debating Lord Hardwicke's Act, efforts were also being made to regulate marriage in Scotland, where Hardwicke had less influence than in England. 'The awful Hardwicke was a busybody, ignorant of Scottish society, who would have liked to have a great deal to say in its management; but, whatever his influence in Whitehall, he was well-nigh powerless in Scotland.'[33] On 17 April 1753, while the English bill was before the House of Commons, Parliament ordered the Scottish judges to draft a bill for Scotland.[34] The bill was presented for first reading on 23 April 1755.[35]

The clauses in the bill mandate

- that underage marriages were void,
- that banns be read in the established church in the parish three times,
- that underage weddings that took place without the father's consent or without banns were void, and
- that those who wed or celebrated weddings without following the proper procedures would be punished.[36]

Specific provision is made for Scottish church government, allowing for the 'Meeting of the Elders' in a parish to authorise banns to be called. And the bill eliminated actions for breach of promise and so abolished the legal force of promises *per verba de praesenti* and *de futuro cum copula*. These are substantial departures from the existing Scottish law, which required no parental consent for marriage, established the legal age for marriage at twelve for girls and fourteen for boys, and recognised promises to marry, either *de praesenti* or *cum copula*, as binding.[37]

The preamble to the bill makes it clear that like the English act, it is concerned primarily with protecting class and property:

> The Laws and Regulations now in force in . . . Scotland against clandestine and irregular Marriages, and the seducing of persons into improper Marriages during their tender Years, have been found not sufficient to prevent the great Mischiefs and Inconveniencies arising from the same.

In correspondence with Charles Erskine (Lord Tinwald) of the Scottish Court of Session, Hardwicke expressed concern that the bill nullified all marriages without consent of the father, including those of the lower classes. Unlike the English bill, the Scottish bill makes marriages void *either* when the parents did not consent *or* when banns were not called. This eliminated the possibility of a marriage between two underage people, by banns, in a rapidly growing Scottish city, as was available to poor, young English couples. Thus, even though an underage marriage was not void in England if banns were called in Birmingham, it was void in Scotland even if they were called in Glasgow, if the father had not consented.[38] Hardwicke wrote:

If I rightly Comprehend it, it makes all Marriages of any Person under the Age of 21 years which shall be had without Consent of Parents, if living, or, if dead, of Curators, to be null and void to all intents and purposes. As this Clause extends to Persons of all Degrees, even the lowest, in that Part of the United Kingdom, it may possibly deserve a reconsideration Whether that Clause ought not to be in some measure limited.[39]

No such limit was ever imposed, because the bill never received a second reading. One reason comes from another letter from Hardwicke, who returned the bill to the Scottish judges and asked that they not send it back to him for several weeks:

If the Bill relating to Clandestine Marriages in Scotland should be proceeded upon this Session, a handle will be taken from thence to attempt alterations in that former Act [i.e. the English Clandestine Marriages Act], and a new Spirit and Flame endeavoured to be excited thereupon, which may be attended with Inconveniencies.[40]

Another act, relating to the naturalisation of Jews, had been passed in 1753 and then had to be repealed because of popular resentment.[41] Hardwicke seemingly feared a similar fate for his English act if its opponents were able to attack a Scottish measure on the same subject. In addition, the bill's failure was also related to Hardwicke's declining political power.[42] Henry Pelham, the Prime Minister, died in 1754, just days before the revised Scottish bill reached Hardwicke. The succeeding government had to defend itself against early reversals in the Seven Years War (known in the US as the French and Indian War). Little time was left for domestic affairs, particularly in Scotland.

To these two reasons must be added three more. First, as we have emphasised, Scotland was a religiously diverse nation, with different forms of Presbyterianism and an episcopal church that could perform weddings: references to the 'established church' in the bill could not have included the episcopalians. And among others, seceder Presbyterians held weddings outside the Church of Scotland, and their marriages were valid under the existing law.[43]

These seceders would be difficult to regulate, particularly as their theology emphasised their independence from the state even more than the established church did. In addition, seceders had political power. Less than a decade earlier the monarchy had enjoyed their support in the rising of 1745. Following its collapse the 4th Marquess of Lothian wrote to Ebenezer Erskine, one of their original number: 'The noble stand which the people of your profession have made for the religion and liberties of the country, must endear them to all true Christians.'[44] It would have been politically unwise to alienate such a substantial sector of the religious population in the 1750s. Finally, the ecclesiastical judge Sir William Wynne wrote that the bill had been blocked because 'by the Act of Union the state of religion [in Scotland was] not to be touched, [but] was to remain exactly as it was, and therefore there was a difficulty arising out of the Act of Union in applying the marriage act to that country'.[45] Imposing legal regulations on marriage in the Church of Scotland from the parliament in Westminster at this time would have been politically divisive and vulnerable to complicated constitutional arguments about the union itself.

All of these reasons reinforce one another. It seems entirely conceivable that Lord Hardwicke's concern with his political opponents was based on someone's explaining that while political economy arguments had prevailed in 1753, a Scottish bill would meet with much broader, constitutional ones. It is also unlikely that he had a very good understanding of church–state relationships in Scotland. He might also have realised that even if the bill succeeded in Westminster it would have been unenforceable in Scotland, because practice there differed so much from English practice. While the eighteenth-century Church of Scotland benefited from a legal privilege over other denominations, in reality it was much weaker than the Church of England. Passing the bill would have been politically hazardous and possibly pointless, given the fact that the Scottish state was a weak one, and the proposals were a radical departure from established practice. Hardwicke's abandonment of the Scottish bill makes a great deal of sense in historical context.

The failure of Lord Hardwicke's Act left the system as it was in Scotland, where the law recognised promises *per verba de praesenti*, one of which formed the basis for a famous case in the nineteenth century. In 1804 nineteen-year-old John Dalrymple, a cornet in His Majesty's Dragoon Guards, travelled to a new post in Edinburgh.[46] Dalrymple was the son of General William Dalrymple and the heir to the 6th Earl of Stair, to whose title he would succeed in 1821. In Edinburgh he met Johanna Gordon, the daughter of 'a gentleman in a respectable condition of life', who was in her twenties. In late May they signed a document stating that they were married, which was evidence of a promise *de praesenti* under Scottish law. They spent nights together and wrote to one another referring to themselves as husband and wife. Eventually, General Dalrymple found out about the liaison and packed John off to Malta. Before he left, John wrote to Johanna, asking her to keep their marriage a secret until he had inherited his fortune.

When he returned to England after his father had died, despite Johanna having cooperated up to this point, John Dalrymple married Lady Laura Manners. Johanna sued for a declaration that she was Dalrymple's wife. Dalrymple responded, claiming that he had been under duress when he signed the document: he was away from his regiment without leave, and he claimed Johanna had threatened to turn him in if he did not sign the document (a claim that was not credible given the amount of correspondence between them). He appealed to 'considerations that apply to the indiscretions of youth, to the habits of a military profession and to the ignorance of the law of Scotland, arising from a foreign birth and education'. But the judge would have none of it. He ordered Dalrymple to take Johanna into his home and to 'treat her with conjugal affection'. In spite of the order, the couple divorced in 1820. Lady Laura, whose marriage had been annulled by the court's judgment for Johanna, lived the rest of her life as a recluse at Hamworth Park with a parrot, her dogs and a female companion.[47]

This case shows the disadvantages inherent in a less formal marriage regime than the one imposed by Lord Hardwicke's Act. Johanna could not be certain of her status while John's father was living, although she undoubtedly took the risk, knowing that she might benefit from John's fortune. John, a son of a wealthy and influential family, first acted impulsively in marrying Johanna, and then assumed that he could act without regard for her wishes when he married Lady Laura.

Gretna Green weddings

The lack of regulation of weddings north of the Scottish border also had an impact on England akin to the impact of Scottish divorces discussed in the last chapter. The first case to reach Lord Hardwicke as a judge after passage of the English act involved the eighteen-year-old heir to 'a considerable estate', who had been seduced by a shopkeeper's wife's sister and had married her in Antwerp.[48] Lord Hardwicke was predictably irritable: 'As to such marriages (I was going to call it robbery), there is door open in the statute, as to marriages beyond seas, and in Scotland.' Because the young man in the case had been a ward of the court and had married without the court's permission, Hardwicke confined both the shopkeeper and the woman to the Fleet for several months, despite an outbreak of smallpox there. Antwerp was one of many places available to those who wanted to travel to escape Hardwicke's regulations. According to the *Gentleman's Magazine*, boats stood waiting at Southampton to carry runaways to Guernsey, where clandestine marriages were still legal.[49] And marriages on the continent were also common among the well-to-do.

Numerous Scottish villages just over the border, including Halidon Hill, Coldstream Bridge and Lamberton Toll Bar, provided marriages for those who could travel.[50] But the most famous of these was Gretna Green, located on the road from Carlisle to Glasgow (now the A74(M) motorway). Since promises *de praesenti* continued to be binding when Hardwicke's Scottish bill failed, reciting the words 'I take thee . . .' was sufficient to make a Scottish marriage that would be valid in England. Early on, these weddings were less common, but as roads improved in the late part of the 1700s, it became easier to cross the border, and the numbers increased. Lord Hardwicke anticipated this danger, as his papers contain a bill that would have imposed a thirty-day residency requirement before a Scottish marriage would be recognised under English law.[51]

Early on, questions were indirectly raised about whether these marriages would be recognised under English law at all, particularly when it could be shown that a couple had travelled to Scotland to evade it.[52] However, the question was supposedly settled in favour of recognition in *Brook* v. *Oliver* (1759) and *Bedford* v. *Varney* (1762).[53]

Nevertheless, judges found other ways of punishing English couples who married in Scotland. A particularly telling example is *Wade* v. *Scruton* (1837),[54] in which the seventeen-year-old heiress Anne Wade, a ward in chancery, was taken away by Charles Baseley through the assistance of her governess and servants. They wed at Gretna Green in May 1815 and again two months later, just to be sure, in the Episcopal church in Edinburgh. Initially Charles Baseley refused to appear before the court, and when he did Lord Eldon committed him to the Fleet prison, where he stayed until Anne reached the age of twenty-one. By that time they had three children. The settlement on Anne put her assets into a trust, with an allowance to Charles and a lump sum of £1,500 to pay off his debts from before the marriage. If she predeceased him, he was to have an income for life, but with that exception she retained the power to dispose of her property by will. If he had married her to get her money, he was only partially successful. Marrying a ward in chancery was not a sure way to obtaining her fortune.

Although they were popular among those who wanted to marry across economic, social or other boundaries, Gretna Green marriages were also popular among workers. John R. Gillis says: 'The principal clients of Gretna Green and other border marriage shops were not the few rich runaways enshrined in legend, but thousands of quite ordinary folk who, for a variety of reasons, wished a cheap, quick, and private union.'[55] Although hard figures are difficult to come by, the number of weddings supposedly taking place in Gretna Green from 1850 to 1855 averaged 747 per year.[56] This is an insignificant number compared to the total number of weddings in Scotland (19,680 in 1855).[57] And it is impossible to tell what proportion of the weddings were between Scots, as opposed to English couples. The notoriety of these marriages likely came from prominent ones, like that of Edward Gibbon Wakefield to the fifteen-year-old heiress Ellen Turner in 1826.[58] Wakefield took Turner from her boarding school by claiming her mother wanted to see her, then went to Gretna Green, married her and travelled on to Calais. They were caught, their marriage was annulled, and Wakefield went to prison. He later became active in colonial politics.

They may have been in decline before, but Gretna Green weddings were virtually eliminated in 1856 by a statute that became known as

Figure 3.1 An eloping couple are married in the smithy at Gretna Green
Source: Gretna Wedding, c. 1850 (Hulton Archive/Getty Images).

Lord Brougham's Act, which imposed a 21-day residence requirement before a Scottish wedding could take place that would be recognised by English law.[59] (Brougham had himself married an heiress
at Coldstream Bridge.) He had introduced bills on the subject since
1835, but it had now become urgent, as the advent of the railways
threatened to inundate Gretna Green with floods of clients from all
over England.[60] Brougham's Act effectively ended cross-border marriages in Gretna Green, at least for the time being.

However, the practice of irregular marriage between Scots and
some English couples slowly increased in the late nineteenth century
and once again gained currency in 1890 when a man named Mackie
purchased the smithy at Gretna Green, fitted up a room with an anvil
and started performing marriages there without scrupulous inquiry
into the residence of the people he was marrying.[61] Trade grew,
particularly during World War I when munitions factories were

built there. In 1935 Parliament appointed a committee to investigate, which recommended that all marriages by promise *de praesenti* be abolished, which happened in 1939.[62] The departmental committee heard testimony and reported that the availability of irregular marriages before the blacksmith had led to impulsive marriages and to couples who did not know for certain whether they were married or not, including a woman from Carlisle who had had a breakdown when she found out that her marriage to her husband, who had deserted her, was invalid.[63]

Gradually during the nineteenth and twentieth centuries, Parliament eliminated the anomalies in Scottish marriage law. In 1916, the procedure that had originally been a tax avoidance scheme was dropped, so that it was no longer possible to go to the sheriff, confess to a clandestine marriage, and use the evidence of conviction for the crime as a marriage certificate.[64] In 1929 the legal age for marriage was set for the first time for both Scotland and England at sixteen for both sexes.[65] Following the report by the government committee mentioned in the previous paragraph, civil marriage was regularised in Scotland, marriage by promise *de verba de praesenti* and *de futuro cum copula* were abolished, and Lord Brougham's Act was repealed.[66] The entire marriage regime was systematised in 1977, and this now governs the law of marriage there.[67]

Nevertheless, Gretna Green weddings enjoyed a resurgence in the late twentieth century, which continues to the present. In the 1970s, only a few hundred couples married there, but that number increased to over 5,000 in 2000: over one in six of the total weddings in Scotland.[68]

Civil and Nonconformist weddings (1836)

Quakers and Jews, as we have said, were exempted from Lord Hardwicke's Act.[69] Another group, the Unitarians, could not be exempted because they were not included in the Toleration Act 1689, which allowed Nonconformists to have their own places of worship, provided that they swore oaths of allegiance (and denied the truth of the Roman Catholic doctrine of transubstantiation, which eliminated Roman Catholics, as well). The Toleration Act extended only to Trinitarian Protestants, and Unitarians believe that Jesus is a teacher and prophet but not the son of God except in a metaphorical sense. In 1813 Parliament passed the Doctrine of the Trinity Act, which made Unitarianism legal. Once they had become a recognised religious group, the Unitarians began to campaign to be exempted from Lord Hardwicke's Act. The problem for them was that the Church of England's prayer book wedding ceremony included a blessing following the couple's vows: 'God the Father, God the Son, God the Holy Ghost, bless, preserve and keep you.'[70]

William Smith (MP for Norwich), who had sponsored the 1812 Unitarians bill, introduced a series of bills on the subject of marriage.[71] These would have permitted the Unitarians either to register their places of worship separately to conduct weddings or to have weddings in front of a justice of the peace. The first of these succeeded in the House of Commons but was thrown out in the Lords; the second advanced as far as committee in the House of Lords but died there when the session ended. One argument concerning the first bill, advanced by Alexander Robertson (MP for Grampound), went like this:

> He thought that the church of England was essential to the safety of the throne of England. Pull down the one, and the other could not stand. The safety of such establishments ought not to be endangered, in order to satisfy the scruples of a small minority of dissentients from the established church.[72]

No one had worried in 1753 about exempting a minority denomination like the Quakers from Lord Hardwicke's Act; however, unlike Quakers, Unitarians did not practice endogamy. Thus their intermarriage with those from other social classes could threaten the hierarchy in ways that Quakers did not. Besides, the emphasis on a 'small minority of dissentients' may reflect the growth of evangelicalism in England in the early 1800s.

In the debates on the second bill, Sir Robert Peel (then an opponent of Catholic emancipation, who would have seen the bill as the thin end of the wedge) distinguished Unitarians from Quakers and Jews. Peel did not worry about giving relief to sincere Unitarians, but he worried about imposters who professed Unitarianism solely to escape the requirements of Lord Hardwicke's Act:

The Jew and the Quaker could be easily discerned by their garb, and their manners. The moment they were seen they were known. They could not practise deceit with any hope of success. But, if a stolen match were intended between a Protestant and an Unitarian, for the purpose of securing a property, it would be difficult, from the garb or manner of either, to discover that any clandestine proceeding was contemplated.[73]

Peel returns to the tone from 1753, arguing for protection from intermarriage between young people who might marry those above or beneath them. Jews and Quakers are sufficiently recognisable, and their marriage practices protect other groups. But Unitarians might be able to lure wealthy children into improvident matches.

In the following decade, proposed exemptions from Church of England weddings were broadened to include all Nonconformists. Peel, who objected more to having Roman Catholics perform weddings on behalf of the state than he did to the weddings themselves, proposed that any denomination (other than the Church of England) might have marriage ceremonies, but only after there had been a civil ceremony before a justice of the peace.[74] This proposal was of course unacceptable to Nonconformists, who wanted religious marriage equality and objected to being relegated to second-class status. Intriguingly, Peel's bill eliminated banns for all ceremonies. Banns, he argued, were no longer suited to a society where different people attended different churches on Sunday; indeed, most clandestine marriages took place after banns had been read.[75] Peel's bill was not well received by Nonconformists, and it died a month after it was introduced, when his ministry fell.

A more successful precursor to the English Marriages Act was one that granted religious marriage equality in Scotland. From the time of the Stuart Restoration (and before), it had been illegal for clergy of the non-established church to perform wedding ceremonies there.[76] A bill was introduced in 1834 which repealed the prohibitions on Roman Catholic priests conducting wedding ceremonies, which was amended to include all clergy of non-established churches.[77] The bill was justified based upon the facts that a Roman Catholic priest had actually been prosecuted in 1815 for conducting an illegal marriage and that the state of the law, recognising promises *de praesenti*, encouraged irregular marriages and immoral behaviour among Roman Catholics and others:

> [Sir George Murray] was asking for something to enable the Roman Catholics to do properly what they could not now do in a country where marriages were contracted so loosely – in a country where persons might write to one another, proposing marriage, and then go to bed; after which, such a mode of matrimony would be considered valid in the eye of the law.[78]

The phrase 'write to one another' refers here not to correspondence but to so-called 'marriage lines', a writing which was not formally required but which made the marriage easier to prove in court if necessary. The bill's sponsor, Murray (a Tory supporter of Roman Catholic civil rights), argued for access to religious marriage for Roman Catholics, to whom it had been denied, so that they could act like responsible members of society.

Lord John Russell's bill

The debate on Lord John Russell's bill to permit Nonconformist weddings in 1836 began with his description of the proper interest of government in weddings and marriage:

> [Russell] thought that the law regarding marriages was a law which had been justly described as creating great confusion between things regarded by the State as important for the well government of the country, and for the due succession of property, and things which were mere matters of conscience. It was of importance that the State should have a certain degree of security in order to prevent marriages being clandestinely performed between persons able to enter into a contract of the kind, and also that the contract should, after certain circumstances had been fulfilled, be considered as finally closed; and that the relative position in which the parties stood to each other should be perfectly understood.[79]

Russell returns to a focus on the contractual aspect of marriage. But here it is opposed to conscience; the status that goes with it is assumed. Room must be made for those who wished to wed in a religious way different from the rites offered by the Church of England. The state's interest was limited to matters that had to do with clandestinity (which could allow for opportunism and therefore a lack of real consent) and certainty, so that the relative status of the couple was understood by them and society at large.

The bill proposed to introduce two new ways to wed, outside the Church of England: through a celebration in a Nonconformist church, including a Roman Catholic one, provided that a civil registrar was present; and through a wedding in a register office, with no religious element at all. The new machinery of the poor law was used to provide personnel for registering the marriages, along with the births and deaths that they were already being required to register under the new act. In addition, the buildings had to be specially registered to conduct weddings, just as they were to conduct other Nonconformist religious services. Quakers and Jews were exempted, so that they did not have to register their buildings, although they were required to comply with the notice and registration process other Nonconformists had to abide by, submitting their registration books to the district registrar on a periodic basis.

The bill was introduced on 12 February and received its second reading on 15 April.[80] Following some skirmishing concerning whether Nonconformists should have to swear that they had scruples about being wed in the established church (they would not), the bill passed on third reading and went on to the House of Lords, which was a dangerous place given the history of the previous marriage bills. Henry Phillpotts, the Bishop of Exeter, led the opposition. Phillpotts is satirised as Archdeacon Grantly's second son Henry in Anthony Trollope's novel *Barchester Towers*. He enjoyed pamphleteering, litigation and making speeches in the House of Lords.[81] He signed more protests against bills successful in the House of Lords than any other nineteenth-century bishop and all but two peers.[82]

Phillpotts objected that members of the Church of England would be tempted into civil marriage 'without uttering a syllable as to the nature of the contract, beyond that they desired to live together as man and wife. They would not even be obliged to say that it was a contract for life.'[83] He proposed an amendment that would have remedied these defects by making the marriage vows to be used in civil ceremonies religious ones.[84] Lord Melbourne, the Prime Minister, explained that the entire purpose of the bill was to meet the demand of those who believed that marriage was a civil contract only: 'The declaration was simply to inform the State what marriages were contracted, and by whom, without reference to any religious ceremony.' Indeed, he objected that Phillpotts's proposal was likely to be fatal to the bill. Supported by the Archbishop of Canterbury, Phillpotts pressed the amendment to a division, which he won 19–15, with two archbishops and six bishops voting in the majority. Had they not voted consistently with their vested interests, they would have lost and the bill would have been successful. Nevertheless, Melbourne won reconsideration of the amendment the following week, and it was removed on a vote of 72 to 29.[85] The Lords did, however, restore the ability of Church of England clergy to call banns before marriage.

Civil weddings

The procedure of going through a civil wedding in the early nineteenth century was an unpleasant one.[86] One of the couple was required to submit a notice to the superintendent registrar, and the notices were read out at meetings of the poor law guardians, who formed part of the larger machinery introduced in 1834 to provide accurate statistics on births and deaths. They contributed to an overall programme to standardise administration of the poor rates and unify local government – including by building work-houses. The guardians undertook an inquiry to ensure that there were no impediments to the marriage. In addition, however, they were supposed to avoid spending excess money on relief. Thus, they had an incentive to forbid marriages either when the couple were likely to have children who would be a burden on the district or when one of the spouses might add to the expense of relief in the district.

The superintendent registrar was also normally clerk of the guardians, a person appointed through patronage, with a reputation for low character and conduct. They discouraged civil marriages, as they were not compensated for them. And the register office itself was a room in the poor-house. All of these circumstances were designed by the House of Lords to discourage civil marriages.

Many have emphasised the small number of overall civil marriages

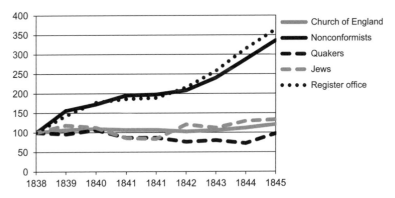

Figure 3.2 Normalised number of marriages 1838–45 (1838=100)

Source: Registrar General [of England and Wales], *Eighth Annual Report*, P.P. (1847–48) vol. 25, p. 28 (967). The year 1841 is included twice because the dates for the reports changed in that year from ending 30 June to ending 31 December. Both figures are annual.

that took place when they were first introduced in 1836. However, they have focused on the absolute number of these marriages, not on the increase in their frequency. It is useful instead to normalise the number of marriages performed, with the 1838 figures being 100 for all denominations, irrespective of the actual number of marriages that took place, and measure their rate of increase from that benchmark. Seen this way, civil marriages increased from 1838 to 1845 by two and a half times, more than any other kind of marriage (see Figure 3.2), although Nonconformist marriages increased nearly as much. This shows that when these kinds of marriage were introduced there was substantial demand for them.

Nevertheless, there were substantial regional differences, which were based upon local customs. A higher incidence of civil marriage tended to occur in districts with a town with a strong radical party, either of the old 'country' sort (Ipswich, Colchester, Norwich) or of the newer, manufacturing-town, class-conscious variety (Burnley, Keighley, Haslingden).[87] The old 'country' radical party from East Anglia had been the seed-bed of resistance to authority from the time of the Peasant's Rebellion (1381) through to the English Civil War and was a source of the great Puritan migration to New England in 1629–40, where place names such as Groton, Lynn and Newton reflect the origins of their inhabitants.[88] Olive Anderson concludes that despite the substantial obstacles, civil marriage became a form of protest. Some of the disadvantages to civil marriage were removed in 1856, when notice ceased to be read at the meeting of the poor law guardians, and in 1898, when registrars were no longer be required to be present at Nonconformist weddings.[89] The simplification of civil weddings in 1856 coincided with Lord Brougham's Scottish residency requirement, discussed above, and the effects were complementary. In Berwick-on-Tweed there were only four register office weddings in 1856, but in 1857 there were fifty-three.

The English and Welsh law of marriage was consolidated into a single act in 1949, which was a product of the Labour government's effort to clean up unwieldy areas in the statute book.[90] Along with a number of nineteenth-century statutes, the act clarified the situation concerning incestuous marriage. During the late nineteenth and early twentieth centuries, one of the annual entertainments in the House of Lords was blocking any effort at making it legal for a widower to marry his late wife's sister. Marriages of this kind were forbidden in 1835 but had been an 'annual blister' from that time and were the object of levity for Gilbert and Sullivan, as shown in the epigraph to this chapter.[91] In 1907 the Liberal government was finally able to pass legislation that permitted such marriages. However, because of objections to the law by clergy in the Church of England, they were exempted from its operation and were permitted to refuse to marry these couples. The act said:

> No clergyman in Holy Orders shall be liable to any suit, penalty or censure, whether civil or ecclesiastical, for anything done or omitted to be done by him in the performance of the duties of his office, to which suit, penalty or censure he would not have been liable if this Act had not been passed.[92]

This clumsy language seems to mean that clergy of the Church of England could ignore the act without being punished; in reality, it means that clergy did not need to marry a man to his deceased wife's sister.[93] One unfortunate clergyman learned this the hard way. Among his parishioners was a man married to his deceased wife's sister; the minister refused the man communion and argued that in the absence of the act he could have done so to a 'notorious evil liver' (that is, one who entered into such a marriage). He spent a great deal of money and continued to fight even after he retired, but he was never vindicated. Although he did not have to marry them, in other respects he had to treat them like any other couple, according to the law. The opening sections of the 1949 Act define who cannot be married because of their relation by blood or marriage, and who can (including deceased wife's sisters).

Divorce

Before 1857 it was possible to divorce in England and Wales, but it was not easy. Divorce as we know it (known as divorce *a vinculo matrimonii* – 'from the chains of marriage'), which released a spouse from all marital obligations, was only possible through three separate actions: one for separation in the ecclesiastical courts; a second for 'criminal conversation' by the husband against his wife and a third party, with whom she was supposedly having an affair; and third, a private divorce bill in the House of Lords for the actual divorce.[94] The second action made it necessary for the husband to divorce his wife in nearly all cases, as no action existed for a wife against her husband and his mistress. Other forms of dissolution were also available, although none carried with it the right to remarry. These included divorce from bed and board (*a mensa et thoro*) and private separation agreements, which allocated property and support between the spouses but which were of doubtful enforceability.[95]

The Matrimonial Causes Act 1857, which simplified the procedure for divorce, was a profoundly conservative statute. It began its life as a judicial reform law, intended to abolish the ecclesiastical courts' jurisdiction over divorce and marriage law by establishing a central divorce court in London unattached to the church. This it accomplished. In addition, it allowed men to divorce their wives based upon adultery; women could divorce their husbands but the adultery had to be accompanied by aggravated circumstances: incest, bigamy or cruelty (narrowly defined to include conduct that posed a threat of bodily harm).[96] In addition, the bill was intended to make divorce less costly (reducing it from as much as £5,000 (£350,000 in today's money) to £40–£60 (£2,800–£4,200) and easier, and thus available to the upper-middle classes. But because a centrally located court was less accessible than the ecclesiastical courts, the difficulty of obtaining a divorce actually increased. The bill also made judicial separation (*a mensa et thoro*) without divorce more expensive and therefore rarer, and kept both judicial separation and divorce inaccessible to the lower-middle class and the poor.[97]

Supporters of the bill included those who advocated women's rights, including one group led by Lord Brougham. Opponents ranged from pious Christians, who believed that marriage was a life-long commitment, and married women who feared that easier divorce would enable husbands to leave their wives when they became tired of them. Among the proposals the bill failed to accomplish was recognition that married women could hold their own property. At the same time, it allowed women who had been deserted by their husbands to apply to a magistrate for an order protecting their property; this was the only measure in the bill that affected those of the lower classes.[98]

The bill is the first that we have examined to be argued on strongly religious grounds. Gladstone, one of its strongest opponents, who later referred to it as one of three 'actual misdeeds of the legislature', argued:

> It is a matter of the deepest consequence to take care that in our legislation with respect to matrimony we do not offer profanation to that religion [Christianity] by making its sacred rites – designated by apostles themselves with the very highest appellations – the mere creatures of our will, like some turnpike trust or board of health, which we can make to-day and unmake to-morrow.[99]

Indeed, in this same speech he even flirted briefly with the idea of offering divorce for civil but not religious marriages, and in committee he proposed an amendment that would have allowed remarriage of divorced persons only in the register office.[100]

In response to Gladstone's proposal, the government offered a compromise. Clergy of the Church of England were allowed an exemption from remarrying divorced persons, which persists to the present day. Section 57 of the act reads:

No clergyman in Holy Orders of the United Church of England and Ireland shall be compelled to solemnise the Marriage of any Person whose former Marriage may have been dissolved on the ground of his or her Adultery, or shall be liable to any Suit, Penalty, or Censure for solemnizing or refusing to solemnize the Marriage of any such Person.

The act also ensures that people otherwise qualified would be permitted to marry in their parish church with another clergyman officiating.

The inequality between men and women in the divorce act remained the law in England and Wales until 1937.[101] In that year, A. P. Herbert (Independent MP for Oxford University) sponsored legislation that made the grounds for divorce the same for men and women and expanded them to include desertion for three years and cruelty (defined more leniently than in 1857). The act preserved the exemption for Church of England clergy, broadening it to include all divorced persons, not just those divorced for adultery. The final comprehensive change to the divorce laws came in 1973, when the Matrimonial Causes Act made 'irretrievable breakdown' of the marriage the sole basis for divorce. Irretrievable breakdown can be proven through adultery, desertion (two years), separation (two years if both parties consent, otherwise five years), or most commonly 'that the respondent has behaved in such a way that the petitioner cannot reasonably be expected to live with the respondent'.[102]

Conclusion

When marriage is heavily regulated, as it was in England from 1753 to 1836, two problems arise. First, individuals find a way to evade the regulations entirely. Some went to Gretna Green to be married; others went to large parishes in Birmingham, where no one would hear the banns being called or know who the couple were if they did. When divorce was allowed in Scotland but not in England, Lolley and his wife travelled from Liverpool to Edinburgh to divorce. In addition, the more comprehensive the regulation, the more necessary it is to limit its operation. While it was possible to regulate marriage strictly in England, the government lacked the power (particularly in the

1700s) to impose those rules in Scotland and on small but powerful groups like the Quakers and Jews. The best explanation for allowing exemptions like these is not a principled one about religious equality, although those arguments may have been made at the time. Rather, it is about the scope of government power. The costs of imposing the rules on Scots, Quakers and Jews were too great to justify any benefits that might have been gained.

The regulations themselves can also be manipulated, used for purposes they were not intended for. From 1753 to 1822 marriages that violated the regulations imposed by Lord Hardwicke's Act were void. But that led to divorce by agreement. No couple had a reason to bring an underage marriage to the attention of the authorities, once it had been celebrated, unless the marriage broke down. Effectively, couples could build in an option to divorce by marrying when one or both of them were younger than twenty-one (or could figure out later that they had been). But the results could also be devastating to their children.

Both evasion and manipulation undermine the authority and legitimacy of the state. Even if only a few hundred couples went to Gretna Green to evade English marriage law, once a prominent scoundrel like Edward Gibbon Wakefield gained notoriety, the rule of law was undermined.

By adjusting itself to widespread social practice, including divorce, the law moves toward an increasingly accommodationist position, adapting to the real practices of individuals and groups, so that threats to its rule are less serious. The Church of England, acting on behalf of the state, enforced existing social structures in the late 1700s and early 1800s, but as fewer people conformed, it became less viable as a way of regulating marital behaviour. Once regular marriage in Scotland became possible outside the Kirk in 1834, irregular marriages became virtually non-existent. Neither the Marriage Act 1836 nor the Matrimonial Causes Act 1857 achieved economic, social, religious or gender equality in marriage, but they began to frame questions in ways that might make such equality possible. This way of framing the questions is a liberal one, which presupposes that policies will be justified to non-Anglicans and even to people outside England, which was impossible in 1753.

During the 1700s and 1800s marriage was increasingly defined in 'thinner' ways that relied only upon the public reasons that could be agreed upon by all relevant groups, within, if not outside, the affected group. If marriage were 'thick', for example an exclusively Anglican rite, then non-Anglicans would do something else, and indeed that was what Sir Robert Peel proposed in his bill making all non-Anglican marriage civil marriage. But the proposal was unrealistic, because Unitarians, Baptists and Roman Catholics all considered their marriages to be just as religious as those conducted in the Church of England, and they did not want a kind of second-class marriage. A fudge was necessary from 1836 to 1898, when civil registrars had to be present at non-Anglican weddings, and the fudge continues into the present in England, in so far as Church of England clergy are the only ministers of religion who are permitted to call banns. But those are fudges, and nothing more.

More than the marriage ceremony changed. Lord Hardwicke's Act was intended to limit the choices available to young people, to discourage inter-class marriages. Bishops were concerned in 1836 that Anglicans might marry Unitarians. And the argument was even made at that time that members of the Church of England might be tempted to marry in a civil ceremony: that kind of wedding was seen as leading to a different kind of marriage, of less social value than a wedding in the Church of England. Even bigger changes were involved when divorce was introduced in 1857 and, fifty years later, a man was permitted to marry his deceased wife's sister. Victorian conceptions of marriage as a life-long union and the need for a strong prohibition in order to avoid temptations brought on by an attractive sister-in-law were both abandoned. These are changes in the underlying principles of marriage, not just in the way that one entered into the relationship.

All this returns us to the question of status and contract introduced at the beginning of this chapter. Contract is the aspect of marriage that concerns only the couple. The economic and class structure imposed upon spouses in the 1700s is now a thing of the past. Whom one marries has become a question of contract, and it is solely a matter of choice. Religious traditions may impose limits on that choice, for example, by requiring that a member of a faith group marry only another member of that faith group (like the endogamy practiced in the 1700s by Quakers and Jews). But that limitation is a question of religious status, and no longer of civil law. In the next chapter we will examine the laws in other countries that differ in what they regulate, how they regulate it, and why.

Notes

1. John T. Noonan, 'Marriage in the Middle Ages: Power to Choose', *Viator* 4 (1973), p. 430.
2. Immanuel Kant, *Metaphysics of Morals*, tr. Mary Gregor (Cambridge: Cambridge University Press, 1996), 6:277; G. W. F. Hegel, *Philosophy of Right*, tr. T. M. Knox (Oxford: Clarendon Press, 1942), § 163.
3. Edward H. Milligan, *Quaker Marriage* (Kendal: Quaker Tapestry Booklets, 1994), pp. 16–17.
4. See debate on the Dissenters' Marriage Bill, Parl. Debs (1827), vol. 17, c. 1412 (26 June 1827); *R.* v. *Millis* (1833–4) 10 Cl & Fin 534 at 864, 8 ER 844 at 966 ('[Jews] are treated . . . as a distinct people, governed, as to this subject [of marriage] by their own religious observances and institutions . . .').
5. See *Middleton* v. *Janverin* (1802) 2 Hag. Con. 436, 161 ER 797.
6. Lawrence Stone, *Road to Divorce: England, 1530–1987*, new ed. (Oxford: Oxford University Press, 1992), p. 20.
7. Ibid., p. 115–16.
8. Ibid. p. 122.
9. Rebecca Probert, *Marriage Law and Practice in the Long Eighteenth Century: A Reassessment* (Cambridge: Cambridge University Press, 2009), pp. 219–20.
10. R. B. Outhwaite, *Clandestine Marriage in England, 1500–1850* (London: Hambledon Press, 1995), pp. 29, 47; Roger Lee Brown, 'The Rise and Fall of the Fleet Marriages', in R. B. Outhwaite (ed.), *Marriage and Society: Studies in the Social History of Marriage* (London: Europa, 1981).
11. See generally, David Lemmings, 'Marriage and the Law in the Eighteenth Century: Hardwicke's Marriage Act of 1753', *Historical Journal* 39(2) (1996), pp. 339–60.
12. William Cobbett (ed.), *Cobbett's Parliamentary History* (London: T. C. Hansard, 1813), vol. 15, cols 2–3.
13. Ibid., col. 11.
14. Ibid., col. 8.
15. Ibid., col. 9.
16. Ibid., col. 6.
17. Patrick Woodland, 'Nugent, Robert Craggs, Earl Nugent (1709–1788)', *Oxford Dictionary of National Biography* (Oxford: Oxford University

Press, 2004; online ed., January 2008), http://www.oxforddnb.com/view/article/20399 (last accessed 10 May 2013).

18. Cobbett, *Cobbett's Parliamentary History*, vol. 15, cols 14–15.
19. Ibid., col. 13.
20. Peter Luff, 'Fox, (Georgiana) Caroline [Lady (Georgiana) Caroline Lennox], suo jure Baroness Holland of Holland (1723–1774)', *Oxford Dictionary of National Biography* (Oxford: Oxford University Press, 2004), http://www.oxforddnb.com/view/article/48888 (last accessed 10 May 2013). See also Peter Luff, 'Fox, Henry, first Baron Holland of Foxley (1705–1774)', *Oxford Dictionary of National Biography* (Oxford: Oxford University Press, 2004; online ed., Oct 2005), http://www.oxforddnb.com/view/article/10033 (last accessed 10 May 2013).
21. Cobbett, *Cobbett's Parliamentary History*, vol. 15, cols 68–9.
22. Ibid. col. 17.
23. Ibid.
24. Ibid.
25. Ibid., col. 20 ('I tremble to think of, I disdain to name the nasty, the abominable crime, which this bill may be the cause of rendering as frequent in this country as it is in too many others.')
26. E. Tavor Bannet, 'The Marriage Act of 1753: "A Most Cruel Law for the Fair Sex"', *Eighteenth Century Studies* 30(3) (1997), p. 235.
27. William Blackstone, *Commentaries on the Laws of England* (University of Chicago Press, [1765] 1979), vol. 1, p. 426.
28. Probert, *Marriage Law and Practice in the Long Eighteenth Century*, ch. 7.
29. Stone, *Road to Divorce*, p. 132.
30. Lemmings, 'Marriage and the Law in the Eighteenth Century', p. 360. Marriage Act 1822; Clandestine Marriages Act 1823; Marriage Act 1823.
31. Hardwicke Papers, BL Add. Mss. 35880, f. 110.
32. Deborah A. Symonds, 'Death, Birth and Marriage in Early Modern Scotland', in Elizabeth Foyster and Christopher A. Whatley (eds), *A History of Everyday Life in Scotland, 1600–1800* (Edinburgh: Edinburgh University Press, 2010), p. 95.
33. Quoted in Brian Dempsey, 'The Marriage (Scotland) Bill 1755', in Hector L. MacQueen (ed.), *Miscellany Six* (Edinburgh: Stair Society, 2009), p. 87 n. 96.
34. Ibid., p. 86.
35. Ibid., p. 91.
36. A Bill Entitled, An Act for the Better Preventing of Clandestine Marriages in that Part of Great Britain called Scotland, Hardwicke Papers, British Library, Add. Mss. 35880, ff. 84–91; see also House of Lords Sessional Papers, 1714–1805, vol. 1, p. 63. For analysis of the

individual clauses and the insertions in the bill, see Dempsey, 'The Marriage (Scotland) Bill'.

37. L. Leneman and R. Mitchison, 'Clandestine Marriages in the Scottish Cities, 1660–1780', *Journal of Social History* 26(4) (1993), pp. 845–61.

38. Cf. Probert, *Marriage Law and Practice in the Long Eighteenth Century*, p. 227.

39. Letter from Hardwicke to Tinwald dated 4 February 1754, reprinted in Dempsey, 'The Marriage (Scotland) Bill', pp. 111–12.

40. Letter from Hardwicke to Tinwald dated 4 February 1754 (marked 'Private'), reprinted in Dempsey, 'The Marriage (Scotland) Bill', p. 113.

41. Paul Langford, *A Polite and Commercial People: England, 1727–1783* (Oxford: Oxford University Press, 1989), pp. 224–5.

42. Dempsey, 'The Marriage (Scotland) Bill', p. 91. Dempsey also argues that the lack of a serious problem with clandestine marriage in Scotland undermined the bill.

43. James Scott Marshall, 'Irregular Marriage in Scotland as Reflected in Kirk Session Records', *Scottish Church History Records* 37 (1972), p. 19.

44. Letter dated 20 January 1746, in John M'Kerrow, *History of the Secession Church* (Glasgow: A. Fullarton, 1841), p. 205.

45. *Middleton* v. *Janverin* (1802) 2 Hag. Con. 437, 448, 161 ER 797, 801. Brian Dempsey discounts this reason based on the absence of available evidence that the argument was actually made.

46. The facts are taken from *Dalrymple* v. *Dalrymple* (1811) 2 Hag. Con. 54, 161 ER 665, supplemented by John Dodson (ed.), *A Report of the Judgment Delivered in the Consistorial Court of London . . . in the Cause of Dalrymple the Wife against Dalrymple the Husband* (London: Butterworth, 1811).

47. Ruth Elvish Mantz and J. Middleton Murry, *The Life of Katherine Mansfield* (London: Constable, 1933), pp. 20–1.

48. *Butler* v. *Freeman* (1756) Amb. 301, 27 ER 204; see also *Butler* v. *Dolben* (1756) 2 Lee 265, 161 ER 336.

49. Stone, *Road to Divorce*, p. 130.

50. Outhwaite, *Clandestine Marriage in England*, p. 132.

51. 'Some Observations on the Act for the Better Prevention of Clandestine Marriages . . .' (n.d., c. 1754), Hardwicke Papers, BL Add. Mss. 35880, ff. 93–109.

52. *Grierson* v. *Grierson* (1781) Dick. 588, 21 ER 400.

53. Probert, *Marriage Law and Practice in the Long Eighteenth Century*, p. 266, citing L. Shelford, *A Practical Treatise of the Law of Marriage and Divorce and Registration* (London: S. Sweet, 1841), ch. 2.

54. (HL) 4 Cl. & Fin. 378, 7 ER 145.

55. John R. Gillis, *For Better, for Worse: British Marriages, 1600 to the Present* (New York: Oxford University Press, 1985), p. 195.

56. Outhwaite, *Clandestine Marriage in England*, p. 132.
57. *Report of the Departmental Committee Appointed to Enquire into the Law of Scotland Relating to the Constitution of Marriage* (1937), Cmd 5354, Appendix I.
58. Abby Ashby and Audrey Jones, *The Shrigley Abduction: A Tale of Anguish, Deceit and Violation of the Domestic Hearth* (Stroud: Sutton, 2003).
59. Marriage (Scotland) Act 1856.
60. Stone, *Road to Divorce*, p. 134. Gretna station was opened by the Glasgow, Dumfries & Carlisle Railway in August 1848.
61. Brian Dempsey, 'Making the Gretna Blacksmith Redundant: Who Worried, Who Spoke, Who Was Heard on the Abolition of Irregular Marriage in Scotland?', *Journal of Legal History* 30(1) (2009), pp. 23–52. For the details of this history see *Report of the Departmental Committee*.
62. Marriage (Scotland) Act 1939.
63. *Report of the Departmental Committee*, pp. 10–11.
64. Marriage (Scotland) Act 1916. It was still possible to apply to the sheriff for a warrant, but the couple also had to complete a Schedule of Particulars, giving their names, ages and other information, as well as the names of the witnesses to the marriage.
65. Age of Marriage Act 1929.
66. *Report of the Departmental Committee*.
67. Marriage (Scotland) Act 1977.
68. General Register Office for Scotland, 'Marriages at Gretna Green, 1975–2000', 2001.
69. Quakers were exempted once again in the Places of Religious Worship Act 1812, which made it legal for them to meet without registering their meeting houses. This exemption has been carried through all subsequent legislation.
70. *Book of Common Prayer* (London: Everyman's Library, [1662] 1999), p. 303.
71. A Bill for Granting Relief to Certain Persons Dissenting from the Church of England in Relation to the Solemnization of Marriages, P.P. 1825 ii, p. 35 (Bill 56); P.P. 1826–27 ii, p. 21 (Bill 336).
72. Hansard, HC Deb, 25 March 1825, vol. 12, col. 1237.
73. Hansard, HC Deb, 25 March 1825, vol. 12, col. 1243.
74. A Bill Concerning the Marriages of Persons not Being Members of the United Church of England and Ireland, and Objecting to be Married According to the Rite Thereof, P.P. 1835 vol. iii p. 314 (Bill 96); Hansard, HC Deb, 17 March 1835, vol. 26 col. 1073.
75. Hansard, HC Deb, 17 March 1835, vol. 26, cols 1086–7.
76. Act against Clandestine and Unlawful Marriages, RPS, 1661/1/302,

http://www.rps.ac.uk/trans/1661/1/302 (last accessed 10 May 2013); Act against Irregular Baptisms and Marriages, RPS, 1695/5/118, http://www.rps.ac.uk/trans/1695/5/118 (last accessed 10 May 2013); see also Act against Clandestine and Irregular Marriages, RPS, 1698/7/113, http://www.rps.ac.uk/trans/1698/7/113 (last accessed 10 May 2013).

77. A Bill to Amend the Laws Relative to Roman Catholic Marriages in Scotland, P.P. (1834) vol. iii, pp. 663, 665 (Bill 38).

78. Hansard, HC Deb, 12 March 1834, vol. 22, col. 101.

79. Hansard, HC Deb, 12 February 1836, vol. 31, cols 371–2.

80. Hansard, HC Deb, 15 April 1836, vol. 32, col. 1093.

81. 'Henry was indeed a brilliant boy . . . Henry could box well and would never own himself beat; other boys would fight while they had a leg to stand on, but he would fight with no leg at all . . . The ring was the only element in which he seemed to enjoy himself; and while other boys were happy in the number of their friends, he rejoiced most in the multitude of his foes. His relations could not but admire his pluck, but they sometimes were forced to regret that he was inclined to be a bully; and those not so partial to him as his father was, observed with pain that, though he could fawn to the masters and the archdeacon's friends, he was imperious and masterful to the servants and the poor' (Anthony Trollope, *Barchester Towers* (Oxford University Press, [1857] 2008), ch. 8). For a full description of his character see Owen Chadwick, The Victorian Church (London: Adam & Charles Black, 1966), vol. 1, p. 217.

82. Arthur Burns, 'Phillpotts, Henry (1778–1869)', *Oxford Dictionary of National Biography* (Oxford: Oxford University Press, 2004; online ed., May 2006), http://www.oxforddnb.com/view/article/22180 (last accessed 10 May 2013).

83. Hansard, HL Deb, 21 July 1836, vol. 35, col. 376.

84. Hansard, HL Deb, 28 July 1836, vol. 35, col. 605.

85. Hansard, HL Deb, 1 August 1836, vol. 35, col. 688.

86. Olive Anderson, 'The Incidence of Civil Marriage in Victorian England and Wales', *Past & Present* 69 (1975), p. 64.

87. Ibid., p. 63.

88. David Hackett Fischer, *Albion's Seed: Four British Folkways in America* (New York: Oxford University Press, 1989), pp. 38, 44.

89. Marriage and Registration Act 1856; Marriage Act 1898.

90. Marriage Act 1949.

91. Nancy F. Anderson, 'The "Marriage with a Deceased Wife's Sister Bill" Controversy: Incest Anxiety and the Defense of Family Purity in Victorian England', *Journal of British Studies* 21(2) (1982), pp. 67–86. The Levitical rules concerning marriage, which had been adopted by Protestant churches at the Reformation, arguably prohibited such marriages, although Martin Luther disagreed. Martin Luther, 'The

Estate of Marriage', in Helmut T. Lehmann (ed.), *Luther's Works* (Philadelphia: Muhlenberg Press, 1962), pp. 23–4. The prohibition became statutory and was removed from the ecclesiastical jurisdiction by the Marriage Act 1835 (Lord Lyndhurst's Act). The prohibition did not apply to Scotland.

92. Deceased Wife's Sister's Marriage Act 1907, § 4.

93. Bruce S. Bennett, '*Banister* v. *Thompson* and Afterwards: The Church of England and the Deceased Wife's Sister's Marriage Act', *Journal of Ecclesiastical History* 49(4) (1998), pp. 668–82. The act was repealed by the Marriage (Enabling) Act 1960, which also abolished the clerical exemption.

94. Stone, *Road to Divorce*, p. 355.

95. Ibid., p. 158.

96. A. James Hammerton, 'Victorian Marriage and the Law of Matrimonial Cruelty', *Victorian Studies* 33(2) (1990), pp. 269–92. The list of grounds in the act includes incestuous adultery; adultery with bigamy; rape, sodomy or bestiality; or adultery coupled with desertion for at least two years.

97. Stone, *Road to Divorce*, pp. 355–6, 372; Gail L. Savage, 'The Operation of the 1857 Divorce Act, 1860–1910: A Research Note', *Journal of Social History* 16(4) (1983), pp. 103–10.

98. Mary Lyndon Shanley, '"One Must Ride Behind": Married Women's Rights and the Divorce Act of 1857', *Victorian Studies* 25(3) (1982), p. 370.

99. H. C. G. Matthew, *Gladstone, 1875–1898* (Oxford: Clarendon Press, 1995), pp. 86*ff.*; Hansard, HC Deb, 24 July 1857, vol. 147, col. 394.

100. Hansard, HC Deb, 18 August 1857, vol. 147, col. 1785.

101. Matrimonial Causes Act 1937.

102. Matrimonial Causes Act 1973, § 1(2).

4

Marriage across the Seas: Ireland, South Africa, Canada and the United States

Almighty God created the races white, black, yellow, malay and red, and he placed them on separate continents. And but for the interference with his arrangement there would be no cause for such marriages. The fact that he separated the races shows that he did not intend for the races to mix.[1]

Commonwealth v. *Loving* (1959)

The exclusion of same-sex couples from the benefits and responsibilities of marriage ... reinforces the wounding notion that they are to be treated as biological oddities, as failed or lapsed human beings who do not fit into normal society, and, as such, do not qualify for the full moral concern and respect that our Constitution seeks to secure for everyone. It signifies that their capacity for love, commitment and accepting responsibility is by definition less worthy of regard than that of heterosexual couples.[2]

Justice Albie Sachs, *Minister of Home Affairs* v. *Fourie* (2005)

In the last two chapters we examined the development of marriage law in Great Britain – England, Scotland and Wales – from the Reformation to the twentieth century. We showed that religious and social cleavages defined policy, so that people's choices were frequently limited: they could not marry whomever they wanted.

In this chapter, we broaden the scope of our analysis to include other nations: Ireland, South Africa, Canada and the United States. All four were colonised at one time or another by England or Great Britain. All four have cleavages that extend beyond those that we have included up to this point, including far more divisive religious conflict in Ireland, and racial cleavages in South Africa and the United States. All four have also engaged in the recent debates about same-sex marriage. South Africa and Canada have adopted same-sex marriage as national policy; Ireland has rejected it; the United States has allowed it to proceed on a state-by-state basis. The continuing theme in this chapter, however, is that limitations on whom one marries have generally been based upon social factors. Some religious and other groups practise endogamy, and when those groups' divisions are reflected in politics, the state may enforce the practice. But those limitations on choice are highly local and depend upon the power of groups and upon the power of the state to enforce those groups' values and preferences.

Ireland

The most important social division that underlies marriage in Ireland is religious. The impact of the penal laws which imposed substantial civil disabilities on Roman Catholics in the 1600s and 1700s is debated.[3] However, they certainly drove Roman Catholicism underground by limiting Catholics' ability to hold office or own property. Laws also prohibited Roman Catholic clergy, who were not even supposed to be in the country, from conducting weddings for couples when one or both were Protestants.[4] The clergy who celebrated the weddings were subject to the death penalty – at least one Catholic priest was put to death for marrying Protestants[5] – and Protestants' marriages to Catholics were void. Ireland also had an early version of Lord Hardwicke's Act, which made underage marriage without a father's consent void, but only if one of the couple had real estate with an income of £100 or personal property worth £50; otherwise, the marriage was valid even without paternal consent. This provides further evidence for the importance of class to these acts. All of these laws were gradually abandoned and repealed during the nineteenth century. The penalties for clergy who married Protestants were removed in 1833, after Catholic emancipation. And the ban on intermarriage was eliminated, although not until 1870.[6] Nevertheless, it is important to recognise that even in the early 1830s, six Catholic priests were fined or imprisoned for celebrating weddings involving Protestants: one had been convicted four times for the offence.[7]

One reason for the continuing persecution of Catholic clergy was that they performed marriages for men who abducted women, a practice that continued well into the 1800s. 'Couple beggars' were clergy, either Roman Catholic or defrocked Protestants, who would, for a fee, marry all comers. James Kelly tells us that these marriage abductions were conducted principally for financial gain.[8] Even if the couple were both Protestant, the man might choose to be married by a Roman Catholic priest, as the marriage would still be valid, and the priest might be easier to find and more cooperative. Kelly describes the case of Jack O'Bryan, a Catholic, who in 1707 abducted Margaret Macnamara, a Protestant heiress, brought her before a priest and obtained her 'consent' by threatening rape. Unlike Mary, Queen of Scots (Chapter 2), she refused to marry her abductor, and her mother appealed to the Irish House of Commons, which strengthened the law and kept O'Bryan from reaping the benefits of his misconduct.

Ireland seems to have retained the statute of Henry VIII, which made consummation necessary before a marriage could have priority over a consummated precontract (a promise *de praesenti*).[9] Although the population of Ireland was nearly all Roman Catholic, the decree from the Council of Trent that prohibited marriage without a priest was never formally promulgated in Ireland – possibly to avoid conflict with the Protestant civil authorities there.[10] And banns were regularly waived in the south of the country, so that the safeguards on Roman Catholic marriage were much weaker than those for Protestants. As a result, the legal status of promises *de praesenti* had to be recognised, and regulated, by the civil law where property rights were concerned. Since most property of importance was owned by Protestants, Roman Catholic marriage was only minimally regulated in Ireland until the mid-1800s.

The trigger for the first comprehensive regulation of Irish marriage from Westminster was a case decided by the House of Lords: *R. v. Millis*.[11] George Millis and Hester Graham were married in January 1829 in Banbridge, County Down, by a Presbyterian minister in his home. Millis was a member of the Church of England and Ireland, and Graham was a Presbyterian. On 24 December 1836, while Graham was still living, Millis married Jane Kennedy in Stoke, Devon, in the Church of England. Millis was charged with bigamy but acquitted in Ireland, and the Attorney General appealed to the House of Lords. The six lords divided evenly, and the decision of the lower court, that Millis's marriage to Graham was void, stood.

The decision effectively invalidated all marriages between Presbyterians and Anglicans that had been celebrated by Presbyterian ministers, making it possible for a large group of men to 'marry' a second wife with impunity. To remedy this, Parliament passed a statute in 1844 which permitted intermarriage between Presbyterians and other Protestants in Presbyterian meeting houses.[12] Roman Catholic marriages with Protestants, however, remained illegal. In *Yelverton* v. *Yelverton*, Maria Longworth, a Catholic, and William Charles Yelverton, a Protestant who later became the 4th Viscount Avonmore, were engaged when he was serving as a major in the Crimean War and she was a nurse.[13] They were married in Edinburgh, where he read to her the Church of England wedding ceremony (a promise *de praesenti*), and then again in a Roman Catholic ceremony in Ireland. The year after the Irish wedding, Yelverton married Emily Forbes. When Longworth sued to confirm her marriage, Yelverton successfully claimed that the Irish prohibition on marriage between Roman Catholics and Protestants applied to them.[14] In a second case, an Irish court confirmed their marriage, but a third case in Scotland annulled it again. This last decision was affirmed by the House of Lords in 1864. Longworth's and Yelverton's travails were the subject of two novels, *Gentle Blood* by J. R. O'Flanagan and *A Wife and Not a Wife* by Cyrus Redding. Longworth made money by publishing her letters but died having spent it all on the lawsuits. The bar on intermarriage between Catholics and Protestants was finally lifted in 1870, in part because of the notoriety of this case.[15]

In the twentieth century, marriage and the family have become constitutional questions in Ireland. In Chapter 1 we discussed the proposed home rule statute that would have protected religious freedom and non-establishment in a devolved Ireland in 1888. Modelled on the first amendment to the US constitution, Gladstone's bill from 1886 provided that 'the Irish Parliament shall not make a law so as to either directly or indirectly establish or endow any religion, or prohibit or restrict the free exercise thereof'. Following Irish independence in 1922, that provision only applied to Northern Ireland, not to the state in the south.

In the Irish Free State (later the Republic) in 1937 a new constitution was adopted, which defined the state in expressly religious terms. At this time the Catholic-dominated Fianna Fáil party was in power and had abandoned compromises that would have been necessary to unite with Northern Ireland. The preamble to the constitution says:

> In the name of the Most Holy Trinity, from Whom is all authority and to Whom, as our final end, all actions both of men and States must be referred,
>
> We, the people of Éire,
>
> Humbly acknowledging all our obligations to our Divine Lord, Jesus Christ, Who sustained our fathers through centuries of trial,
>
> Gratefully remembering their heroic and unremitting struggle to regain the rightful independence of our Nation,
>
> And seeking to promote the common good, with due observance of Prudence, Justice and Charity, so that the dignity and freedom of the individual may be assured, true social order attained, the unity of our country restored, and concord established with other nations,
>
> Do hereby adopt, enact, and give to ourselves this Constitution.[16]

It continues in Article 41:

> The State recognises the Family as the natural primary and fundamental unit group of Society, and as a moral institution possessing inalienable and imprescriptible rights, antecedent and superior to all positive law ... The State pledges itself to guard with special care the institution of Marriage, on which the Family is founded, and to protect it against attack ... No law shall be enacted providing for the grant of a dissolution of marriage.[17]

Éamon de Valera, the leader of the government, consulted with the Vatican when the constitution was being drafted, and it reflects Catholic social teaching of the 1930s, including the importance of women not working and remaining in the home.[18] Until it entered the European Economic Community in 1973, Ireland had a bar against married women being employed in the public sector.[19] The constitution also limits the recognition of foreign divorces.[20] Under the prevailing rules concerning residency, a husband could avoid divorcing his wife simply by remaining in Ireland. Since her domicile followed him, however, he could obtain a divorce if he went abroad, even if she remained at home in Ireland.

The constitutional prohibition on divorce was removed by the fifteenth amendment to the constitution, which was approved in a referendum in 1995.[21] At present divorces may be granted if a court finds that the couple has lived apart for four of the previous five years and that there is no reasonable prospect for reconciliation. The amendment took two tries before it passed: the first referendum, held in 1986 on a slightly different amendment, was defeated by 63 per cent to 36 per cent on a 60 per cent turnout.[22] On the second try, the amendment passed by 50.1 per cent on a 62 per cent turnout. The changes that were made between the votes included the following:

- passage of a liberalised law concerning legal separations, which permitted them to be based on six grounds, including 'unreasonable behaviour';[23]
- a less prominent role for the Catholic Church in opposing the amendment (based upon the church–state separation encouraged by Vatican II and clergy sex scandals during the campaign);
- increased government support for the amendment, to the extent that it was challenged as excessively partisan; and
- social liberalisation brought about by Ireland's membership of the European Union.[24]

The situation before 1996 had led to a practical breakdown of marriage, in spite of the legal, constitutional commitment to protect it. It was estimated that 70,000 couples in Ireland were living together without being married in 1986, and spouses regularly 'divorced' one another through abandonment, separation and divorces in foreign countries.[25] Moreover, the children of these unmarried couples were denied inheritance rights based upon their legal illegitimacy.[26] This legal disparity was eliminated in 1987 when the Status of Children Act permitted the children of unmarried parents to establish property rights, as well as guardianship and support. Also in 1986, following the failure of the constitutional referendum, the Irish parliament passed a law broadening the recognition of foreign divorces.[27] That act allowed divorces to be recognised if they had taken place in a specified jurisdiction (including England and Wales), as long as one spouse planned to live there permanently.

Although the Irish constitution does not specify that marriage is between a man and a woman, the Irish courts have refused to extend the constitutional protections afforded to families to same-sex couples.[28] Katherine Zappone and Ann Louise Gilligan, both Irish citizens, met while they were studying at Boston College in the United States.[29] They had been together for thirty years when they travelled to Canada to be married in 2003. When they returned they asked to be allowed to claim tax allowances available to married couples. Relying on the *Oxford English Dictionary*'s definition of 'husband' and 'wife', the Revenue Commissioners rejected their request, and the couple brought an action in the High Court. There, the judge found:

> Marriage was understood under the 1937 constitution to be confined to persons of the opposite sex. That has been reiterated in a number of the decisions . . . Judgment in [a recent] case was given as recently as 2003. Thus it cannot be said that this is some kind of fossilised understanding of marriage. I fully appreciate that changes have been made; indeed, some far-reaching changes have been made to the institution of marriage as it was understood in 1937. Changes in relation to capacity in respect of the marriage age have been made and the most fundamental change of all has been the change in relation to the indissolubility of marriage. I accept that the constitution is a living instrument . . . I also accept the arguments of Mr O'Donnell to the effect that there is a difference between an examination of the constitution in the context of ascertaining unenumerated rights and redefining a right which is implicit in the constitution and which is clearly understood. In this case the court is being asked to redefine marriage to mean something which it has never done to date.

She rejected the couple's claims.

The problem with the judge's reasoning is that it fails to take account of the entire history of Irish marriage law, which we have described in this section. The 'meaning' of marriage at the time of the adoption of the 1937 constitution was between a man, who would work and earn a living, and a woman, who would stay at home and have children. That meaning had to be abandoned when Ireland became a member of the EEC. As the judge acknowledges, the meaning of marriage also changed from a life-long commitment in 1996, although that change was made through a constitutional amendment. More importantly, however, historically Irish marriage law, or its absence, has been a way of keeping different religious groups separate and reinforcing divisions in society. Because Catholic marriages could not be formally acknowledged by the Protestant civil authority, they had to be treated informally. And for nearly a century clergy who refused to comply with the existing sectarian divisions and married Protestants to Catholics were subject to the death penalty. This history warrants more attention from those who argue that marriage has a 'meaning' that cannot change along with changes in social practice.

In 2006 the All-Party Oireachtas Committee on the Constitution (*oireachtas* is Gaelic for 'parliament', including both houses) reported on its investigation into potential changes to the Irish constitution's treatment of the family.[30] It recommended legislative changes to respect both cohabiting opposite-sex and same-sex couples. The committee pointed out that while 75 per cent of the 'family units' responding to the 2002 census were married couples, either with (55 per cent) or without (20 per cent) children, another 8.4 per cent were unmarried cohabitants, and 3.2 per cent had children. While there were few same-sex cohabiting couples (1,300), their number had grown from 150 in 1996.

That report made a number of recommendations. It recommended that cohabiting couples be granted similar rights to married couples and that civil partnership be offered to same-sex couples. Both were done in 2010 when a single act extended some of the rights enjoyed by married couples both to cohabiting opposite-sex and cohabiting same-sex partners.[31] There is a certain logic to this: those who do not marry are part of one legal regime, which is different from those who do marry. The latter category receives full benefits of joint adoption, tax benefits and other status-related classifications that are linked to marriage. Those who do not marry but register their relationships have a different legal status. But the important difference is that opposite-sex couples can choose either status; same-sex couples can choose only one. Ireland has a history of marriage being offered to different groups which were either favoured or disfavoured by those in power: first the Protestant ascendancy, later the Roman Catholic majority. Asymmetric rules concerning marriage are embedded in the political culture there, and it has been difficult to overcome historical patterns in current thinking about marriage law.

In 2012 the national parliament convened a constitutional convention, consisting of twenty-nine of its own members, four representatives of Northern Ireland's political parties and sixty-six randomly selected citizens.[32] The convention first met on 1 December 2012. Among the proposals it is to comment on is whether provision should be made for same-sex marriage. At the time of writing, the submissions to the convention have been strongly divided, pro and con.[33] According to a poll conducted by the firm Millward Brown Lansdown for an Irish equal marriage group, support for same-sex marriage increased from 51 per cent to 75 per cent between 2006 and 2012.[34] Support is highest among the age cohort 18–24 (88 per cent) and lowest among those over sixty-five, but even there it rose from 27 per cent to 43 per cent in four years, from 2008 to 2012.[35] It seems plausible that this trend will lead to popular acceptance of same-sex marriage in Ireland in the near future, even if a minority continues to object and even if the courts refuse to intervene. In April 2013 79 per cent of the constitutional convention voted in favour of holding a referendum on same-sex marriage.[36]

South Africa

The Republic of South Africa's political history has been based on ethnic and racial conflict. The territory was originally colonised in the 1600s, when the Dutch East India Company established an outpost on the Cape of Good Hope, to supply sailors engaged in the spice trade.[37] When the First French Republic invaded the Dutch Republic in 1795, Britain took over the area. It annexed the Cape Colony in 1806, driving the original European settlers, known as Boers, into what became the Natal, Orange Free State and Transvaal regions of the country. The effect of the British takeover was the importation of Christian missionaries and British settlers, along with abolition of the slave trade, but also increased conflict with the indigenous peoples.[38]

The Boer Wars (1880–1 and 1899–1902) were fought between the

British and the Boers and resulted in South Africa, including the Boer republics, becoming a British colony with some degree of independence. The wars, and particularly the latter one, led to hostility between the Afrikaans-speaking Boers and the British, which brought about serious resistance to South Africa joining the Allies during World War II. Following the war, the National Party was elected, and in 1961 South Africa became an independent republic, with a president replacing the British monarch as head of state.

Although there had been racial tensions in South Africa since it was colonised, the government of the republic made racial segregation part of the law in the system known as apartheid. Like the British in Ireland, the minority white government in South Africa imposed civil disabilities on the non-white population there, including strict separation of the races, legal disabilities, and labour and housing restrictions.[39]

One of South Africa's main marriage laws dates from the period of apartheid. Adopted in order to make marriage law uniform throughout the country, this law provides that marriage officers, including ministers of religion, are appointed by the Minister of Home Affairs to celebrate weddings. At present no licence or banns are required, and marriages are recorded with the Department of Home Affairs.[40] Those who are under eighteen must have parental consent, and males under eighteen and females under sixteen must also have the consent of the Minister of Home Affairs. Divorce has been available since 1979, based upon the irretrievable breakdown of the marriage, with no fault attributable to either spouse.[41]

At the time this marriage statute was enacted, marriages between whites and non-whites were void.[42] Marriage officers who conducted weddings for whites and non-whites were subject to fines. Marriage and even sexual relations outside marriage between whites and non-whites were punishable with jail terms of up to seven years. African customary marriages were recognised for limited purposes, but spouses married in this way did not enjoy the full civil status afforded to marriage under the general marriage act.[43] Nor were they systematically registered.[44]

The system of apartheid ended in the 1990s.[45] In 1996 South Africa adopted a new constitution.[46] Its preamble is very different from the preamble to the Irish constitution:

We, the people of South Africa,
Recognise the injustices of our past;
Honour those who suffered for justice and freedom in our land;
Respect those who have worked to build and develop our country;
and
Believe that South Africa belongs to all who live in it, united in our
diversity.

We therefore, through our freely elected representatives, adopt
this Constitution as the supreme law of the Republic . . .

May God protect our people.

The constitution reflects this emphasis on diversity. Chapter 12 explicitly recognises the authority of traditional leaders and of customary law and requires that courts apply customary law when it applies to a case before them. Section 15(3), which concerns freedom of religion, belief and opinion, expressly provides for legal recognition of 'systems of personal or family law under any tradition, or adhered to by persons professing a certain religion'. Meanwhile, the constitution also has broad prohibitions on discrimination, including on the basis of gender or sexual orientation.[47] Customary law must be interpreted consistently with the rights in the constitution, including these protections from discrimination.[48]

In 1998 South Africa legislated to recognise customary marriages: marriages according to African, rather than European, customs.[49] It also imposed an age requirement on who could marry and protected the property of wives in polygamous marriages by requiring that the husband obtain a court-approved agreement concerning their property.[50] It also required that customary marriages be dissolved in court rather than according to customary law.[51] All this was to protect the interests of wives. The treatment of customary marriages remains a difficult legal problem in South Africa, as it involves balancing the collective interests of groups that have historically been oppressed with the individual interests of the members of those groups, based, among other things, upon gender.[52] In addition, the problem with AIDS in South Africa makes sexual exclusivity a question of public health.

Along with statutory civil and religious marriages and customary marriages, South African courts have also shown a willingness to move beyond monogamous marriage in the context of Islam. An apartheid-era case, *Ismail* v. *Ismail*, had refused to enforce support and other rights of a spouse in a Muslim marriage, because the marriage was potentially polygamous, even though in fact it was monogamous.[53] *Khan* v. *Khan*, decided after apartheid, took the opposite position, holding that spouses in a polygamous marriage could receive court-ordered support:

> The purpose of the [Marriage] Act would be frustrated rather than furthered if partners to a polygamous marriage were to be excluded from the protection the Act offers, just because the legal form of their relationship is not consistent [with it].[54]

Nevertheless, Muslim marriages, and particularly polygamous ones, are generally not recognised by South African law.

The South African Constitutional Court, which only deals with constitutional cases, has been an active interpreter of civil rights, finding that the death penalty was unconstitutional and even that the government has an obligation to provide housing for citizens under certain conditions.[55] In 2002 a lesbian couple, Marié Fourie and Cecelia Bonthuys, challenged the definition of marriage under South African law: 'the legally recognised voluntary union for life of one man and one woman to the exclusion of others while it lasts'.[56] The case eventually reached the South African Constitutional Court, which decided that the definition violated the constitution.[57] In his decision, Justice Albie Sachs pointed out the importance that society places on the status of marriage, by regulating the rites that surround it and the obligations it imposes on spouses. He then wrote, in a passage preceding the epigraph to this chapter:

> The exclusion of same-sex couples from the benefits and responsibilities of marriage ... is not a small and tangential inconvenience resulting from a few surviving relics of societal prejudice destined to evaporate like the morning dew. It represents a harsh if oblique statement by the law that same-sex couples are outsiders, and that their need for affirmation and protection of their intimate relations as human beings is somehow less than that of heterosexual couples.[58]

The decision then goes on to address arguments by those who opposed integrating same-sex couples into South African marriage law based upon the fact that same-sex couples cannot procreate and the claim that same-sex marriage is inconsistent with Christian values.[59] Sachs called arguments based on the importance of pro-creation 'demeaning' (a) to those who could not have children, (b) to adoptive parents, by implying that their marriages were less entitled to respect, and (c) to those who decide, for reasons protected by privacy interests, not to have children.[60] While emphasising the need to respect religious beliefs, Sachs wrote: 'It is one thing for the Court to acknowledge the important role that religion plays in our public life. It is quite another to use religious doctrine as a source for interpreting the constitution.'[61] In this context he emphasised that under South African law no minister of religion could be compelled to celebrate a same-sex wedding.[62]

In the *Fourie* decision the Constitutional Court gave the government a year, until 1 December 2006, to provide equal legal status for same-sex couples in South Africa. The required law was passed on 29 November 2006, and it came into effect the following day.[63] The civil union act allows either same-sex or opposite sex couples to form a union, with duties and obligations identical to those under the Marriage Act of 1961.[64] The process that one goes through to attain the status is either a 'civil partnership' or a 'marriage', and the parties are 'partners' after the first and 'spouses' after the second.[65] There is no difference in the legal status that depends upon the name used; the status itself is a 'civil union'. All marriage officers (magistrates and civil servants) who were not ministers of religion were automatically authorised to conduct civil partnerships and marriages, although they could request an exemption from conducting them based upon conscience, religion or belief.[66] Religious organisations were permitted to apply to have their ministers registered as marriage officers, and once they were approved, individual ministers could apply. Thus, to perform a same-sex marriage or civil partnership religious marriage officers must both be in a religious organisation that approves of same-sex marriage, and must also individually wish to conduct such ceremonies.[67]

Marriage in South Africa is essentially pluralistic. Polygamous marriages are different in nature; they are not merely a different way of entering into marriage. As in Ireland, the range of choice available to potential marriage partners is governed primarily by historical circumstances. Whereas in Ireland the long-standing oppression of Roman Catholics has created an environment where that religion has much influence over the law of marriage, in South Africa marriage has had to accommodate native cultures and practices that are inconsistent with Western practices and beliefs. Ireland has adhered to marriage practices that no longer apply in most European countries, including its rejection of divorce. South Africa has engaged in an ongoing effort to legitimise alternative ways of thinking about marriage in order to accommodate a highly pluralistic culture. The two countries' treatment of same-sex marriage is consistent with these cultural foundations.

Canada

Rather than being alternately colonised by the Dutch and the English, as South Africa was, Canada was alternately colonised by the French and the English.[68] However, the alternation caused similar problems: an ethnic-religious minority (in South Africa the Boers, in Canada the French Canadians) and military conflict. One military conflict in Canada was a proxy war between France and England, which made up part of what the English and Canadians call the Seven Years War (1756–63), along with conflicts in India, west Africa and other places. People from the US call it the French and Indian War. Another similarity with South Africa is that colonists in Canada did not encounter an unoccupied land; numerous aboriginal peoples were already there. In Canada these peoples are called First Nations. During the colonial era fur traders in remote areas married women members of the First Nations and were assimilated into these cultures.[69] Under the Indian Act of 1869, any woman who married a European lost her native status. By then these marriages had become increasingly rare.

Canada received its first constitution in 1867, known as the Constitution Act 1867 in Canada but still known as the British North America Act 1867 in Britain. The country was established as a federal state, in recognition of the differences between the French Canadians in Quebec, who were largely Roman Catholic, and the other, English-dominated provinces. The Constitution Act gives the federal government power over 'Marriage and Divorce' and provincial governments power over 'Solemnization of Matrimony'.[70] In general terms, this has meant that the federal government has power to determine who has the *capacity* to marry, and the provinces have the power to determine *what forms* must be observed in the ceremony.[71]

Under federal law, the rules of consanguinity and affinity have been relaxed, so that the only prohibited relationships are lineal (between children, parents, grandparents and so on) and sibling (brothers and sisters, including half-siblings and adoptive siblings).[72] The age of consent, however, has not been regulated by the federal government but has been left to the provinces, even though this seems inconsistent with the constitutional distinction described above. In Ontario young people must have their parents' consent to marry if they are under eighteen; in British Columbia, parental consent is necessary up to the age of nineteen.[73] Provincial law has regulated, for example, whether civil marriages are available, with the three most western provinces offering it from the nineteenth century.[74] Ontario did not offer civil marriage until 1950, and Newfoundland did not offer it until 1974.

In the interwar period, a number of Canadian provinces became concerned with the decline of the family and attempted to impose harsh regulations to protect it. Among other things, they nullified marriages between minors who had failed to obtain the permission of their parents, an attack on clandestine marriages.[75] In addition, they began requiring doctor's certificates attesting to the sound health and normal mentality of the man and woman as a prerequisite to marriage. These measures were promoted primarily by religious groups, asserting their own authority and the values that they represented. They died out in the 1930s, partially because of popular resistance to the regulations and partially because of the churches' withdrawal into regulating religious, as opposed to civil, marriage.

In a rapid series of cases in 2003–4, courts of appeal in Ontario, British Columbia, Quebec and other provinces determined that not allowing marriage to same-sex couples violated the equality provisions of the Canadian Charter of Rights and Freedoms, which had been adopted when the constitution was patriated in 1982.[76] In one case, the trial court had applied an originalist interpretation to the constitution, defining marriage according to the common law at the time that the Constitution Act 1867 was enacted.[77] That court found that while the court could change the common law, it could only do so incrementally, and that a change to same-sex marriage would not be incremental.[78] The judge went on to say that the Canadian constitution granted power over 'marriage' to the federal government but that it would be necessary to amend the constitution to change the definition of marriage that was implicit in the constitution.[79] The court of appeal disagreed. First, it held that the definition of marriage was not an entrenched part of the Canadian constitution; instead, it was a term that referred to a class of subjects that the legislature had power to regulate.[80] The term did not have an 'internal frozen in time meaning that reflect[ed] the presumed framers' intent as it may have been in 1867'. Finally, the court found that failure to extend marriage to same-sex couples violated the Charter of Rights and Freedoms' protection of lesbians, gay men and bisexuals and that the breach was not justified.[81]

In its findings the court of appeal followed the divisional court in *Halpern* v. *Canada (Attorney General)*.[82] There the court had also decided that the common law definition of marriage, as being between one man and one woman, was inconsistent with the Charter of Rights and Freedoms. Justice LaForme found that a different form of recognition for same-sex partners would not be adequate under the charter, referring to decisions, such as *Brown* v. *Board of Education* in the United States, which had prohibited racial segregation:

> It should be recalled that at one time African-Americans were entitled to sit on the same bus as 'whites' and in seats that were equally comfortable to other seats. They just could not sit at the front of the bus because those equal seats were reserved for 'white people'. As well, African-Americans were entitled to drink water and to use toilet facilities that were in all other respects equal to those used by white people. Once again, they could not do so from the same fountain or use the same toilet as whites. Each of those were – although once seemingly credible concepts – discredited and rejected by courts in the United States.[83]

Justice LaForme also responded to an argument about procreation being central to the meaning of marriage. He made the following observations:

I do not agree that the evidence . . . supports the AGC's [Attorney General of Canada's] proposition that procreation is the essential objective of marriage. Indeed, the evidence actually demonstrates that it was only recently – when same-sex couples began to advance claims for equal recognition of their conjugal relationships – that some courts began to infer that procreation was an essential component to marriage. There is simply no evidence that convinces me that those earlier courts, when developing the common law rules regarding the validity of marriage and capacity, viewed procreation as the purpose of marriage.[84]

In support of this finding, he relied upon the fact that under Canadian law a marriage remains valid and not voidable when one spouse refuses to have sexual intercourse, is infertile or insists on using contraceptives. In support of the last point, he referred to the UK House of Lords case *Baxter* v. *Baxter*, in which the court refused to grant an annulment when the wife insisted that the husband use a condom.[85]

On appeal, the decision was affirmed. The government, defending the common law definition, argued that 'marriage' did not distinguish between same-sex and opposite-sex couples, because it was a unique descriptor that relates only to opposite-sex couples.[86] The court of appeal responded:

If marriage were defined as 'a union between one man and one woman of the Protestant faith', surely the definition would be drawing a formal distinction between Protestants and all other persons. Persons of other religions and persons with no religious affiliation would be excluded. Similarly, if marriage were defined as 'a union between two white persons', there would be a distinction between white persons and all other racial groups.[87]

These decisions are an example of a bandwagon, where an early decision by a judge gains credibility with other judges, who follow it. Here, one of the most influential was Justice LaForme. Referring to the earlier decisions in support of same-sex marriage, the Ontario Court of Appeal said:

We want to record our admiration for the high quality of the reasons prepared by all of the judges in these cases. As will become clear, we agree with a great deal of their reasoning and conclusions on the equality issue. Our reasons can be shortened, given the clarity and eloquence of our judicial colleagues.[88]

With the exception of the trial court in British Columbia, all the courts' findings and conclusions were fundamentally consistent.

Following the decisions in Ontario and British Columbia, the federal government announced that it would refer a bill opening marriage to same-sex couples to the Supreme Court of Canada.[89] The questions referred to the court were (1) whether the proposal to extend marriage to same-sex couples was consistent with the Charter of Rights and Freedoms, (2) whether the proposed legislation was within the exclusive competence of the federal legislature under the constitution, and (3) whether the protection of religious freedom enshrined in the charter would allow religious officials to opt out from performing same-sex marriages. While the court considered these questions, the Prime Minister, Jean Chrétien, was replaced by Paul Martin (both were from the Liberal Party). Martin came out in support of same-sex marriage, but because an election was due the next year he attempted to give same-sex marriage opponents a fair hearing. He added a fourth question: whether the existing exclusion of same-sex partners from marriage was consistent with the charter.

The court found that the proposed bill was constitutional and that ministers of religion would be adequately protected by the charter from being forced to conduct same-sex weddings.[90] The bill defined marriage, contrary to existing Canadian common law, as 'the lawful union of two persons to the exclusion of all others'. The Supreme Court held that the constitutional definition of marriage was not fixed. Considering the case that had defined marriage before, *Hyde* v. *Hyde*,[91] the court found its references to 'Christendom' to have become outdated and inapplicable. Relying on cases decided under the Canadian constitution that had permitted women as well as men to be appointed to the Canadian senate, the court rejected original- ist reasoning: 'The "frozen concepts" reasoning runs contrary to one of the most fundamental principles of Canadian constitutional interpretation: that our constitution is a living tree which, by way of progressive interpretation, accommodates and addresses the realities of modern life.'[92] Opponents of same-sex marriage argued that allowing it would violate the principle of equality respecting those who opposed it for religious reasons or those who were married to spouses of the opposite sex. The Supreme Court was dismissive:

> No submissions have been made as to how the proposed act, in its effect, might be seen to draw a distinction [that violates Section 15 of the charter], nor can the court surmise how it might be seen to do so. It withholds no benefits, nor does it impose burdens on a differential basis.[93]

However, the court refused to answer the fourth question: whether the existing system, as it was before the earlier cases had been decided, was inconsistent with the charter. The government's lawyers had 'reiterated the government's unequivocal intention' to introduce same-sex marriage during argument before the court.[94] It had accepted the earlier judicial rulings by the lower courts, and five provinces and one territory had begun to offer marriage to same-sex couples. Because the parties to the previous lawsuits (and other same-sex couples) had been married based on the earlier decisions, and their status had been settled in one way, a decision that the common law rule was consistent with the charter would throw that status into doubt. As marriage was a personal decision that had 'implications for a complex interplay of social, political, religious, and financial considerations', and given that the government had already decided to introduce a bill that was consistent with the charter, revisiting the past was a dangerous enterprise that the court refused to undertake.[95] The bill was considered by the Canadian House of Commons in the summer of 2005, and the bill passed by a 155–133 margin.[96]

Canada's acceptance of same-sex marriage, like South Africa's, has been judicially driven. One commentator has argued that the change in public attitude towards same-sex marriage in Canada has also been driven by the courts, which can stabilise those attitudes because the courts are themselves relatively stable.[97] We would extend this argument, however, to point out that judges can be particularly adept at differentiating between good arguments and bad ones, and they can be good at deciding what counts as proper evidence. (This

Marriage across the Seas

does not mean that all of them do so all of the time in every legal system.) Irrespective of one's position on the outcome of *Fourie* and the Canadian appellate cases, the logical basis for the decisions is well grounded in liberal, secular logic. Good arguments can be made by opponents of same-sex marriage, as we will argue in the next chapter, but when judges are confronted with bad ones, they tend to dismiss them.

United States

The social and political cleavages of the United States are complex and overlapping. We cannot undertake an extended analysis of them here, except to recall from Chapter 1 that patterns of immigration from Great Britain had an important influence on the way that marriage developed in New England, the Hudson valley (New York, Pennsylvania), the South (eastern Virginia) and the backcountry (western Virginia and Tennessee, for example). In addition to these geographical divisions, we address four other divisions briefly in this chapter. First, we address those between settlers and Native Americans, whom the settlers encountered when they landed. Second, we examine treatment of other immigrant groups, such as the Chinese. Next, we discuss the problem of polygamy and religious freedom, which arose when the Mormons were settling the Utah Territory. Finally, we look at the question of African-American intermarriage.

Although Native Americans did not share a common language or culture during the colonial period, some peoples dominated certain areas of the continent, such as the Iroquois in the east. They did not make the family as central as it was to the European groups in North America that we examined in Chapter 1.[98] Instead, women were economic actors, and polygamy and divorce with remarriage were accepted. In addition, Native American culture included the *berdache*: a male who was treated as a female in the community but who was highly integrated into the religious, ritual and sacred lives of the group.[99] Although in places where Europeans lived transient lives, for example as trappers, they could marry Native American women, just as the early Canadian settlers did, it was not acceptable for Native American men to marry non-Native women.[100] As in

135

Canada, laws were passed to make Native American women citizens if they married non-Native men; however, in the United States this was done to prevent the men from using marriage to escape from criminal charges, as Native Americans were subject to different laws from whites.[101] As the Native Americans were forced from their land, the United States government engaged in a programme of domesticating them.[102] This included creating faithful domestic households with husbands who were farmers, and integrating them into society as citizens. Marriage, for Native Americans, was something imposed from outside based upon a need to normalise them so that they could be integrated into society in the United States.

In addition to writing about Native Americans, Nancy Cott has also pointed out that Chinese suffered from similar prejudice when they immigrated to the United States, first during the California gold rush and then in greater numbers when they were in demand as low-cost labour for building railways and for mining.[103] Along with their competition with higher cost, non-immigrant labour, their marriage practices offended those in power and the electorate: 'They were not Christians; their inherited culture accepted polygamy; their livelihoods showed them to be enemies of the civilization embraced by the American nation.'[104] In the 1870s, many female Chinese immigrants to California were, in fact, prostitutes or second wives.[105] In 1875 the Page Act was passed, the first federal statute to restrict immigration into the United States.[106] Previous state statutes limiting immigration had been rejected by courts as infringing the national government's power to control foreign policy. And federal legislators were bound, where the Chinese were concerned, by the Burlingame Treaty, which prohibited restrictions on Chinese immigration.[107] However, by putting the question in terms of morals and the protection of the nuclear family, the bill's sponsors were able successfully to regulate Chinese sexual conduct.

Another group that has experienced prejudice in the United States is the Mormons. The Latter-Day Saint movement originated in western New York with Joseph Smith, Jr.[108] After migrating through Ohio and Missouri, the Mormons regrouped in Nauvoo, Illinois. There, Smith approved the practice of plural marriage, polygamy, as a restoration of the practice found in the Old Testament. Religious conflicts between conventional Christians and Mormons became violent in Nauvoo, and Smith was lynched by a mob on 27 June 1844. Brigham Young, one of the senior governing members of the church, led church members out of Illinois in 1846, and they arrived in the Salt Lake Valley in July 1847, where they founded Salt Lake City.

When the Mormons arrived in Salt Lake, no federal law prohibited polygamy, because such matters (bigamy as a crime; marriage) were reserved to the states.[109] Only in 1862 did Congress pass the Morrill Act, legislation clearly directed at the Mormons.[110] The act banned polygamy, repealed a law passed by the territorial legislature that had permitted the practice and restricted property ownership by churches and non-profits to $50,000.[111] This statute led to one of the first decisions by the US Supreme Court concerning the first amendment of the US constitution, which provides: 'Congress shall make no law respecting an establishment of religion, or prohibiting the free exercise thereof . . .' The case is *Reynolds* v. *United States.*

The Mormons had been able, because of their political power, to ignore the Morrill Act until 1874, when George Reynolds, a church leader, was indicted and charged; he was convicted and sentenced to two years' hard labour and a fine of $500.[112] Reynolds claimed that he had been exercising his religion, which permitted polygamy. Chief Justice Waite rejected the religious freedom claim. He engaged in an originalist analysis, looking to the history of the enactment of the first amendment (as well as the history of bigamy going back to the time of James VI/I), and then for the first time in Supreme Court history quoted from Thomas Jefferson's message to the Danbury Baptists:

> I contemplate with sovereign reverence that act of the whole American people which declared that *their* legislature should 'make no law respecting an establishment of religion or prohibiting the free exercise thereof,' thus building a wall of separation between church and State.[113]

Jefferson's 'wall' has become the focus of innumerable debates about how much religious freedom should be allowed in the United States.[114] In this case the judge went on to ignore the wall and hold that Reynolds could not defend a criminal charge of bigamy based upon his religious beliefs; his reasoning was conclusory:

So here, as a law of the organization of society under the exclusive dominion of the United States, it is provided that plural marriages shall not be allowed. Can a man excuse his practices to the contrary because of his religious belief? To permit this would be to make the professed doctrines of religious belief superior to the law of the land, and in effect to permit every citizen to become a law unto himself. Government could exist only in name under such circumstances.[115]

Although there was a wall of separation between church and state, the state could disregard the wall when it was passing laws for the 'organization of society' in a way that was consistent with the way that society had been organised since James VI/I.

Persecution of the Mormons continued. In 1881 Congress passed the Edmunds-Tucker Act, which took away the corporate status of the church, expropriated its assets, disenfranchised women in the territory and imposed an anti-polygamy oath on voters, jurors and public officials.[116] The act was upheld by the US Supreme Court on 19 May 1890.[117] By that time, the federal government had expropriated most of the property of the church and had deprived it of much of its political power in the territory. Five months later, in October 1890, the church adopted the 1890 Manifesto, which abandoned the teaching of polygamy.[118]

In all three of these cases – Native Americans, Chinese and Mormons – the US government used its power to regularise marriage. In the first and last cases, it was doing so because it had authority over an area without its own state government. With respect to California, its power was contested by the state, but policy ultimately came from Congress, because the problem involved foreign immigrants. In Utah, the federal government's power was limited in the 1850s and 1860s by political forces similar to those that constrained the UK parliament when it was unable to regulate marriage in Scotland: there were simply too many Mormons, and they were too far away. Indeed, in 1857–8 the US government sent an unsuccessful military expedition to suppress the church.[119] It became known as Buchanan's blunder, named after the president who had authorised it based on inaccurate information and popular demand. Eventually the Mormons gave in, however, and in 1896, when Utah applied for statehood the application was approved by Congress. But it is difficult to find another case in US history where a religious group was persecuted so forcefully over such an extended period of time.[120] The official website of the Church of Jesus Christ of Latter-Day Saints is remarkably candid about the connection between the persecution the church suffered and its abandonment of polygamy. Viewed from the perspective of the government, however, the cost was high as well. And its efforts were not entirely successful; Mormon groups practice polygamy to the present day.[121] Polygamous Mormon families have recently become popular in US television programmes such as *Sister Wives* and *Big Love*. The Mormons from one of these television programmes have brought an action in federal court, challenging Utah's anti-polygamy statute as unconstitutional, and thus far they have not been thrown out of court.[122]

The mistreatment of African-Americans in US history needs neither introduction nor explanation, but the racial divide had a long-term impact on marriage law and practice there. From the early 1700s the North American colonies prohibited intermarriage between 'Negroes or mulattoes' and 'her Majesty's English or Scottish subjects [and] of any other Christian nation'.[123] In the south, such laws would have been redundant, but states such as Illinois, Maine and Michigan, where slavery was outlawed, had laws against intermarriage before the American Civil War.[124] More laws concerning racial intermarriage were passed during the civil war and the Reconstruction that followed than in any comparably short period.[125] These laws were subject to the same kind of manipulation that we have seen before, with respect to consummation and the age qualification, under Lord Hardwicke's Act. For example, on 21 March 1921 Joe Kirby took his wife Mayellen to court.[126] Instead of a divorce, which would have involved a division of property, he asked for an annulment under Arizona's law against racial intermarriage, claiming that the couple's marriage was void. At the trial, he testified that he was a 'Mexican' (which counted as white under the law); Mayellen did not need to testify, as her physical characteristics spoke for themselves: she was an African American. The judge found that the couple had never been legally married. The trial testimony reflects the difficulty of basing legal classifications on socially constructed characteristics like race. Like many Americans, Joe was of mixed race, which combined Irish and what he called 'Mexican' elements.

California's ban on interracial marriage was adopted when it became a state.[127] Over the years it was amended to include 'Mongolians' and 'Malays'.[128] By 1948, the statute forbade 'marriages of white persons with negroes, Mongolians, members of the Malay race, or mulattoes'.[129] Andrea Perez, a Mexican American, and Sylvester Davis, an African American, met while working in the defence industry in California. When their application for a marriage licence was rejected by the Los Angeles county clerk, they claimed that the law infringed violated the first amendment's protection of their free exercise of religion. They were both Roman Catholics, and the Catholic church had no prohibition on interracial marriage, but the state did. In the first case invalidating a ban on interracial marriage in the United States, the Supreme Court of California held that the ban was unconstitutional.

The court refused to analyse the question purely in terms of religious liberty, because of the decision in *Reynolds*, discussed above, which permits state regulation of marriage. However, it examined the couple's rights in terms of whether the racial bar was irrational and found that the statute was, in fact, both arbitrary and irrational. Justice Roger Traynor wrote that the statute was arbitrary, because the legislature could define 'racial intermarriage' in any way it liked: states differed as to whether 'Indians' or 'Hindus' were included in such bans.[130] The bans were also arbitrary because they had to identify the amount of racial admixture necessary to disqualify someone from marrying a white person.[131] He also rejected the state's claim that African Americans were 'socially inferior' and that 'the progeny of a marriage between a Negro and a Caucasian [would] suffer not only the stigma of such inferiority but the fear of rejection by members of both races'.[132] In response to the argument that African Americans were less intelligent than whites, the court asked whether it wouldn't be more appropriate to give applicants for a marriage licence an intelligence test, if that were the real concern.[133]

Twenty years later this rejection of bans on interracial marriage became mandatory federal law in the United States. Mildred Jeter, who was black, and Richard Loving, who was white, were residents of Virginia, which had a law prohibiting interracial marriage.[134] In 1958 they went to Washington DC, which did not prohibit interracial marriage, married and returned to Virginia, where they were convicted of violating the law.

At trial the judge said:

Almighty God created the races white, black, yellow, malay and red, and he placed them on separate continents. And but for the interference with his arrangement there would be no cause for such marriages. The fact that he separated the races shows that he did not intend for the races to mix.[135]

He sentenced the Lovings to a year in prison, which would not be enforced if they left the state for twenty-five years. They left the state but continued to challenge the law in court.

The US Supreme Court found the Virginia law unconstitutional, which meant that the sixteen remaining state prohibitions on inter-racial marriage could no longer be enforced.[136] Among other things, supporters of the ban argued that the statute did not discriminate between the races, because it punished both blacks and whites who intermarried. They also claimed that since scientific evidence concerning whether African Americans were inferior was in doubt, the court should defer to the legislature on the question and let the laws stand. The court rejected the first argument, because Virginia's law was based upon a racial *classification*. The constitution's protection of equal treatment bars 'arbitrary and invidious' discrimination, and race is a classification that requires careful examination, to be sure that it is not being used for bad purposes. As a result, the doubtful scientific evidence could not be used to justify the state's law. It would matter only if the law had to be examined less carefully.

The court framed the right to marry in broad terms, based on the constitution's fourteenth amendment, which prohibits states from depriving people of 'life, liberty or property without due process of law':

Marriage is one of the 'basic civil rights of man', fundamental to our very existence and survival . . . To deny this fundamental freedom on so unsupportable a basis as the racial classifications embodied in these statutes, classifications so directly subversive of the principle of equality at the heart of the Fourteenth Amendment, is surely to deprive all the State's citizens of liberty without due process of law. The Fourteenth Amendment requires that the freedom of choice to marry not be restricted by invidious racial discrimination. Under our Constitution, the freedom to marry or not marry, a person of another race resides with the individual and cannot be infringed by the state.[137]

During the past decade, this argument has been advanced by those advocating same-sex marriage. We will return to those arguments in Chapter 5.

Conclusion

This chapter has expanded the focus from Great Britain and has included more varieties of marriage and different kinds of conflict than the previous chapters. Imposing the death penalty on Irish Catholic clergy who performed marriages between Protestants and Catholics is far more extreme than ignoring them, as was generally done in England in the 1700s and 1800s. Sending the US Army after Mormon polygamists in Utah is even more serious, although their disenfranchisement and deprivation of property is reminiscent of the UK's treatment of Irish Catholics. Once again, however, we note the importance of politics and culture to marriage and the enforcement of 'normality' on the family. What is 'normal' has generally been decided by those with political power.

In the United States, African Americans have been disenfranchised, and bans against interracial marriage protected whites, whatever that meant at a particular time, from the dilution of their power at the hands of a disadvantaged racial group. The same can be said of Roman Catholics in Ireland. Before independence Roman Catholics were treated badly, and that treatment produced a backlash reflected in the constitution, which gives precedence to theories of the family that were prevalent in the Republic of Ireland of the 1930s. Even when there is true majority rule, James Madison's warning holds: when a population is less diverse and lacks indirect, representative government, it is more likely to oppress minorities.[138] Ireland's political institutions, which include a bicameral legislature, provide some safeguards against minority oppression, but the homogeneity of Ireland has in the past made it difficult to protect minorities.

In three of the cases in this chapter it has been necessary for judges to intervene, either to permit interracial marriage (in the US) or to permit same-sex marriage (Canada and South Africa). In these cases, personalities are important. Earl Warren, chief justice of the US Supreme Court and the author of the majority opinion in *Loving*, had by 1967 acquired the reputation of a reformer. He had begun political life as a Republican prosecuting attorney in California, and during World War II he had been instrumental in the programme of confining Japanese Americans in camps, disrupting families and homes based upon their ancestry rather than on any real war-time threat.[139] He apologised for this in 1977.[140] By 1967, however, Warren was well known as the chief justice of the US Supreme Court who had abolished racial segregation in schools, had abolished school prayer and had introduced protections for defendants in criminal cases.[141] The *Loving* case had legitimacy based upon the reputation of this court and its chief justice.

Albie Sachs's career has been more heroic than Earl Warren's.[142] He served on the South African Constitutional Court from 1994, as one of its founding members, until he retired in 2009. His support for equal civil rights for non-whites in South Africa began when he was a law student at the University of Cape Town. He worked as a lawyer defending clients who were charged under the racist laws of the apartheid regime, and then went into exile in 1966. He was seriously injured in 1988, when a bomb placed in his car by South African security agents exploded: he lost an arm and the use of an eye. He helped the African National Congress with its organisation, and he was a major participant in the negotiations that ended with South Africa becoming a constitutional democracy. Both Warren and Sachs were closely involved in the changes in race relations in their respective countries, and both had moral authority that made it possible for them to open up marriage to excluded groups: African Americans in the United States and same-sex couples in South Africa.

Up to this point, we have been building up data. In Chapter 1 we described different, largely inconsistent theories of what marriage means. Chapters 2 and 3 examined the history of marriage law in England and Scotland, and in this chapter we have expanded our analysis to include marriage laws in Ireland, South Africa, Canada and the United States, including the first three countries' debates about same-sex marriage. In the next chapter we distil these data into policy recommendations. What matters about marriage, and what does not? What count as good arguments in favour of same-sex marriage, and which arguments do not make sense in light of the theories and facts that we have discussed up to now?

Notes

1. Quoted in *Loving v Virginia* (1967) 388 US 1, 3.
2. *Minister of Home Affairs* v. *Fourie* [2005] ZACC 19, para. 71.
3. W. P. Burke, *Irish Priests in the Penal Times (1660–1760)* (Shannon: Irish University Press, [1914] 1969); Ian McBride, *Eighteenth-century Ireland: The Isle of Slaves* (Dublin: Gill & Macmillan, 2009), p. 194 and works cited.
4. An Act to Prevent Marriages by Degraded Clergymen and Popish Priests etc. 1725 (Ireland).
5. Burke, *Irish Priests in the Penal Times*, pp. 188–9.
6. Marriages by Roman Catholics (Ireland) Act 1833, § 1; Matrimonial Causes and Marriage Law (Ireland) Amendment Act 1870.
7. Returns of Marriages Celebrated by Persons in Holy Orders in the Church of Rome, P.P. 1831–32 vol. 30, p. 65 (589).
8. James Kelly, 'The Abduction of Women of Fortune in Eighteenth-century Ireland', *Eighteenth-century Ireland* 9 (1994), pp. 7–43.
9. Marriage Act 1542 (Ireland), re-enacted in the Marriage Act 1725 (Ireland), § 21.
10. McBride, *Eighteenth-century Ireland*, p. 148.
11. (1843–4) 10 Cl & Fin 534, 8 ER 844.
12. Marriages (Ireland) Act 1844.
13. Albert Nicholson, 'Longworth, Maria Theresa (1833–1881)', rev. Catherine Pease-Watkin, *Oxford Dictionary of National Biography* (Oxford: Oxford University Press, 2004), http://www.oxforddnb.com/view/article/16998 (last accessed 11 May 2013); E. I. Carlyle, 'Yelverton, William Charles, fourth Viscount Avonmore (1824–1883)', rev. K. D. Reynolds, *Oxford Dictionary of National Biography* (Oxford: Oxford University Press, 2004), http://www.oxforddnb.com/view/article/30216 (last accessed 11 May 2013).
14. (1859) 1 Sw & Tr 574, 164 ER 866.
15. Matrimonial Causes and Marriage Law (Ireland) Amendment Act 1870.
16. Preamble, Constitution of Ireland, http://www.taoiseach.gov.ie.
17. Constitution of Ireland, Article 41, §§ 1.1, 3.1, 3.2.
18. Constitution of Ireland, Article 41, §§ 2.1–2.2.

19. 'The EU and Irish Women', European Commission website, http://ec.europa.eu/ireland/ireland_in_the_eu/impact_of_eu_on_irish_wom en/index_en.htm (last accessed 11 May 2013).

20. Constitution of Ireland, Article 41, § 3.3.

21. Christine P. James, 'Céad míle fáilte? Ireland Welcomes Divorce: The 1995 Irish Divorce Referendum and the Family (Divorce) Act of 1996', *Duke Journal of Comparative & International Law* 8(1) (1997), pp. 175–228.

22. *Referendum Results, 1937–2012* (Dublin: Department of the Environment, Community and Local Government), http://www.environ.ie/en/Pub lications/LocalGovernment/Voting/FileDownLoad,1894,en.pdf (last accessed 13 May 2013).

23. Judicial Reform and Family Law Reform Act 1989.

24. Lindsay L. Abbate, 'What God Has Joined "Let" Man Put Asunder: Ireland's Struggle between Canon and Common Law Relating to Divorce', *Emory International Law Review* 16(2) (2002), pp. 617–18.

25. Ibid., p. 597, n. 59.

26. Succession Act, No. 27 (1965); *O'B.* v. *S.* 1984 IR 316, 329–31; Kathleen M. Dillon, 'Divorce and Remarriage as Human Rights: The Irish Constitution and the European Convention on Human Rights at Odds in *Johnston* v. *Ireland*', *Cornell International Law Journal* 22(1) (1989), pp. 63–90.

27. Domicile and Recognition of Foreign Divorces Act 1986; see also Family Law Act 1995.

28. Brian Tobin, 'Gay Marriage – A Bridge Too Far?', *Irish Student Law Review* 15 (2007), pp. 175–96.

29. *Zappone and Gilligan* v. *Revenue Commissioners* [2006] IEHC 404, available online at http://www.bailii.org/ie/cases/IEHC/2006/H404.html (last accessed 13 May 2013).

30. All-Party Oireachtas Committee on the Constitution, *Tenth Progress Report: The Family* (Dublin: Stationery Office, 1996), https://www.con-stitution.ie/Documents/Oireachtas%2010th-Report-Family%202006.pdf (last accessed 13 May 2013).

31. Civil Partnership and Certain Rights and Obligations of Cohabitants Act 2010 (effective 1 January 2011).

32. 'Constitutional Convention: Government Proposals', Merrion Street (Irish Government News Service) website, 28 February 2012, http://www.merrionstreet.ie/index.php/2012/02/constitutional-convention-government-proposals-28-february-2012 (last accessed 13 May 2013). The convention's website is at https://www.constitution.ie.

33. https://www.constitution.ie/Submissions.aspx (last accessed 13 May 2013).

34. '75% support same-sex marriage: poll', *Irish Times*, 28 January 2013,

http://www.irishtimes.com/news/75-support-same-sex-marriage-poll-1.1072147 (last accessed 13 May 2013).

35. 'Millward Brown (Lansdown) Polling Highlights', Marriage Equality website, http://www.marriageequality.ie/getinformed/polling2012.html (last accessed 13 May 2013).

36. Henry McDonald, 'Ireland to hold gay marriage referendum', *The Guardian*, 14 April 2013, http://www.guardian.co.uk/world/2013/apr/14/ireland-hold-gay-marriage-referendum (last accessed 13 May 2013).

37. Iris Berger, *South Africa in World History* (Oxford: Oxford University Press, 2009), ch. 2.

38. Ibid., ch. 3.

39. Deborah Posel, *The Making of Apartheid, 1948–1961: Conflict and Compromise* (Oxford: Clarendon Press, 1991).

40. Marriage Act No. 25 of 1961. The requirement that banns be read was eliminated in the Marriage Amendment Act No. 51 of 1970.

41. Divorce Act No 70 of 1979. Before 1979, divorce had to be based upon adultery, malicious desertion, incurable mental illness lasting at least seven years or imprisonment for at least five years after having been declared a habitual criminal. Jacqueline Heaton et al., 'Marriage', in *The Law of South Africa* (Durban: Butterworths, 2006), vol. 16, § 161.

42. Prohibition of Mixed Marriages Act No. 55 of 1949, § 1(1); see also Immorality Act No. 23 of 1957 (subsequently renamed Sexual Offences Act 1957) as amended by Immorality Amendment Act No. 57 of 1969, and Immorality Act No. 5 of 1927 as amended by Immorality Amendment Act No. 21 of 1950.

43. For example, the Black Laws Amendment Act No. 76 of 1963 permitted a widow to claim damages for loss of support arising from her husband's death.

44. Deborah Posel, 'State, Power and Gender: Conflict over the Registration of African Customary Marriages in South Africa, c. 1910–1970', *Journal of Historical Sociology* 8(3) (1995), pp. 223–56.

45. The ban on interracial marriage was repealed in 1985 by the Immorality and Prohibition of Mixed Marriages Amendment Act No. 72.

46. The 1996 constitution of South Africa is available online at http://www.constitutionalcourt.org.za/site/theconstitution/english-09.pdf (last accessed 13 May 2013).

47. Constitution of South Africa (1996), § 9.

48. Ibid., § 39(2).

49. Recognition of Customary Marriages Act No. 120 of 1998.

50. Ibid., §§ 3(1), 7(6).

51. Ibid., § 8(1).

52. See e.g. *Recognition of Customary Marriages* (Cape Town: Women's

Legal Centre, 2011), http://www.wlce.co.za/morph_assets/theme lets/explorer/relationship%20rights/general/Recognition%20of%20 Customary%20Marriages.pdf (last accessed 13 May 2013); Nicola Barker, 'Ambiguous Symbolisms: Recognising Customary Marriage and Same-sex Marriage in South Africa', *International Journal of Law in Context* 7(4) (2011), pp. 447–66.

53. *Ismail* v. *Ismail* 1983 (1) SA 1006 (A).

54. 2005 (2) SA 272 (T), at paras 11.12–11.13.

55. *S.* v. *Makwanyane and Another* (CCT3/94) [1995] ZACC 3; *Government of the Republic of South Africa and Others* v. *Grootboom and Others* (CCT11/00) [2000] ZACC 19.

56. Heaton et al., 'Marriage', § 12.

57. *Minister of Home Affairs v Fourie.*

58. Ibid., para. 71.

59. He also addressed arguments based upon international law (paras 99–105) and justified discrimination against same-sex couples (paras 110–13).

60. Ibid., para. 86.

61. Ibid., para. 92.

62. Ibid., para. 97, citing Marriage Act of 1961, §§ 31, 34.

63. Civil Union Act No. 17 of 2006.

64. Ibid., § 13.

65. Ibid., § 1.

66. Ibid., §§ 4, 6.

67. Ibid., § 5.

68. Scott W. See, *The History of Canada* (Westport, CT: Greenwood Press, 2001).

69. Sylvia van Kirk, 'From "Marrying-in" to "Marrying-out": Changing Patterns of Aboriginal/Non-Aboriginal Marriage in Colonial Canada', *Frontiers: A Journal of Women Studies* 23(3) (2002), pp. 1–11.

70. Sections 91(26) and 92(12), respectively.

71. Peter W. Hogg, *Constitutional Law of Canada*, 4th ed. (Toronto: Carswell, 1997), § 26.3.

72. Marriage (Prohibited Degrees) Act 2005 SC, ch. 46.

73. Marriage Act, RSO 1990, ch. M.3, § 5(1); Marriage Act, RSBC 1996, ch. 282, § 28(1); see also Age of Majority Act, RSBC 1996, ch. 7 (establishing the age of majority at nineteen in British Columbia).

74. James G. Snell and Cynthia Comacchio Abeele, 'Regulating Nuptiality: Restricting Access to Marriage in Early Twentieth-century English-speaking Canada', *Canadian Historical Review* 69(4) (1988), p. 482.

75. Ibid., p. 475.

76. See, *History of Canada*, pp. 177–9. See also *EGALE Canada Inc.* v. *Canada (Attorney General)* 2003 BCCA 251 (CanLII), (2003), 225 DLR

(4th) 472, 2003 BCCA 251; *Halpern* v. *Canada (Attorney General)* 2003 CanLII 26403 (ON CA), (2003), 65 OR (3d) 161 (C.A.); *Hendricks* v. *Québec (Procureur général)*, 2002 CanLII 23808 (QC CS), [2002] RJQ 2506 (Sup. Ct.). For a detailed discussion of this litigation see Martha Bailey, 'Regulation of Cohabitation and Marriage in Canada', *Law and Policy* 26(1) (2004), pp. 165–6.

77. *EGALE* v. *Canada* (2001) BCSC 1365, [2001] 11 WWR 685; 88 CRR (2d) 322; 19 RFL (5th) 59; 95 BCLR (3d) 122, para. 75, citing *Hyde* v. *Hyde and Woodmansee* (1866), LR 1 P&D 130.

78. Ibid., paras 92–7.

79. Ibid., para. 124.

80. *EGALE Canada Inc.* v. *Canada (Attorney General)*, paras 69–71.

81. Ibid., paras 95, 135.

82. 2002 CanLII 42749 (ON SCDC), http://canlii.ca/t/7bf5 (last accessed 13 May 2013).

83. Ibid., para. 195.

84. Ibid., para. 238.

85. Ibid. para 241, citing *Baxter* v. *Baxter* [1948] AC 274 at 290, [1947] 2 All ER 886.

86. *Halpern* v. *Canada*, para. 66.

87. Ibid., para. 70.

88. Ibid., para. 34.

89. Bailey, 'Regulation of Cohabitation and Marriage in Canada', p. 166. The Supreme Court of Canada is permitted to hear and consider 'important questions of law or fact concerning . . . the powers of the Parliament of Canada . . . whether or not the particular power has been or is proposed to be exercised'. Supreme Court Act, RSC 1985, ch. S-26, § 53(1).

90. *Reference re Same-Sex Marriage*, 2004 SCC 79 (CanLII), [2004] 3 SCR 698, http://canlii.ca/t/1jdhv (last accessed 13 May 2013).

91. (1866) LR 1 P&D 130, at p. 133.

92. *Reference re Same-Sex Marriage*, para. 22.

93. Ibid., para. 45.

94. Ibid., para. 65.

95. Ibid., paras 67–71.

96. J. Scott Matthews, 'The Political Foundations of Support for Same-sex Marriage in Canada', *Canadian Journal of Political Science* 38(4) (2005), pp. 841–66.

97. Ibid., p. 862.

98. Nancy F. Cott, *Public Vows: A History of Marriage and Nation* (Cambridge, MA: Harvard University Press, 2000), p. 25.

99. John Curra, *The Relativity of Deviance*, 2nd ed. (Thousand Oaks, CA: Pine Forge Press, 2011), p. 233; James Steel Thayer, 'The Berdache

of the Northern Plains: A Socioreligious Perspective', *Journal of Anthropological Research* 36(3) (1980), pp. 287–93.

100. Margaret D. Jacobs, 'The Eastmans and the Luhans: Interracial Marriage between White Women and Native American Men, 1875–1935', *Frontiers: A Journal of Women's Studies* 23(3) (2002), pp. 29–54.

101. Cott, *Public Vows*, p. 264 n. 45.

102. Ibid., p. 121.

103. Ibid., pp. 135–7.

104. Ibid., p. 137.

105. Kerry Abrams, 'Polygamy, Prostitution, and the Federalization of Immigration Law', *Columbia Law Review* 105(3) (2005), p. 643.

106. Act of Mar. 3, 1875 (Page Law), ch. 141, 18 Stat. 477.

107. Abrams, 'Polygamy, Prostitution, and the Federalization of Immigration Law', p. 644.

108. Claudia L. Bushman and Richard L. Bushman, *Building the Kingdom: A History of the Mormons in America* (New York: Oxford University Press, 2001), ch. 1.

109. US Constitution, Amendment X.

110. Carol Cornwall Madsen, '"At Their Peril": Utah Law and the Case of Plural Wives, 1850–1900', in John S. McCormick and John R. Sillito (eds), *A World We Thought We Knew: Readings in Utah History* (Salt Lake City: University of Utah Press, 1995), p. 69.

111. Act of July 1 1862 (Morrill Anti-Bigamy Law), ch. 126, 12 Stat. 501.

112. *Reynolds* v. *US*, 98 US 145 (1878). Measured conservatively, the amount would be about £6,900 ($10,600) in today's currency.

113. Quoted at 98 US at 164. See Thomas Jefferson, *Writings*, ed. Merrill D. Peterson (New York: Literary Classics of the United States, 1984), p. 510 (emphasis in original).

114. See, e.g., Philip Hamburger, *Separation of Church and State* (Cambridge, MA: Harvard University Press, 2002); Noah Feldman, *Divided by God: America's Church–State Problem – and What We Should Do about It* (New York: Farrar, Straus & Giroux, 2005).

115. 98 US at 167.

116. Act of March 3, 1887 (Edmunds-Tucker Law), ch. 397, 24 Stat. 635.

117. *Late Corporation of the Church of Jesus Christ of Latter-Day Saints* v. *US*, 136 US 1 (1890).

118. Church of Jesus Christ of Latter-Day Saints, Doctrine and Covenants, Official Declaration 1, http://www.lds.org/scriptures/dc-testament/od/1 (last accessed 13 May 2013).

119. R. D. Poll, '"Buchanan's Blunder" the Utah War, 1857–1858', *Military Affairs* 25(3) (1961), pp. 121–31.

120. This is not to minimise religious persecution of Roman Catholics, Jews

or other smaller groups; however, military force has not been involved in these other cases.

121. Cardell K. Jacobson and Lara Burton (eds), *Mormon Polygamy in the United States: Historical, Cultural, and Legal Issues* (New York: Oxford University Press, 2011).

122. *Brown* v. *Herbert* (D UT 2012) 850 F.Supp. 2d 1240.

123. Act for the Better Preventing of a Spurious and Mixt Issue, Acts of the Province of Massachusetts Bay, 1705–6 3rd session, ch. 10, § 4.

124. Cott, *Public Vows*, pp. 40–1.

125. Ibid., p. 99 and note 64. Laws were passed in Alabama, Arizona, Colorado, Idaho, Mississippi, Nevada, Ohio, Oregon, South Carolina and West Virginia.

126. The case is described in Peggy Pascoe, 'Miscegenation Law, Court Cases, and Ideologies of "Race" in Twentieth-century America', *Journal of American History* 83(1) (1996), pp. 44–69. See also Peggy Pascoe, *What Comes Naturally: Miscegenation Law and the Making of Race in America* (New York: Oxford University Press, 2009).

127. 'All marriages of white persons with negroes or mulattoes are declared to be illegal and void. Whoever shall contract marriage in fact, contrary to the prohibitions in the two preceding sections, and whoever shall solemnize any such marriage shall be deemed guilty of a misdemeanor and upon conviction shall be punished by fine or imprisonment, or both, at the discretion of the jury which shall try the case; . . . the fine to be not less than $100 nor more than $10,000 and imprisonment to be not less than 3 months nor more than 10 years.' An Act Regulating Marriages, Cal. Stats. 1850, §§ 53–4, p. 424.

128. Irving G. Tragen, 'Statutory Prohibitions against Interracial Marriage', *California Law Review* 32(3) (1944), p. 272 n. 17.

129. *Perez* v. *Lippold*, 32 Cal.2d 711, 198 P.2d 17 (1948) at 198 P.2d 18.

130. 198 P.2d at 22.

131. Ibid. at 27–8.

132. Ibid. at 26.

133. Ibid. at 25. The court also rejected the factual basis for this claim.

134. *Loving v Virginia*, 388 US 1 (1967).

135. 388 US at 3.

136. Besides Virginia, the states in question were: Alabama, Arkansas, Delaware, Florida, Georgia, Kentucky, Louisiana, Mississippi, Missouri, North Carolina, Oklahoma, South Carolina, Tennessee, Texas and West Virginia. *Loving*, 388 US at 6 n. 5.

137. 388 US at 12.

138. Sean Nicholson-Crotty, 'Reassessing Madison's Diversity Hypothesis: The Case of Same-sex Marriage', *Journal of Politics* 68(4) (2006), pp. 922–30.

139. G. Edward White, *Earl Warren: A Public Life* (New York: Oxford University Press, 1982), p. 67.

140. Melissa Cully Anderson and Bruce E. Cain, 'The Warren Court and Redistricting', in H. N. Scheiber (ed.), *Earl Warren and the Warren Court: The Legacy in Foreign and American Law* (Berkeley, CA: Lexington, 2007), p. 41.

141. *Brown* v. *Board of Education*, 347 US 483 (1954); *Engel* v. *Vitale*, 370 US 421 (1962); *Gideon* v. *Wainwright*, 372 US 335 (1963) (right to counsel); *Miranda* v. *Arizona*, 384 US 436 (1966) (right to be informed of rights and need for voluntary waiver).

142. 'Justice Albie Sachs', Constitutional Court of South Africa website, http://www.constitutionalcourt.org.za/site/judges/justicealbiesachs/index1.html (last accessed 13 May 2013).

5

Current Policy Questions: Fighting Fair about Same-sex Marriage

It's gude to be merry and wise,
It's gude to be honest and true,
And afore you're off wi' the auld love
It's best to be on wi' the new.

Old Scottish song[1]

It's gude to be merry and wise;
It's gude to be honest and true;
It's gude to be aff wi' the auld love,
Before ye be on wi' the new.

Robert Burns[2]

Whether in literature, law or politics, some arguments make more sense than others. That holds particularly true in the debate about same-sex marriage, where people's positions can become quite emotional. According to one recent story, a group of conservative Russian Orthodox Christians sued to void the sale of Alaska to the US in 1867.[3] They said that they were trying to rescue Orthodox Christians in Alaska from the immorality of the United States' approval of same-sex marriage. Their claim was based on the US government's payment for the Russian territory with a cheque, instead of with gold as had been promised in the treaty. Their case was thrown out of a Russian court for technical reasons. In this chapter we turn more explicitly to the debate about same-sex marriage than we have in previous chapters, and our objective is to narrow the argument, so that people focus on what matters and not on what doesn't.

We are not claiming that any of the arguments about same-sex marriage we examine here are as silly as the ones by these Russian plaintiffs. But we do claim that some arguments are worth spending time on, and others are not. Among those that need not detain us, and we will show why not, are arguments about sex and natural law. A more borderline question, which we still think should be disposed of without too much discussion, is the question of plural marriage: polygyny or polyamory.

But there are serious questions about how same-sex marriage should happen and what interests need to be protected. The first of these is about religious freedom. Religious organisations and faith groups should be treated equally. They should be free to celebrate and recognise those marriages that are legitimate in their particular faith traditions – the question is how far that freedom should extend beyond the marriage ceremony itself. Equally important is the point that marriage should be portable. Spouses' rights and obligations should not vary drastically from one legal jurisdiction to another, and they should know where they stand when they travel, whether on holiday or for work. These policy questions are the subject of this chapter.

What doesn't matter

Private sexual behaviour

The word 'privacy' is not used in the United States constitution, but it is in the European Convention on Human Rights (ECHR), which was adopted by the Council of Europe following the Second World War.[4] Article 8 ECHR says: 'Everyone has the right to respect for his private and family life, his home and his correspondence.' The article also says that this protection is not absolute; indeed, it can be infringed for purposes such as public safety, economic well-being and even the protection of health and morals. So a court must determine whether a law or government conduct that infringes on privacy or family life is *necessary* for one of these purposes on a case-by-case basis.

The most recent authoritative statements about the privacy interests protected by the US constitution are to be found in the Supreme Court's decision in *Lawrence* v. *Texas*, which found a state anti-sodomy law unconstitutional.[5] Sexual privacy has been an issue in American law since at least 1965 when the court decided *Griswold* v. *Connecticut*, saying that a married couple had the right to use contraceptives and that a law banning them infringed their privacy. Underpinning that decision, which famously rested on a 'penumbra' of associational rights, is also the fourth amendment, which like Article 8 ECHR protects people's security in their 'persons, houses, papers and effects'.[6] The similarity to ECHR Article 8 is fairly obvious.

The principle of *Griswold* was extended outside the marital bedroom in *Eisenstadt* v. *Baird*, where the court said that unmarried people also had the right to obtain contraceptives.[7] Together, these cases limit the government's ability to regulate private sexual behaviour between consenting adults.[8] In *Lawrence*, the court recognised 'an emerging awareness that liberty gives substantial protection to adult persons in deciding how to conduct their private lives in matters pertaining to sex' and overruled its previous decision, *Bowers* v. *Hardwick*, that states could criminalise same-sex sexual behaviour.[9] Among other things, it relied upon a case from the European Court of Human Rights, applying Article 9 of the ECHR, to contradict a statement in its earlier decision, that condemnation of same-sex conduct was uniform, historical and international.[10]

Privacy is not enough to justify same-sex marriage, or even non-discrimination against LGBT people in employment or the provision of goods or services.[11] However, it is at the root of one of the discussions about whether same-sex marriage should be legal: the relative importance or unimportance of consummation and/or adultery to marriage. In English law, consummation is the penetration of a vagina by a penis.[12] Adultery is comparable to consummation: 'Adultery cannot be proved unless there be some penetration. It is not necessary that the complete act of sexual intercourse should take place.'[13] Our colleague Leslie Green has summarised the common law cases about consummation as 'nothing less, but emphatically nothing more, than the penetration of a vagina by a penis to a sufficient depth and duration to please the trier of fact'.[14] The same summary applies to adultery.[15]

Nevertheless, public officials, including former judges, have objected to British proposals for same-sex marriage based upon the fact that neither consummation nor adultery is possible for a same-sex couple, who by definition lack one of the required sexual organs. (This does not apply to bisexuals, who could commit adultery outside their same-sex marriage. But that need not detain us here.) Even some progressives have argued that not including these concepts in same-sex marriage statutes violates principles of equality.[16] But these arguments should be dismissed. First of all, as Lord Justice Hodson pointed out in *Dennis* v. *Dennis*, 'adultery, being a secret matter, as a rule has to be inferred from evidence of inclination and opportunity'.[17] Adultery and consummation fall into the same trap as the Fleet registers discussed in Chapter 2: they are difficult to reliably prove. Also recall the Tudor repeal of the statute requiring consummation, also discussed in Chapter 2. The requirement led to unintended consequences and had to be abandoned. Today a requirement to prove either adultery or consummation, in order to prove a valid marriage or to prevail in a divorce, should fall foul of Article 8 ECHR or of the privacy provisions of the US constitution.

Neither consummation nor adultery is important until a marriage relationship has broken down. In earlier times, a man might have the option of proving his ability to consummate by having sex with a prostitute before witnesses.[18] Less intrusive trials still became a way of selling pornography to the public.[19] Practices like these seem not only antiquated but outright offensive today. Proof of private sexual conduct as a basis for making legal decisions about people's status is incoherent with modern ideas of privacy and human dignity.

Likewise, adultery is today one sub-class of a single requirement for divorce in England and Wales under the Matrimonial Causes Act 1973: irretrievable breakdown.[20] Desertion is also a basis for showing irretrievable breakdown. As we have seen, these bases date from the 1500s in Scotland, and they were among the first grounds for divorce in England when Parliament approved judicial divorce (Chapter 3). But adultery is no longer a crime. Non-consummation is an adaptation of the ecclesiastical law's impediment to marriage, which made a marriage voidable when the man was impotent.[21] Now both of these problems arise only if one of the spouses becomes unhappy with the marriage. Either spouse may tolerate adultery, and no one need know of non-consummation unless the other spouse complains.[22] By agreement spouses can contract out of any supposed obligations about sex. All this is a consequence of the modern conception of privacy.[23]

Divorcing couples' behaviour is further evidence of this point. Figure 5.1 compares two of the legal bases for divorce, both of

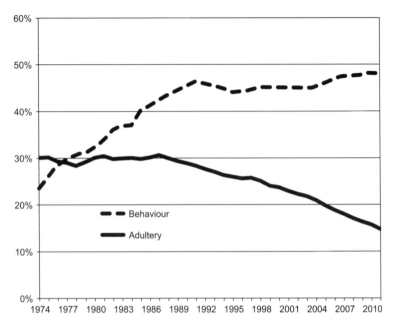

Figure 5.1 Divorce petitions in England and Wales granted based upon an allegation of adultery and unreasonable behaviour as a percentage of all petitions granted.

Source: Office of National Statistics, Divorces in England and Wales 2011, available at http://www.ons.gov.uk/ons/rel/vsob1/divorces-in-england-and-wales/2011/rft-divorces--number-of-divorces-age-at-divorce-and-marital-status-before-marriage.xls (last accessed 13 May 2013).

which count as 'irretrievable breakdown': adultery and a catch-all category called 'unreasonable behaviour'.[24] In 1977 approximately equal percentages accounted for divorces in these two categories; the others available to divorcing couples were 'desertion' or 'separation'. Since then the incidence of adultery as a basis for divorce has steadily declined, so that in 2011 fewer than 15 per cent of divorces were granted for adultery. It does not seem plausible that less adultery is happening now than in 1977. What does seem plausible is that married people consider their sexual conduct a private matter (even when they divorce) and believe that a judge knows enough about their relationship if one party thinks the other has 'behaved unreasonably'. Most couples seem to think that sex should be a private matter, and judges, who have other things to worry about than married adults' sex lives, should get on with other pursuits than hearing evidence about matters like these.

Sex is not part of the public, legal conception of marriage. Reproductive sex has not been part of marriage in the United States since *Griswold*. A state's investigation into a person's past sexual conduct should violate Article 8 ECHR.[25] Arguments about the sexual aspect of the marital relationship are not ones that couples normally want the state to investigate. And they are not ones that should detain policymakers who are serious about respecting people's dignity and human rights.

Natural law

Natural law has existed in many forms over the centuries, and at bottom its central claim is non-controversial: legal rules must be rational. So far, so good. One leading post-war natural law theorist was Lon L. Fuller.[26] He believed that law had to be founded on certain principles, including non-contradiction, prospectivity (no *ex post facto* laws) and certainty. Again, this seems to be fairly common sense, although it led to a vigorous dispute with the legal philosopher H. L. A. Hart, who was a positivist and believed that laws are rules of different kinds, independent of any required 'principles'.[27] In recent decades, however, natural law theory has gone beyond Fuller's formal requirements to argue more forcefully for substantive moral foundations for law, to show that law has a moral purpose.

The debate over same-sex marriage has attracted many of these natural lawyers, who oppose it because it is inconsistent with human nature and moral law.[28] They begin by identifying certain human goods, which include marriage (or possibly 'life' in John Finnis's work) and friendship and which are independent. Each has multiple purposes, including human fulfilment and benefits for society. These add up to human flourishing. According to the new natural law (NNL) theorists, confusing one with another confuses the particular purposes and benefits of each. Marriage and friendship are independent goods, which benefit spouses, friends and society in different ways. A married couple may also be friends, but to confuse those two relationships is to detract from both. Marriage is an essentially pro-creative relationship; friendship is not. Both relationships are ones where people care deeply about one another, but the purpose of the relationships is different. A married couple enjoys raising children together; friends enjoy doing things like going to the movies and playing golf together. Moreover, both relationships can be corrupted in parallel but different ways. People who treat their spouses badly by only caring about sex or about the children (and not about their collective enterprise, 'raising a family') offend the dignity of the spouse or the children. Friends who treat one another instrumentally, for example as networking contacts for business or social purposes, do so at the other's expense.

From these premises, NNL draws some very specific conclusions about same-sex relationships and particularly about same-sex marriage. Because human beings are 'embodied', it is necessary that their bodies join in a procreative act for them to be really complete in marriage:

> Our claim is that a marital act is an act in which a man and woman, as complementary, become bodily and organically one, in that they jointly perform a single act, single in that it is an act that is biologically oriented to procreation, though some other condition in the agents may prevent the completion of that orientation in this act.[29]

Other sexual acts (including all sex acts that do not involve penetration as defined above) simply will not do, as they offend the dignity of those involved, just as it offends the integrity of a friendship to use it primarily for social or business networking. Rearing children is not sufficient for this kind of relationship; any two people (siblings, for example) can raise a child. Indeed, we might add, single people may do so, as may institutions such as orphanages. The child must be the biological product of the relationship in order to offer the fulfilment of a family. Marriage can be defined in no other way than as potentially procreative: involving a penis and a vagina and coitus.

Many have pointed out the incoherence of this position.[30] The first problem is that natural law cannot comply with John Rawls's requirement that law be justifiable with public reasons. By the time the NNL argument arrives at the goods that define human flourishing, it has become a reasonable comprehensive doctrine. Recall the definition of reasonable comprehensive doctrines from Chapter 1: 'they include conceptions of what is of value in human life, and ideals of personal character, friendship, and familial and associational relationship, amongst other things'. NNL fits squarely into this category. While NNL is entitled to compete for political goods in the debate about same-sex marriage, it is not entitled to deference, and its adherents have a duty to express policy objectives in terms that can be agreed to by those who do not accept the entire doctrine. Simply put, others participating in the debate can take NNL or leave it. But more needs to be said in defence of the NNL position, to make it plausible for those who do not accept this particular view of 'human goods'. What makes that more difficult today is the concept of complementarity that is used to justify the need for an opposite-sex couple in a marriage. Once one accepts the premise, then other kinds of gender discrimination become acceptable, including traditional breadwinner/homemaker gender roles in the house (think of the Irish constitution in Chapter 4).

Besides these problems, the goods that NNL depends upon so heavily are difficult to define in mutually exclusive, collectively exhaustive ways, so that they are analytically satisfactory; indeed, they seem somewhat arbitrary. To return to the good of friendship, friendships are defined by 'unions of minds and wills, by which each friend comes to know and seek the other's good'. Scholarly relationships 'are most embodied in joint inquiry, discovery, and publication'.[31] But what other relationships count? Are business relationships of a similar kind, so that the two (or more) participants seek mutual benefit from economic surplus? If not, why not? And if this is the case, then is it not possible that different kinds of marriage have their own goods, including same-sex marriages (where the gender equality improves the marriage by reducing the potential that the spouses will take on breadwinner/homemaker roles) or even plural marriages (which might promote something like 'sexual unselfishness')?

NNL also advances the 'one-flesh' argument quoted above, which is related to the notion of complementarity. Recalling Plato's Aristophanes, however, which we discussed in Chapter 1, the one flesh could also be a same-sex flesh, according to a more classical theory. Some women might understand themselves as part of an entirely female whole, and some men might be sliced from an entirely male whole, so that they become 'one flesh' when they engage in same-sex sexual conduct. And a third category of both sexes might be separated from an opposite-sex whole, so that they have a desire to reunite with someone of the opposite sex. Certainly, NNL theorists can find support for their general theory from Genesis 2:21–2: 'So the Lord God caused a deep sleep to fall upon the man, and he slept; then he took one of his ribs and closed up its place with flesh. And the rib that the Lord God had taken from the man he made into a woman and brought her to the man.' NNL theorists point out that other classical authors support the Genesis view. But a public reason must accommodate *competing* reasonable comprehensive doctrines, not just those that are consistent. And the Plato–Aristophanes view competes with the view of the NNL.[32]

The NNL theorists also focus on the importance of biological children, as is evident from their emphasis on procreation and coitus. As we saw in Chapter 4, however, Justice Albie Sachs was dismissive of the argument that marriage is defined by procreation:

> [The argument is] deeply demeaning to couples (whether married or not) who, for whatever reason, are incapable of procreating when they commence such relationship or become so at any time thereafter. It is likewise demeaning to couples who commence such a relationship at an age when they no longer have the desire for sexual relations or the capacity to conceive. It is demeaning to adoptive parents to suggest that their family is any less a family and any less entitled to respect and concern than a family with procreated children. It is even demeaning of a couple who voluntarily decide not to have children or sexual relations with one another; this being a decision entirely within their protected sphere of freedom and privacy.[33]

Finally, the legal history of marriage, as we have described it in Chapters 2 to 4, does not support the NNL view. Historically, marriage has been important because procreation was a possible consequence, not because it was the essence of marriage. Not one of the legal regimes we have discussed made it necessary for a couple to be able to procreate in order to marry, for example by excluding post-menopausal women. The law of marriage has taken a number of forms. But it seems implausible to argue that Henry Fox was concerned about anything other than freedom to marry someone of another class (for money and political power), or that Lord Hardwicke was worried about anything other than stopping Fox. Those who opposed the extension of legal marriage to include weddings by Nonconformist clergy in 1836 were concerned with preserving established religion, if not a religious monopoly. Historically, almost no one has been concerned with whether procreation was part of the law of marriage or not. Policymakers should not become preoccupied with it either.

Polygamy

As we have seen (Chapter 4), polygamy was practised in Utah in the mid- to late-1800s based upon Old Testament principles, and it is currently practised in African customary marriages. Both are based upon religious belief. Joseph Smith, for example, relied upon the polygyny of Abraham and David as authority for his commendation of the practice.[34] Recent scholars have also argued that the number of spouses that a person marries should be more flexible and should avoid any 'amatonormative' idealisation of the romantic couple. Instead it should include support for friendships and care networks, including 'urban tribes'.[35] Some critics of same-sex marriage believe that relaxation of marriage laws to include same-sex couples will also lead to relaxation of the same laws to permit polygamy.[36]

Perhaps because of the history of Mormonism and polygamy in the United States, the practice is actually less tolerated in law there today than it is in the UK. The nineteenth-century case *Hyde* v. *Hyde* defined marriage in the following terms: 'I conceive that marriage, as understood in Christendom, may for this purpose be defined as the voluntary union for life of one man and one woman, to the exclusion of all others.'[37] In this case, a Mormon had travelled from London, where he met his wife, to the then territory of Utah, where they were married according to Mormon rites. They fell out, he was divorced under Utah law, and he returned to Britain. He asked the court for a divorce based upon his wife's adultery. She had married and lived with a man named Joseph Woodmansee. But because their Utah marriage was potentially polygamous, even though they had remained monogamous during their marriage, the court refused to recognise it or to grant a divorce.[38]

Current law, however, allows a court in England or Wales to grant legal relief (including a divorce and financial settlement) to spouses in a polygamous marriage, as long as the marriage took place in a place where polygamy was legal and the spouses were not domiciled (living permanently) in England or Wales when they were married.[39] In the United States, such broad recognition of polygamous marriages is not offered, and bigamy is illegal everywhere. However, Utah, for example, has a policy of not prosecuting criminal charges against polygamists unless other crimes, such as underage sex or incest, are present.[40] Just as in the early North American colonies, where local communities could recognise informal divorces, local practice may depart from the formal requirements of law.

As we saw in Chapter 1, David Hume had compelling arguments against polygamy. First, it skews the marriage market, and creates jealousy among those who have fewer wives. Judge Richard Posner goes further and argues that it limits the supply of spouses and creates queuing, so that men at the back of the line create demand for prostitution.[41] Second, historically, women have been segregated in order to protect them against this jealousy. Third, Hume argues that children will not be raised well. Updating his third argument slightly, we can point out that if all the spouses are responsible for raising all the children, principal-agent problems will arise, so that it is difficult to determine exactly which spouse is responsible for any one child's problems. Hume hints at this when he says that that a spouse of one sex must use tactics to divide and conquer multiple spouses of the other sex: hierarchy is a structural necessity in a plural marriage.

Stephen Macedo has summarised the arguments against polygamous marriage, which do not read across to same-sex marriage.[42] He rightly emphasises the distinction between legal recognition of multiple-partner relationships and people who choose to live in plural marriages without legal recognition: 'Consenting adults should be able to sleep with, eat breakfast with, and maintain a household with whom they want, so long as there is not a distinct harm to others.' In so far as legal recognition is concerned, however, he points out, first, that a desire to have multiple, simultaneous spouses is not an orientation, a deep-seated and limiting feature of human personality, in the same way that same-sex attraction is. Instead, it is a preference. Second, historically, anthropologically and even currently, polygamous families have been associated with women's inequality, domestic violence and poorer outcomes for children. Third, marriage is already a relationship that requires a great deal of negotiation between two partners to make it workable, in terms of personal and social roles and responsibilities. Bringing in a third party makes the negotiations more complex and the relationship less stable.

The fact is that little actual support exists for expanding marriage to include multiple partners. Government resources are limited, and democratic choices do not favour a move in this direction. Things may change in the future – the history of marriage shows that it is not an institution frozen in time. And there is a great deal to be said for the integration of foreign polygamous marriage into British law. But no evidence supports a claim that one change in the law of marriage (allowing same-sex marriage) will inevitably lead to another (polygamy).

What matters a lot

In this part of the chapter, we are concerned with public policy matters that are susceptible to debate in a liberal democracy based upon public reason. There are no clear, self-evident answers to the questions we ask, and policymakers and voters must make decisions between competing values, which may be based upon individual preferences, local circumstances, history or political culture. The answers to these questions may also be driven by powerful, well-organised groups, so that the results reflect their preferences rather than any popular notion of what the right outcome should be. Nevertheless, these are issues that we think must be addressed in any sensible debate about same-sex marriage, and if a person is making a decision about how to vote or is writing to her legislator, she should consider carefully her position on these questions.

Religious freedom

The most vigorously contested values that crop up in discussions of same-sex marriage are religious freedom and religious equality. Roman Catholic theology is, at present, incompatible with same-sex marriage and appears likely to remain so for the foreseeable future. However, Liberal Jews, Unitarians and Quakers in the UK have all decided that they would like to be able to perform religious wedding ceremonies for same-sex couples. In the US, the groups that are most supportive of same-sex marriage include the Quakers, the Metropolitan Community Church (a denomination based upon acceptance of sexual minorities), the United Church of Christ and some parts of the Episcopal Church, the non-established US version of the Church of England. All of these groups have their own reasonable comprehensive doctrines, but none should prevail over the others in a liberal democracy.[43] If Quakers are allowed to perform wedding ceremonies for opposite-sex couples and wish to do so for same-sex couples, then it seems obvious that if the state allows same-sex marriage at all, it must extend the power to celebrate same-sex marriages to Quakers (and Liberal Jews and Unitarians, too). At the same time, the Roman Catholics and others should be allowed to refuse to marry same-sex couples, just as they are currently allowed to refuse to marry those who are divorced and whose spouses are still living.

It does not seem coincidental that these three British religious organisations are the first to ask to perform same-sex marriages. As we showed in Chapter 3, Quakers and Jews have been exempt from many general laws about marriage in the UK since 1753, and Unitarians were the first denomination to aggressively seek an exemption from Lord Hardwicke's Act in the early 1800s. One difference is that in 1753 Quakers and Jews both married endogamously, within their own religious denomination. Intermarriage with other, larger and more powerful denominations or religions was not possible, so that the risk to those other groups of loss of membership or financial support was limited. In 1825, however, MPs expressed concerns that Unitarian ministers might marry members of the Church of England. Today, Roman Catholics (and others) can quite reasonably be concerned that their members who want to enter into same-sex marriages will do so (sinfully) in another church, just as they remarry after divorce. But according to modern liberal principles, no one group's reasonable comprehensive doctrine can be systematically favoured over another's, and it is generally accepted that people should be able to choose which religion to adhere to or whether to adhere to one at all. The state can no longer base its policy on the preference of one religion or religious denomination over others, as it could in 1753.

But the principle works the other way, too. According to Rawls a plurality of reasonable comprehensive doctrines is a product of a free, democratic state with a culture of free institutions. Although some, such as Richard Dawkins, might disagree,[44] it seems at least impolite if not malicious to deny that Roman Catholicism is a comprehensive doctrine, which one can understand that other reasonable people might believe in. Indeed, Rawls admired the Roman Catholic jurist and political philosopher Jean Bodin.[45] Rawls considers individuals who recognise religious and moral obligations as being bound absolutely by them.[46] And he offers vigorous defences of freedom of thought and conscience, including religion. Thus, it is in the interests of all to ensure that Catholics and others who disagree with same-sex marriage on principled, moral grounds should not be forced to endorse it. As we said in Chapter 1, government should not interfere in religious practice unless there is a good reason to do so. The question is how much protection should be offered when religious interests conflict with other kinds of interest (particularly those in non-discrimination). Three cases can serve to illustrate this point.

In September 2006 Vanessa Willock contacted Elane Photography in Albuquerque, New Mexico and asked whether her company would photograph her commitment ceremony with her same-sex partner. The owners of the business, Christians who object to same-sex relationships, refused to take the job, although they advertised their business to the public through the internet and the commercial telephone directory. The New Mexico Human Rights Commission found that the photographer had violated New Mexico's sexual orientation anti-discrimination law. The New Mexico Court of Appeals affirmed the Human Rights Commission's decision.[47]

On 4 September 2008 Steven Preddy booked a room with a double bed at the Chymorvah Hotel in Cornwall for himself and his civil partner, Martin Hall. The hotel was owned by Peter and Hazel Bull, devout Christians. The online booking form contains the statement, 'Here at Chymorvah we have few rules, but please note, that out of a deep regard for marriage we prefer to let double accommodation to heterosexual married couples only – thank you.' Unfortunately, Preddy booked by phone, so he did not see the statement, and Mrs Bull was ill when she took the reservation, so she did not follow her normal practice of telling Preddy that the hotel offered double rooms to married couples only. When Preddy and Hall arrived at the hotel, they were told that only opposite-sex, married couples could stay in double rooms, and they were forced to find alternative accommodation. Preddy and Hall brought a legal action, and the courts decided that they had suffered direct discrimination based upon their sexual orientation. They were awarded £1,800 in damages.[48]

In June 2012 a married, same-sex couple negotiated with the Roman Catholic Diocese of Worcester, Massachusetts to purchase a former conference and retreat centre. Same-sex weddings are legal in Massachusetts. After the negotiations broke down, the lawyer for the diocese inadvertently forwarded an email from his client to the couple's broker, which said:

> I just went down the hall and discussed it with the bishop. Because of the potentiality of gay marriages there, something you shared with us yesterday, we aren't interested in going forward with these buyers. I think they're shaky anyway. So just tell them that we will not accept their revised plan and the Diocese is making new plans for the property. You find the language.[49]

The diocese has claimed that the potential buyers could not finance the purchase ('they're shaky anyway'), but the buyers have claimed that the diocese engaged in sexual orientation discrimination, which is illegal under Massachusetts law. The diocese argues that it is entitled to limit sales of its properties to those who will use them for purposes consistent with Roman Catholic doctrine. The property has since been sold to a buyer who has publicly stated that he will not use it for same-sex weddings. No lawsuit has been filed at the time of writing.

These cases are on the boundary of the religious exemptions

that might be allowed for believers who object to same-sex marriage (many would say they are beyond the boundary). Different approaches can be taken to how that boundary is drawn, and at least three models approach the question in different ways. The first of these is a narrow rule that defines which categories of individuals are entitled to protection from having to accept same-sex marriage. The second is more factually oriented and sees the problem primarily from the point of view of the religious believer, while acknowledging that same-sex couples deserve respect as well. The third model shifts the emphasis away from the religious believer, offering more (but still not complete) protection to the same-sex couple from dignitary harms that come from being discriminated against.

In all these models, and in others like them, it is important to emphasise that two comparable interests must be balanced. Both sexual orientation and religious identity share common characteristics: (1) they are reflective of personal autonomy, in the sense that they involve an expression of one's identity; (2) they have a merged identity and conduct dimension, so that Christian belief or sexual orientation cannot readily be separated from acting on that belief or orientation; (3) they are intensely relational, based upon a connection with God or a spouse or partner and recognition of that connection in a broader community; and (4) they create duties and responsibilities.[50] These interests – religious liberty and non-discrimination – are similar in important ways and should be treated that way.

Model 1. Chai Feldblum has advocated allowing exemptions for ministers and churches, so that they do not have to perform same-sex weddings, as well as for enterprises operated by belief communities that are specifically designed to inculcate values in the next generation, such as schools, day-care centres, summer camps and even tours (including, perhaps, religious groups' tours to sacred sites like Jerusalem).[51] None of these organisations should be required to perform or recognise same-sex marriage. Feldblum also tentatively extends this exemption to leadership in enterprises that are broadly commercial: hospitals, adoption agencies and drug treatment centres. Notably, she includes all organisations, whether religious or non-religious, where liberty of belief, not just religious belief, warrants an exemption from general laws prohibiting discrimination. In all of these cases, however, the people and the conduct exempted from anti-discrimination laws are closely connected to maintaining, teaching and passing on adherence to the reasonable comprehensive doctrine. Teaching in a religious school ensures that the religion is passed on to the next generation. In the leadership exemption, broad principles of ethics and morality may be involved, say, in management decisions and the overall business plan.

The religious or moral comprehensive doctrine may be promoted, even if that involves disqualifying some individuals, such as those involved in same-sex relationships, from making those management decisions, since those adhering to the comprehensive doctrine may reasonably believe that people in same-sex relationships cannot consistently adhere to other fundamental tenets of the doctrine. In all other cases, however, Feldblum argues that the requirement of equal treatment should apply to same-sex couples and to all goods and services provided by those who object to same-sex marriage. Feldblum would offer no exemptions to the photographer, the hoteliers or the property seller in the cases above.

Feldblum's model can be thought of as beginning with core cases that must be protected and trying to find the limits for that rationale. 'Leadership' is one line she draws, and the line can be justified by the fact that leaders have to exercise broad discretion, which will be informed by principles, and those principles may be religious ones. What does 'leadership' include? There will be borderline cases, but leaders will not include typists and others who exercise less discretion in their jobs. According to Feldblum's model, there is no justification for broadly commercial enterprises (even non-profits), which are open to the public, to discriminate against typists and janitors in same-sex relationships or marriages.[52] But this raises another question. Should a typist be able to object to particular tasks for religious reasons, including, say, typing the notice of a civil marriage to be published by the registrar?[53]

The next two models can be thought of in a different way, perhaps as extensions of Model 1. Instead of trying to define reasons for exemptions from non-discrimination rules using core cases, these models focus on the periphery. How much religion should the law either force or allow employers to tolerate?

Model 2. Two methods of dealing with peripheral cases are offered by Douglas Laycock, Robin Fretwell Wilson and others.[54] First, they believe that institutional arrangements can minimise the impact of discriminatory exemptions for same-sex couples. Wilson gives the example of a government licensing office where marriages are solemnised by four clerks: Faith, Hope, Charity and Efficiency. Only Faith objects to same-sex marriage. If the clerks serve the public at random, then a problem will arise if Steve comes to the counter and Faith only later realises that he is there with his same-sex partner. If she refuses to serve Steve, he will be harmed. Wilson proposes that Efficiency should serve as the intake clerk, assigning only opposite-sex couples to Faith. In this way she will be able to protect her conscience without offending any members of the public, who will never know that they have been diverted away from Faith. An established institutional arrangement of this kind would have eliminated the conflict in *Ladele* v. *UK*, recently decided by the ECtHR, in which a registrar was fired because of her refusal to participate in civil partnership ceremonies.[55]

Second, in addition to these kinds of institutional arrangement, Wilson and Laycock propose broad legal exemptions for those who oppose same-sex marriage.[56] They have drafted a model statute that protects religious organisations from having to 'provide services, accommodations . . . or privileges related to the . . . celebration of any marriage' and even from being required to treat the marriage as valid. Likewise, their statute offers a blanket exemption to small businesses unless the same-sex couple was 'unable to obtain any similar goods or services, employment benefits, or housing elsewhere without substantial hardship'. They go so far as to allow a conscientious opt-out for state judges who object to performing same-sex weddings. To offer additional protection to protect same-sex couples from being surprised or inconvenienced, these authors consider whether it would be desirable to impose a notice requirement on the discriminatory businesses, so that customers would be able to avoid them. The notice would be like the one that the Bulls had on their online reservation forms.

Laycock and Wilson focus on the reasonable expectations of both parties and point out that same-sex couples probably do not want those who have strong moral objections to their relationships providing flowers or taking photographs at their weddings. It even seems, intuitively, that many couples like Steve Preddy and Martin Hall would prefer not to unknowingly make a reservation to stay in a small hotel with owners who rented the room but then made their disapproval obvious in legal but unpleasant ways. Preddy and Hall objected to being sent to another bed and breakfast, but other couples might want to know before they faced sullen hoteliers and poor service (and perhaps 'misplaced' reservations when they arrived to stay for the night).

It is important to note that many advocates of these broad exemptions, including Wilson and Laycock, are also advocates of same-sex marriage. They believe that because attitudes towards same-sex marriage are changing rapidly, the exemptions will soon be unnecessary and will die out. But they also believe that the exemptions are desirable to protect religious liberty and to make passage of same-sex marriage legislation politically feasible in more states.

These proposals have been criticised.[57] The notice requirement is reminiscent of signs saying that certain racial or ethnic groups were not welcome in commercial establishments such as hotels or restaurants in the last century and before. Laycock hopes that businesses with notices declaring discriminatory intent will lose business from all, including opposite-sex couples, who support same-sex marriage. He admits, however, that if the signs become sufficiently numerous they could encourage similar discrimination by making it acceptable. Moreover, one of the early, basic steps towards equality for same-sex couples was broad anti-discrimination legislation protecting sexual orientation. The Laycock–Wilson statute would substantially weaken that legislation. Indeed, some proposed statutory exemptions for religious belief are not limited to same-sex marriage and could permit other kinds of discrimination based upon marital status, including interracial marriage. Despite these problems Laycock and Wilson have been relatively successful at obtaining religious exemptions in states where same-sex marriage has been adopted by the legislature.[58]

Model 3. A third option might adapt the Wilson–Laycock approach but focus on the perspective of the consumer and the cost to the same-sex couple of being discriminated against, imposing more of the cost on the religious believer than Model 2 does. Such a proposal would shift the burden from the same-sex couple, to prove that they could not obtain goods, services or accommodation without 'substantial hardship', to the business or service provider, to show that alternatives were readily available. Like Model 2, this model would address each situation on a fact-specific basis. Commercial enterprises would have to show that although they refused to provide services to same-sex couples, identical services were available from numerous other businesses and that they made the couple aware of that fact. In addition, Model 3 would impose heavy penalties on those whose customers suffered impermissible discrimination and who were inconvenienced, even if only slightly, because of the dignitary harm that they suffered in the process. Many mechanisms are available to achieve all this. Just by shifting the burden and imposing the potential of a penalty for misconduct, however, the approach would increase the likelihood that a business owner would decide not to engage in discrimination at all.

Although the methods of analysis are similar, the latter two approaches focus more on the decision process than Model 1 does, because it focuses on the core cases, and these focus on peripheral ones. No one thinks that the Roman Catholic Church should be forced to hire openly gay, partnered clergy any more than it should be forced by civil law to ordain women. And most religious organisations do not support discrimination based upon people's sexual *orientation*, only on their conduct. These are both core cases, which have a clear basis in the integrity of the religious believers and those who suffer from discrimination. The real difficulty lies at the periphery: how to make it possible for one group to preserve its integrity, without detracting more than necessary from the integrity of the second group. According to Model 3, for example, if a religious believer is sufficiently convinced of the immorality of same-sex relationships, he or she will be willing to take substantial risks to be sure not to act contrary to his or her reasonable comprehensive (religious) doctrines. The model allows for that but puts a substantial penalty in the way when it disadvantages a same-sex couple to too great a degree.

These are not easy problems to solve with simple models. However, we offer them as ways of thinking about the question. None can be excluded without consideration. As we saw in Chapter 4, South

Africa allows for conscientious objection by its marriage officers. However, the same-sex marriage legislation currently pending in the UK parliament, which would apply to England and Wales, specifically states that registrars are not permitted such an opt-out. And the Scottish consultation concerning same-sex marriage anticipates that no opt-out will be available for registrars there.[59] Both have adopted Model 1, blocking objections from registrars by statute instead of offering the institutional accommodation that Model 2 does.

The same-sex marriage bill for England and Wales amends the Equalities Act 2010, so that people are not obliged to 'participate in' same-sex marriages, and the bill itself provides that 'a person may not be compelled . . . to be present at, carry out, or otherwise participate in' a same-sex marriage.[60] Aside from the 'otherwise participate in' language, which could conceivably be interpreted broadly by a judge sympathetic with religious believers, these exemptions are quite narrow.[61] However, broad exemptions have been included in New York legislation, for example, which allows that a non-profit religious organisation need not provide 'services, accommodations, advantages, facilities, goods, or privileges' for the solemnisation of same-sex marriages, and that religious organisations may take into account their doctrines when selling or renting housing, 'taking such action as is calculated . . . to promote the religious principles for which [they are] established or maintained'.[62] Even the Roman Catholic Diocese of Worcester, described in the third case above, would arguably be exempt under a statute of this kind if a retreat centre is deemed to be 'housing accommodation'.

Portability and predictability

In addition to religious freedom, it is also necessary for policymakers to address the question of portability and predictability. Once there are different laws in different geographic regions, either of a single country like the US or the UK or of a common market like the European Union, conflicting rules about marriage can create problems for a couple. This was clear from the case of Lolley and his wife, in Chapter 2, who were divorced in Scotland. Lolley was convicted of bigamy in England when he returned there and remarried, because the English courts refused to recognise his divorce. In the United

States, many of these concerns fall under the 'full faith and credit' clause of the constitution: 'Full Faith and Credit shall be given in each State to the public Acts, Records and judicial Proceedings of every other State.' Intuitively, marriage and divorce should both be 'public Acts' or 'judicial Proceedings' that require other states to recognise them. The text continues, however, 'Congress may by general Laws prescribe the Manner in which such Acts, Records and Proceedings shall be proved, and the Effect thereof.'[63]

The 'full faith and credit' clause has supposedly included an exception for marriage and divorce, based upon 'public policy'. This allowed states not to recognise other states' marriages when they were 'incestuous' (marriage to a deceased wife's sister, or more likely between cousins) or polygamous.[64] But no state has ever allowed either parent–child or sibling marriage (which really are incestuous), and we have seen what happened when Utah allowed polygamy – the army was sent in.

The only important implementation of the 'public policy' exception to full faith and credit has been in the context of statutes against interracial marriage. The limited number of cases on the point turned out in different ways. Some courts recognised out-of-state marriages.[65] Other courts did not.[66] In one of the few cases refusing to recognise an interracial marriage, the court worried about a slippery slope if the marriage were recognised:

> We might have in Tennessee the father living with his daughter, the son with the mother, the brother with the sister, in lawful wedlock, because they had formed such relations in a state or country where they were not prohibited. The Turk or Mohammedan, with his numerous wives, may establish his harem at the doors of the capitol, and we are without remedy. Yet none of these are more revolting, more to be avoided, or more unnatural than the case before us.[67]

The case was sent back so that Bell, the defendant, could be tried in a criminal court for his illegal, interracial marriage. But enforcement of these laws was not uniform.

In addition to public policy, US courts are also allowed to ask whether there was 'jurisdiction' over at least one of the spouses when the 'public Act' occurred. English judges confronted the same problem when they considered cases of people who married or divorced in Scotland. In the UK the jurisdiction problem has normally been solved with specific statutes.[68] In the US jurisdiction is the subject of a highly technical body of case law developed by the courts (as well as in a number of statutes), including the nightmare of all first-year law students: *Pennoyer* v. *Neff*.[69] These two exemptions to interstate recognition of marriage – public policy and jurisdiction – are extended by Section 2 of the federal Defense of Marriage Act (DOMA), which permits states to refuse to recognise same-sex marriages.[70] We will discuss DOMA in Chapter 6.

These jurisdictional conflicts are clearest when a couple divorces in a state other than the one where they normally live. The US has long had states whose divorce laws made them attractive to those from other states who wanted to leave their marriages. They included Connecticut, Rhode Island and Vermont in the early 1800s, and Utah and the Dakotas after that.[71] But the most infamous divorce mill in the twentieth century was Nevada. The attraction of Nevada for divorcing couples lay in its relatively short residency requirement and in its allowance of service by publication, that is, giving notice of the divorce to defending spouses by publishing it in a newspaper and mailing it to their last known address. This kind of process is a necessity for deserted spouses, who might not be able to deliver papers personally to someone who had left them. But it was not necessary for the deserting ones, who frequently took advantage by going to Nevada. A pair of cases from the US Supreme Court, both involving the same couple, shows how complicated the rules about interstate divorce could be.[72]

O. B. Williams and Lillie Hendrix left their homes and spouses in Granite Falls, North Carolina on 7 May 1940. Williams owned a store where Hendrix's husband had worked as a clerk. The two travelled to Las Vegas and resided for six weeks (the required residence period before filing for a divorce) at the Alamo Auto Court (a motel). They served their spouses with legal papers both by publishing the petitions in a local paper and sending them to their 'last known address' back in Granite Falls. Their divorces became final on 4 October, and on the same day they married one another. They returned to North Carolina and set up home in Pineola, about

50 miles away from Granite Falls. They were convicted of bigamous cohabitation in 1941, when North Carolina refused to recognise the Nevada divorces.

In the first case, the Supreme Court held that every state had an obligation to recognise divorce decrees from other states based upon the 'full faith and credit' clause. Following that decision the Williamses remained in North Carolina, where they continued to 'bigamously cohabit', making it possible to charge them again on a new set of facts, or at least different dates. This time, they were required to prove that they had acquired good-faith residency in Nevada, which they could not do. When the case came back to the Supreme Court, Justice Frankfurter, who had joined in the first judgment requiring recognition of their divorce, found that on the new (lack of) evidence North Carolina did not have to recognise the divorce, since Williams and Hendrix had gone to Nevada solely to obtain one.[73]

The main question here is: how much predictability should these people expect? Thomas Reed Powell, a lawyer and a political scientist, wrote in the 1940s about the Williamses: 'Persons who wish a divorce that will protect them from jail if they remarry have only to get one where they are really at home.'[74] Powell is making the same point that British judges did in past centuries when they refused to recognise marriages and divorces that had been obtained by 'fraud', travelling to a foreign country to marry or divorce. But he is using more precise language. The Lolleys were not 'really at home' in Edinburgh, they just went there to get a divorce. But England had a much stronger interest in their marital status if they were domiciled in Liverpool. What is important is not their intention to evade English law, which is what 'fraud' is all about. What is important is England's interest in their status, for example for purposes of inheritance or other kinds of state support. That is why a court's, and a state's, 'jurisdiction' should mean something.

Adopting a rule like Powell's creates serious problems for same-sex marriage, however, because it invalidates same-sex marriages when the couple travels to another territory, such as Canada, Belgium, the Netherlands or Massachusetts, just to marry, as many did when same-sex marriage first became available in those places. But what about a couple that has permanently moved to another jurisdiction?

J.B. and H.B., a same-sex couple, were married in Massachusetts in 2006.[75] They moved to Dallas County, Texas, where the marriage failed. In 2009 J.B. filed a petition for divorce, which H.B. did not contest. Article I, section 32 of the Texas constitution says: 'Marriage in this state shall consist only of the union of one man and one woman.' The Texas family code says that Texas may not give any effect to any public act, record, or judicial proceeding that creates, recognises, or validates a same-sex marriage in Texas or any other jurisdiction.[76] Although these laws seem contrary to the 'full faith and credit' clause, they are permitted by DOMA. However, the judge took jurisdiction over J.B.'s and H.B.'s divorce. She found that these Texas laws violated the equal protection clause of the US constitution, which says: 'No State shall make or enforce any law which shall . . . deny to any person within its jurisdiction the equal protection of the laws.' She thought that these laws forced her to treat same-sex couples unequally. The state of Texas intervened to stop her from granting the couple's divorce, and the case is on appeal.

The state of Texas has argued in the J.B. case that the proper remedy is a declaration that the marriage is void, which it is under Texas law, and this could even involve division of the couple's property. This means J.B. and H.B. are not entirely without a legal remedy. Texas's constitutional definition of marriage was adopted in a referendum in 2005 and was supported by 76.25 per cent of those voting.[77] Should this be a matter for democracy, or is this exactly what James Madison worried about, that too much democracy (for example, through referenda) would infringe minority rights?

The state did not focus on those kinds of question, although it did rely on other applicable legal principles that are more complicated. What the state also did, though, was to introduce arguments that should not matter:

> Throughout centuries of human history and across diverse human civilizations, societies have recognized – and their governments have given legal effect and enforcement to – the institution of marriage as the union of one man and one woman. And the reason is neither complicated nor controversial: The naturally procreative relationship between a man and a woman deserves special societal support and protection.[78]

As we have seen, the first sentence is empirically false, because it implies that opposite-sex, monogamous marriages are the only ones that have been recognised 'throughout centuries . . . and across . . . civilizations'. The reason given in the second sentence depends upon reasonable comprehensive doctrine(s) that are not authoritative in a liberal, democratic society. These are the kinds of argument that we contend should not be used in disagreements about the law of same-sex marriage. The Texas Court of Appeals did not include this kind of rationale in its decision in favour of the state and against granting J.B. and H.B. a divorce.

Geographical divisions between governments create legal problems, whether the governments are sub-units in a federal or devolved system or independent states that people travel between. The UK now normally anticipates these problems and generally legislates to avoid them. Same-sex marriage is not recognised in Northern Ireland, and will not be in the foreseeable future. As a result, the Marriage (Same-Sex Couples) Bill currently pending before Parliament says that same-sex marriages from other parts of the UK will be recognised there as civil partnerships.[79] This makes the rights of same-sex couples predictable but preserves the competency of the devolved parliament in Stormont, since marriage is a devolved matter.

Like other federal or devolved answers to policy questions, however, this also allows government sub-units to experiment. In the words of Justice Brandeis, 'It is one of the happy incidents of the federal system that a single courageous state may, if its citizens choose, serve as a laboratory; and try novel social and economic experiments without risk to the rest of the country.'[80] One sub-unit may also choose, as Northern Ireland has done, to look on as others try something new, or perhaps recognise fundamental rights, as southern states in the US did with racial integration and intermarriage and with abortion.

One final case about geographical jurisdiction, which has facts analogous to one that we have already discussed, bears examination in this chapter. The reader will recall George Millis from Chapter 4, who married Hester Graham in Ireland in a Presbyterian ceremony and then went on to marry Jane Kennedy in England in a Church of England ceremony. Millis was charged with bigamy. The House of Lords decided that only the second marriage counted, so Millis was not guilty. But Parliament had to pass an act permitting members of the Church of England to marry in Presbyterian meeting houses, because the House of Lords' decision called many Irish marriages into question.[81]

On 19 April 2003 Todd Warnken entered into a same-sex civil union in Vermont with his then partner.[82] At that time Vermont did not have same-sex marriage. On 17 October 2005 Todd married Richard Elia in Worcester, Massachusetts without dissolving the civil union (he changed his surname to Elia-Warnken). Todd and Richard filed for divorce four years later, and during the proceedings Richard found out about Todd's previous civil partnership. He asked the court to void their marriage rather than granting the divorce. (The record does not say why it was in his interest to do so, but it almost undoubtedly was.)

In this case, unlike the Millis case, it was the second marriage that was void, because the civil union was recognised as equivalent to a marriage by the court. Although the court did not say so, there are good policy reasons for this, as well. Todd had evaded his responsibility to his civil partner by marrying Richard in Massachusetts without dissolving a civil union, just as George Millis had abandoned Hester Graham. Richard should not have been penalised, as he did not know of the existing civil union, but Todd should not have profited from his wrong. Thus, the court was establishing a deterrent for misconduct like Todd's. In this book we have encountered a number of similar miscreants, including not only Lolley and Millis, but also Dalrymple and now Elia-Warnken. The civil law of marriage is designed to protect faithfulness, among other things. Just as one should divorce at home, as T. R. Powell suggests, one should also adhere to the second, rather than the first, rhyme in the epigraph to this chapter, and be 'off with the old love, before you are on with the new'.

Conclusion

We have shown in this chapter that some arguments about same-sex marriage really are worth having. Arguments about democracy and human rights, arguments about the effect of inter-jurisdictional travel, and arguments about religious freedom: all of these should attract the attention of those who are on both sides of this issue. What are far less important are the particular sexual activities of the spouses, whether public laws should conform to reasonable comprehensive doctrines such as NNL and whether allowing same-sex marriage will lead inevitably to polygamy (let alone things we haven't discussed like paedophilia and bestiality).

In the next chapter we will analyse some arguments in action. The US Supreme Court has recently handed down its decisions in *Hollingsworth* v. *Perry* and *United States* v. *Windsor*, and both sides had to decide what arguments would be most convincing to the judges in the case. This gives us a way of putting some of the historical and logical claims that we have made in this book in a contemporary context. Similarly, the UK parliament has advanced towards passing a law allowing same-sex partners to marry in England and Wales. Debates in the House of Commons and the House of Lords should be held up against the claims that we have made here, to see whether our focus is one that can advance debate there, so that legislators do not simply talk past one another.

Our concluding chapter is a way of synthesising history and policy, to try to make sense of what outcomes have been reached and what interests underlie those outcomes.

Notes

1. C. N. Douglas, ed., *Forty Thousand Quotations* (London: George Harrap, 1916).
2. Robert Chambers (ed.), *The Scottish Songs* (Edinburgh: William Tait, 1829), vol. 2, pp. 591–2, citing Johnson's *Musical Museum*, part 5 (c. 1798). These two quotes can be traced back further to a Jacobite song, which included the couplet, 'It's good to be aff wi' the auld king | Afore we be on wi' the new.' That is, it's best not to put William III on the throne when James VII/II is still around. Robert Burns parodied that song, replacing the last couplet to support Whig opposition of Charles James Fox: 'It's guid to support Caledonia's cause, | And bide by the buff and the blue.' He also was involved in the preparation of Johnson's *Musical Museum*, a collection of songs, and the second song in the epigraph is the Burnsian one. James Hogg, *The Jacobite Relics of Scotland* (Edinburgh: William Blackwood, 1819), p. 50; Robert Burns, 'A health to them that's awa", in Allan Cunningham, *The Works of Robert*

Burns with His Life (London: James Cochrane, 1834), vol. 5, p. 255; see also R. Chambers (ed.), *The Life and Works of Robert Burns* (Edinburgh: W. & R. Chambers, 1856), vol. 2, pp. 262–5. We are grateful to John Filling and Chris Brooke for these references.

3. 'Russian fundamentalists sue US, want Alaska back', RIA Novosti website, 16 March 2013, http://en.rian.ru/russia/20130316/180055 377/Russian-Fundamentalists-Sue-US-Want-Alaska-Back.html (last accessed 13 May 2013).

4. The official text of the ECHR can be found on the Council's website: http://www.echr.coe.int (last accessed 13 May 2013). The Council of Europe, which currently consists of forty-seven countries, is different from the European Union, which only consists of twenty-eight.

5. *Lawrence* v. *Texas* (2003) 539 US 558.

6. *Griswold* v. *Connecticut* (1965) 381 US 483–5.

7. *Eisenstadt* v. *Baird* (1972) 405 US 438.

8. But see *Williams* v. *Attorney General of Alabama* (11th Cir. 2004) 378 F.3d 1272, upholding a state ban on the sale of sex toys.

9. *Bowers* v. *Hardwick* (1986) 478 US 186.

10. *Lawrence* v. *Texas* (2003) 539 US at 573 citing *Dudgeon* v. *United Kingdom* (ECtHR 1981) App. No. 7525/76, holding that Northern Ireland's prohibition of male homosexual acts violated ECHR Article 8.

11. Nicholas Bamforth, *Sexuality, Morals and Justice: A Theory of Lesbian and Gay Rights Law* (London: Cassell, 1997), pp. 206–20. See also Andrew Sullivan, *Virtually Normal: An Argument about Homosexuality* (London: Picador, 1995), ch. 3.

12. *R.* v. *R. (otherwise F.)* [1952] 1 All ER 1194.

13. *Dennis* v. *Dennis (Others Cited)* [1952] 2 All ER 51 (Singleton LJ). See also *In re Blanchflower* (NH 2003) 834 A.2d 1010.

14. Leslie Green, 'Sex-neutral Marriage', *Current Legal Problems* 64 (2011), p. 15.

15. Masturbation, even by a person of the opposite sex who is not the other spouse, is not adultery (*Sapsford* v. *Sapsford and Furtado* [1954] 2 All ER 373). It follows from Lord Hodson's dictum that there is unlikely to be a trier of fact in the bedroom, armed with a ruler, to determine whether adultery (or consummation) has taken place.

16. See John Bingham, 'Coalition "faffing around with gay marriage"', *Daily Telegraph*, 29 March 2013, quoting Baroness Butler-Sloss objecting to same-sex marriage; Official Report, Marriage (Same-sex Couples) Public Bill Committee, 12 February 2013, col. 63, Q168 (testimony of Sian Payne, director, Lesbian and Gay Foundation); see also ibid. at c. 65, Q172 (Chris Bryant MP).

17. *Dennis* [1955] 2 All ER at 56.

18. Stephanie B. Hoffman, 'Behind Closed Doors: Impotence Trials and the Trans-historical Right to Marital Privacy', *Boston University Law Review* 89(5) (2009), p. 1734.

19. Peter Wagner, 'The Pornographer in the Courtroom: Trial Reports about Cases of Sexual Crimes and Delinquencies as a Genre of Eighteenth-century Erotica', in Paul-Gabriel Boucé (ed.), *Sexuality in Eighteenth-Century Britain* (Manchester: Manchester University Press, 1982).

20. Matrimonial Causes Act 1973, § 1.

21. In rare cases, women too could be 'impotent' if they were unable to have intercourse or habitually refused to do so.

22. This has long been the case under the common law; if the spouses reconciled following a divorce, the guilty party could use that as a defence in a subsequent divorce action. The defence was known as 'condonation'. 'The [Marital Causes Act 1973] "swept away" the absolute bars to divorce such as connivance, collusion, condonation, conduct conducing and the other bars to divorce' (*Kim* v. *Morris* [2012] EWHC1103 (Fam)).

23. Of course, privacy rules no longer apply in cases of spouse abuse or marital rape. 'The marital exemption [from charges of rape] simply does not further marital privacy because this right of privacy protects consensual acts, not violent sexual assaults' (*People* v. *Liberta* (NY 1984) 64 NY 2d 152, 474 NE 2d 567).

24. 'Unreasonable behaviour' is viewed from the perspective of the person seeking the divorce and asks whether she could not reasonably be expected to live with her spouse. The behaviour may include an affair that does not reach the level of adultery/sexual intercourse. *Wachtel* v. *Wachtel* [1973] Fam 72, [1973] 1 All ER 113; *Halsbury's Laws of England*, 5th ed. (London: LexisNexis, 2009), vol. 72, para. 360.

25. Compare *Salmanoğlu and Polattas* v. *Turkey*, Application no. 15828/03 (17 March 2009) and *Yazgül Yılmaz* v. *Turkey*, Application no. 36369/06 (1 February 2011), decided under Article 3 ECHR ('No one shall be subjected to torture or to inhuman or degrading treatment or punishment'), which prohibited virginity tests by legal authorities.

26. Lon L. Fuller, *The Morality of Law*, rev. ed. (New Haven, CT: Yale University Press, 1969).

27. H. L. A. Hart, 'Positivism and the Separation of Law and Morals', *Harvard Law Review* 71(4) (1958), pp. 593–629; Lon L. Fuller, 'Positivism and Fidelity to Law: A Reply to Professor Hart', *Harvard Law Review* 71(4) (1958), pp. 630–72. See also Nicola Lacey, 'Philosophy, Political Morality and History: Explaining the Enduring Resonance of the Hart–Fuller Debate', *New York University Law Review* 83(4) (2008), pp. 1059–87.

28. Examples of the writings of these theorists include John Finnis, 'Law, Morality and "Sexual Orientation"', *Notre Dame Law Review* 69(5) (1994), pp. 1049–76; Robert P. George and Jean Bethke Elshtain, *The Meaning of Marriage: Family, State, Market, and Morals* (Dallas: Spence, 2006); Sherif Girgis, Ryan T. Anderson and Robert P. George, *What Is Marriage? Man and Woman – a Defense* (New York: Encounter, 2012). The following description is drawn primarily from the most recent iteration of Girgis et al., *What Is Marriage?*, ch. 1.

29. Patrick Lee and Robert P. George, *Body–Self Dualism in Contemporary Ethics and Politics* (Cambridge: Cambridge University Press, 2008), p. 204.

30. Sullivan, *Virtually Normal*, pp. 99–107; Nicholas Bamforth and David A. J. Richards, *Patriarchal Religion, Sexuality, and Gender: A Critique of New Natural Law* (Cambridge: Cambridge University Press, 2008); John Corvino and Maggie Gallagher, *Debating Same-sex Marriage* (New York: Oxford University Press, 2012).

31. Girgis et al., *What Is Marriage?*, p. 29.

32. See also Andrew Koppelman, *Careful with That Gun: Lee, George, Wax, and Geach on Gay Rights and Same-sex Marriage* (Chicago: Northwestern University School of Law, 2010), available online at http://ssrn.com/abstract=1544478 (last accessed 14 May 2013), pp. 9–10.

33. *Minister of Home Affairs* v. *Fourie* [2005] ZACC 19, para. 86.

34. Church of Jesus Christ of the Latter-Day Saints, Doctrine and Covenants, § 132, paras 30–9, http://www.lds.org/scriptures/dc-tes tament/dc/132.28-39?lang=eng#27 (last accessed 14 May 2013). See Genesis 16:3, Genesis 21:1–13 and, for example, 2 Samuel 5:13.

35. Elizabeth Brake, *Minimizing Marriage: Marriage, Morality, and the Law* (New York: (Oxford University Press, 2012), pp. 160–3. For Brake this expansion of marriage takes place in an ideal world. See also Tamara Metz, *Untying the Knot: Marriage, the State, and the Case for Their Divorce* (Princeton: Princeton University Press, 2010). Both prioritise the value of 'care'.

36. Michael Reagan, 'Churches: time to fight back', *Ironton Tribune* (Ironton, OH), 2 April 2013, http://www.irontontribune.com/2013/04/02/church es-time-to-fight-back (last accessed 14 May 2013). The author of this article is the son of the late US President Ronald Reagan.

37. *Hyde* v. *Hyde* (1866), LR 1 P&D 130; Sebastian Poulter, '*Hyde* v. *Hyde*: A Reappraisal', *International and Comparative Law Quarterly* 25(3) (1976), pp. 475–508. As in the Puritan definition of marriage in Chapter 3, the emphasis is properly on the word 'one' rather than on 'man' or 'woman', as the concern is with plural marriage, not with the gender of the spouses.

38. This legal doctrine led to bad results for women through to the

mid-twentieth century. See *Janet Amerley Sowa* v. *Benjamin Sowa* [1961] EWCA Civ Jo210-1 (refusing to grant an abandoned wife relief when the couple had been married in Ghana).

39. Matrimonial Causes Act 1974, § 47.

40. *Brown* v. *Herbert* (D. UT 2012) 850 F.Supp. 2d 1240.

41. Richard Posner, *Sex and Reason* (Cambridge, MA: Harvard University Press, 1992), ch. 9.

42. Stephen Macedo, 'The Future of Marriage: Liberal Justice, Love, and the Law', paper presented at the Western Political Science Association, 28–30 March 2013, http://wpsa.research.pdx.edu/papers/docs/macedo. docx (last accessed 14 May 2013). The paper is part of a forthcoming book, Stephen Macedo, *The Future of Marriage?*.

43. This point is developed at length in Eric Alan Isaacson, 'Are Same-sex Marriages Really a Threat to Religious Liberty?', *Stanford Journal of Civil Rights and Civil Liberties* 8(1) (2012), pp. 123–54.

44. Richard Dawkins, *The God Delusion* (London: Black Swan, 2007).

45. John Rawls, 'On My Religion', in *A Brief Inquiry into the Meaning of Sin and Faith*, ed. Thomas Nagel (Cambridge, MA: Harvard University Press, 2009), p. 266.

46. John Rawls, *A Theory of Justice*, rev. ed. (Oxford: Oxford University Press, 1999), p. 182.

47. *Elane Photography* v. *Willock* (NM Ct of Appeals 2012) Docket No. 30,203 (unpublished opinion); *Willock* v. *Elane Photography, LLC* (NM Human Rights Comm'n 2008) Case No. 06-12-20-0685.

48. *Bull* v. *Preddy* [2012] EWCA Civ 83; *Hall* v. *Bull* (2011 Bristol County Court) Case No. 9BS02095.

49. Gary V. Murray, 'Diocese sued for sex bias', *Worcester Telegram & Gazette* (Worcester, MA), 11 September 2012, http://www.telegram. com/article/20120911/NEWS/109119835/1246; Lee Hammell, 'Diocesan retreat in Whitinsville sold for $800K', *Worcester Telegram & Gazette*, 18 October 2012, http://www.telegram.com/article/20121018/ NEWS/110189860 (both last accessed 14 May 2013).

50. Alan Brownstein, 'Gays, Jews and Other Strangers in a Strange Land: The Case for Reciprocal Accommodation of Religious Liberty and the Right of Same-sex Couples to Marry', *University of San Francisco Law Review* 45 (2010), pp. 400–3.

51. Chai R. Feldblum, 'Moral Conflict and Conflicting Liberties', in Douglas Laycock, Anthony R. Picarello Jr and Robin Fretwell Wilson (eds), *Same-sex Marriage and Religious Liberty: Emerging Conflicts* (Lanham, MD: Rowman & Littlefield, 2008).

52. Here Feldblum applies non-discrimination law more broadly than current Supreme Court precedents would seem to extend. *Corporation of the Presiding Bishop of the Church of Jesus Christ of Latter-Day Saints*

v. *Amos* (1987) 483 US 387 (church could dismiss janitor for failure to qualify for church membership). Cf. *Hosanna-Tabor Evangelical Church and School* v. *Equal Employment Opportunity Commission* (2012) 565 US __, 312 S. Ct 694 ('called' teacher not protected by the Americans with Disabilities Act, based upon the ministerial exception to the act).

53. *Salford Health Authority* v. *Janaway* [1989] 1 AC 537 (typist may not claim religious exemption from writing a letter referring a patient for an abortion).

54. Robin Fretwell Wilson, 'The Calculus of Accommodation: Contraception, Abortion, Same-sex Marriage, and Other Clashes between Religion and the State', *Boston College Law Review* 53(4) (2012), pp. 1417–1513; Robin Fretwell Wilson, 'Insubstantial Burdens: The Case for Government Employee Exemptions to Same-sex Marriage Laws', *Northwestern Journal of Law & Social Policy* 5(2) (2010), pp. 318–68; Douglas Laycock, 'Afterword', in Douglas Laycock, Anthony R. Picarello Jr and Robin Fretwell Wilson (eds), *Same-sex Marriage and Religious Liberty: Emerging Conflicts* (Lanham, MD: Rowman & Littlefield, 2008). See also Douglas Laycock and Thomas C. Berg, 'Protecting Same-sex Marriage and Religious Liberty', *Virginia Law Review Online* 99(1) (2013), http://www.virginialawreview.org/content/pdfs/99/Online/LaycockBerg.pdf (last accessed 14 May 2013); Matthew Chandler, 'Moral Mandate or Personal Preference? Possible Avenues for Accommodation of Civil Servants Morally Opposed to Facilitating Same-sex Marriage', *Brigham Young University Law Review* 2011(5) (2011), pp. 1625–68.

55. (2011) App. Nos. 51671/10 and 36516/10 (ECtHR), http://hudoc.echr.coe.int/sites/eng/pages/search.aspx?i=001-111187 (last accessed 14 May 2013).

56. See Wilson, 'The Calculus of Accommodation', p. 1512, Appendix B.

57. Douglas NeJaime, 'Marriage Inequality: Same-sex Relationships, Religious Exemptions, and the Production of Sexual Orientation Discrimination', *California Law Review* 100(5) (2012), pp. 1169–1238; Laura S. Underkuffler, 'Odious Discrimination and the Religious Exemption Question', *Cardozo Law Review* 32(5) (2011), pp. 2069–91; Ira C. Lupu and Robert W. Tuttle, 'Same-sex Equality and Religious Freedom', *Northwestern Journal of Law & Social Policy* 5(2) (2010), pp. 274–306.

58. 'Charting the Success of Same-sex Marriage Legislation: An Appendix to "The Calculus of Accommodation"', available online at http://law.wlu.edu/faculty/facultydocuments/wilsonr/ChartingTheSuccessAppendix.pdf (last accessed 14 May 2013).

59. Marriage (Same-Sex Couples) Bill 2013 (Bill 126), cl. 2(3); Scottish

Government, 'The Marriage and Civil Partnership (Scotland) Bill: A Consultation' (2012), §§ 3.08–3.10. The decision in Scotland not to allow a conscientious opt-out was likely made based on the controversial case of *Ladele* v. *London Borough of Islington* [2009] EWCA Civ 1357, in which a registrar objected to performing civil partnerships on religious grounds.

60. Marriage (Same-Sex Couples) Bill 2013, clauses 2(2), 2(5).
61. See *Salford Health Authority* v. *Janaway*. See also *Doogan & Wood* v. *Greater Glasgow Health Board* [2012] CSOH 32 (midwives cannot invoke conscientious objection to 'participating' in abortion when they supervise or support staff who provide care to the patients; reversed on appeal).
62. NY Domestic Relations Law, § 10(b).
63. US Constitution, Article IV, § 1.
64. Andrew Koppelman, *Same Sex, Different States: When Same-sex Marriages Cross State Lines* (New Haven, CT: Yale University Press, 2006).
65. *Miller* v. *Lucks* (Miss.1948) 36 So. 2d 140; *Bonds* v. *Foster* (1871) 36 Tex. 68.
66. *State* v. *Bell* (1872) 66 Tenn. (7 Baxter) 9.
67. Ibid., at 11. Koppelman hypothesises that this result came about because of the end of the Reconstruction. By 1872 Democrats held a clear majority in the state legislature. Koppelman, *Same Sex, Different States*, p. 168, n. 68 citing Eric Foner, *Reconstruction: America's Unfinished Revolution, 1863–1877* (New York: Harper & Row, 1988), pp. 440–1.
68. Marriage (Scotland) Act 1856 (requiring twenty-one days' residence before a couple could marry in Scotland).
69. (1878) 95 US 714. *Pennoyer* did not involve a marriage. It does, however, involve enough complicated facts and parties that it provides an initiation rite into the mysteries of US civil procedure.
70. Pub. L. 104-199, 110 Stat. 2419 (21 September 1996); 1 USC, § 7; 28 USC, § 1738C.
71. Glenda Riley, *Divorce: An American Tradition* (New York: Oxford University Press, 1991), pp. 62, 94.
72. *Williams* v. *North Carolina* (1942) 317 US 287; (1945) 325 US 226. See also T. R. Powell, 'And Repent at Leisure: An Inquiry into the Unhappy Lot of Those Whom Nevada Hath Joined Together and North Carolina Hath Put Asunder', *Harvard Law Review* 58 (1945), pp. 930–1017.
73. *Williams* v. *North Carolina*.
74. Powell, 'And Repent at Leisure', p. 1017.
75. *In re J.B. and H.B.* (TX App., 5th Cir., slip op. 31 August 2010) No. 05-09-01170-CV. The court of appeal's decision is available online at http://caselaw.findlaw.com/tx-court-of-appeals/1536784.html (last

accessed 14 May 2013). J.B.'s brief and the brief of the state of Texas are available through Westlaw. The parties are identified only by their initials by the courts to protect their privacy.

76. Texas Family Code, § 6.204(c)(1).
77. Office of the Secretary of State, 'Race Summary Report: 2005 Constitutional Amendment Election', http://elections.sos.state.tx.us/elchist.exe (last visited 13 May 2013).
78. *In re J.B. and H.B.*, Brief of Texas at pp. 17–18.
79. Marriage (Same-Sex Couples) Bill, Schedule 2, cl. 2.
80. *New State Ice Co.* v. *Liebmann* (1932) 285 US 262, 311.
81. *R.* v. *Millis* (1843–4) 10 Cl & Fin 534, 8 ER 844; Marriages (Ireland) Act 1844.
82. *Elia-Warnken* v. *Elia* (2012) 463 Mass. 29, 972 NE 2d 17.

Chapter 6
Legislatures Argue and the Supreme Court Decides

Our straightforward legal analysis sidesteps the fair point that same-sex marriage is unknown to history and tradition. But law (federal or state) is not concerned with holy matrimony. Government deals with marriage as a civil status – however fundamental – and New York has elected to extend that status to same-sex couples. A state may enforce and dissolve a couple's marriage, but it cannot sanctify or bless it. For that, the pair must go next door.

Dennis Jacobs, Chief Judge, Second Circuit Court of Appeals
Windsor v. *United States*[1]

A fast-changing situation

In this chapter we review some fast-moving changes during 2013. We cannot track all of them, and we are wary of making predictions. In his informative analysis of same-sex marriage, *From the Closet to the Altar*, the Harvard law professor Michael Klarman wrote (probably in 2012): '[US President Barack] Obama is unlikely to endorse gay marriage before the 2012 [presidential] election.'[2] Events proved Klarman wrong when Vice President Joe Biden announced his support for same-sex marriage on 6 May 2012, virtually forcing the President's hand.[3] Books and articles on this subject currently run these risks, and we have done our best to avoid them. As noted elsewhere in this book, same-sex marriage has been legalised in several jurisdictions even during the short period while we have been writing. So we focus only on the USA and the UK in this chapter.

First, we outline some of the developments in the four nations that make up the United Kingdom, giving some detail of the debates recently held in the UK parliament about same-sex marriage in

England and Wales. These track many of the themes that we have been developing in earlier chapters of this book. We move on to discuss the decisions by the United States Supreme Court in *United States* v. *Windsor* and *Hollingsworth* v. *Perry*, which were handed down on the last day of the court's October 2013 term – 26 June 2013, just as this book was about to go to press. We proceed to analyse some of the politics and history that underlie these two decisions and then move on to some analysis and final thoughts about conclusions that can be drawn from this policy process viewed in the light of history and politics.

Love and law in the UK

The Scottish Government published its Marriage and Civil Partnership (Scotland) Bill 2013 on 26 June 2013 (the day that the US Supreme Court handed down its opinion in *Windsor* and *Perry*).[4] That bill, if enacted, will extend the rights of celebrants, including humanists, to conduct same-sex marriages if they wish to, while protecting ministers and denominations that do not wish to. It is expected to proceed through the Scottish Parliament in autumn 2013. Despite (or perhaps in part because of) two public consultations, it is certain to be controversial and fiercely contested. The first consultation drew the largest number of responses the Scottish Government had ever received, as did the equivalent consultation by the UK government about the bill for England and Wales on the same subject.[5] Very late in the progress of the England and Wales bill, the UK government conceded the principle of allowing humanist weddings there. The terms may remain different to those in Scotland, so Gretna anomalies may continue. However, in most other respects the law in Scotland will resemble that in England and Wales (with minor changes to accommodate Scots law).[6] Northern Ireland has no plans to introduce same-sex marriage. Therefore same-sex marriages from elsewhere in the UK will be treated as civil partnerships there.

To become law in the United Kingdom (or in England and Wales, which have the same parliament as the UK), a bill must be approved by both houses of the legislature (Parliament): the House of Commons (whose elected members, MPs, win a plurality of votes in their constituency elections, which are now normally held every five years) and the House of Lords (whose members are currently primarily 'life peers', selected by the monarch on the advice of his or her ministers – that is, the government of the day).[7] In addition to life peers, the House of Lords includes ninety-two hereditary peers, elected by the aristocracy from their own number, and twenty-six bishops of the Church of England (but no *ex officio* representatives of any other faith groups). Technically, the approval of the monarch (royal assent) is also required, but it has not been withheld since 1708.[8]

In each of the two houses, the bill must pass (1) a largely symbolic first reading, (2) second reading, where the underlying policy behind the bill is debated, (3) committee stage, where amendments are proposed, and (4) report stage, where the amendments are approved or rejected. Finally, at third reading (5), the contents of the bill are once again debated and voted on by the entire house. When the houses cannot agree, they do not form a conference committee to iron out differences as is done in the United States. Instead, they engage in what is known as ping-pong, where one house (usually the Lords) proposes amendments, which are accepted or rejected by the other, and the bill is then passed back to the first house. Normally, one house or the other gives in, but if the Lords prove refractory, then the House of Commons can invoke the Parliament Act and override the Lords' suspensory veto simply by passing the same bill twice in the same parliament (a process that can nevertheless be time consuming).

For England and Wales, the UK Government's Marriage (Same Sex Couples) Bill had cleared the House of Commons and had reached report stage in the House of Lords by our press date. To that date, there were no signs to suggest that it would not clear the Lords and receive royal assent. It is worth tabulating some highlights of the bill's progress (see Table 6.1).

To summarise the information in Table 6.1, the bill, which was supported by the leaders of all three main political parties, passed through the House of Commons unamended, with substantial majorities in free votes (in which the government does not impose its party whip to ensure that it has a majority) at the start and end of the process. In the unelected House of Lords, its first obstacle was a rare motion to deny it a second reading by Lord Dear, a former chief constable of West Midlands Police. That wrecking motion was soundly defeated, even though nine of the fourteen bishops present,

Table 6.1 Marriage (Same Sex Couples) Act for England and Wales: parliamentary progress

Date (all 2013)	Event	Comment
5 February	Commons second reading carried by 400 votes to 175	Free vote. Labour and Liberal Democrat parties heavily in favour. Slight Conservative majority against, although it was a government bill
5 February	Carry-over motion carried by 464 votes to 38	Enabled bill to be carried over into 2013–14 session. Bill was introduced as early as it was, with carry-over motion, so that Commons would have time to carry it under Parliament Act provisions before next general election if Lords should vote it down
12 March	Commons committee stage concluded	No successful amendments made, but an amendment to permit humanist celebrations was defeated on the committee chair's casting vote, according to parliamentary precedent when a committee is tied
21 March	Commons report and third reading stages completed. Third reading approved by 366 votes to 161	No amendments made. Bill passed to Lords
4 June	Lords second reading approved by 390 votes to 148	Second reading votes in the Lords are rare. The vote was on a motion to deny the bill a second reading. A majority of all parties, including Conservatives, opposed the motion. However, nine lords spiritual (bishops) supported the motion to deny a second reading, while five abstained. No lord spiritual supported a second reading
24 June	Lords committee stage concluded	Government amendments made; all others withdrawn or not put. Government promised to consider some issues raised, signalled that it would resist others
10 July	Lords report stage concluded	Government concedes recognition of humanist celebrants
15 July	Lords third reading	No further changes of importance
17 July	Bill enacted	Official text available at http://www.legislation.gov.uk/ukpga/2013/30/contents/enacted

Sources: Hansard for dates shown; bill page at http://services.parliament.uk/bills/2013-14/marriagesamesexcouplesbill/stages.html (last accessed 6 July 2013).

including the Archbishop of Canterbury, supported it. The following day, the convener of the bishops issued a press release stating that the bench of bishops would abandon their attempt to defeat the bill, and would focus instead on attempting to amend it to meet their religious-freedom concerns.[9]

Religious freedom was a central part of the debate in both houses. The government had introduced the bill with what it called a quadruple lock, which (1) offered legal protections to faith groups that did not wish to perform same-sex marriages; (2) afforded further legal protections to individual clergy (even in faith groups that allowed same-sex marriage) who objected to performing the ceremonies; (3) created an exemption from anti-discrimination laws which allowed clergy and faith groups to refuse to conduct, be present at or otherwise participate in a same-sex wedding; (4) required further government action before the Church of England and the Church in Wales could opt in and perform same-sex marriages.[10] These 'locks', while generous, most closely resemble Chai Feldblum's Model 1 in Chapter 5: no protections are afforded to any but religious groups, and marriage registrars like Faith (who is protected in Model 3) are specifically excluded.[11] Opponents of the bill have argued that no protections, no matter how many there may be, can be certain to preclude challenges based upon the European Convention on Human Rights.[12]

The arguments then blended off in some cases to heavy reliance upon reasonable comprehensive doctrines. Edward Leigh (Conservative MP for Gainsborough) quoted from the Roman Catholic catechism for his definition of marriage as being necessarily between one man and one woman.[13] This may have been persuasive to other Roman Catholics who were predisposed to vote against the bill anyway; others almost certainly simply ignored it. Further arguments that were connected with religious values and institutions were even less plausible. Stephen Timms (Labour MP for East Ham) made the claim that 'the Church of England was the custodian of marriage in Britain for hundreds of years', to which Tom Docherty (Labour MP for Dunfermline & West Fife) retorted: 'The Church of England has never been the custodian of marriage in Scotland.'[14] Meanwhile, Sir Tony Baldry (Second Church Estates Commissioner and Conservative MP for Banbury) said:

The Church of England cannot support the proposal to enable all couples, regardless of their gender, to have a civil marriage ceremony. Such a move will alter the intrinsic nature of marriage as the union of a man and a woman as enshrined in human institutions throughout history.[15]

Also evident were arguments based upon new natural law (NNL), which we discussed in Chapter 5. Again, Leigh set out the position fairly comprehensively:

Every marriage has procreating potential in that marriage brings together biologically the two elements needed to generate a child. The very reason that marriage is underpinned with laws and customs is that children often result from it. They need protecting from the tendency of adults to want to break their ties and cast off their responsibilities. Marriage exists to keep the parents exclusively committed to each other, because, on average, that is the best and most stable environment for children. If marriage were solely about the relationship between two people, we would not bother to enshrine it in law, and nor would every culture, society and religion for thousands of years have invested it with so much importance.[16]

The proximity (in the debate reports) between his reference to the catechism and this description of complementarity is telling. As we have previously pointed out, what Leigh cannot address is the fact that once same-sex couples have children, those children are also entitled to the same protection from adults' desire 'to break their ties and cast off their responsibilities'. Our criticisms of these arguments from Chapter 5 hold. Finally, some argued that since consummation and adultery could not apply to same-sex marriage, because of the particular sexual organs involved, it could not be marriage at all.[17]

More generally acceptable arguments, which have a basis in public reason, include those by the Northern Ireland MP Jim Shannon (DUP, Strangford) and others who said that they did not support same-sex marriage because their constituents were opposed to it[18] – an argument simply based on the liberal democratic process. Others argued that economic issues were more important and that

Parliament should not be devoting time to questions like these when the economy was doing poorly, and some queried whether the government had spent enough time on the legislation or paid enough attention to objectors. Such arguments are predictable in any legislative debate and are perfectly fair game, to the extent that they are convincing.

In the House of Lords, the bishops' arguments reflected divisions among the other members. The Archbishop of Canterbury, Justin Welby, expressed the Church of England's long-held, but incomplete, view that 'the majority of bishops who voted during the passage of the Civil Partnership Act . . . were in favour of civil partnerships'.[19] In fact, as the church's secretary for parliamentary affairs has shown in a detailed analysis, the bishops who voted in the civil partnership debate supported a wrecking amendment introduced by Baroness O'Cathain six to one.[20] The Bishop of Leicester, anticipating an argument that would be made by Justice Samuel Alito in the US Supreme Court later in the month, distinguished between a 'traditional and conjugal' view of marriage and a 'privative' one, which is more concerned with the individuals than with their potential to biologically reproduce without artificial assistance.[21] The Bishop of Chester was difficult to understand, arguing that the Submission of the Clergy Act 1533, which prohibits the Church of England from adopting church laws (canons) without royal assent and licence, 'also lays a certain obligation on the state not to pass laws which are contrary to the received canon laws of the Church of England'.[22]

Not all bishops opposed the bill, of course. Lord Harries of Pentregarth, who supported civil partnership in 2004 as Bishop of Oxford, welcomed it, echoing many of the arguments that we have made in this book:

For most of history, among the upper classes, marriage was primarily a way of controlling titles and wealth. Among all classes, it involved the radical subservience of women. Often it went along with a very lax attitude – by males, not females – to relationships outside marriage. Contraception was forbidden and this resulted in many children, and as often as not the wife dying young. Only in the eighteenth century did we get a growth in emphasis on the quality of the relationship of the couple. Now, this mutual society, help and comfort that the one ought to have with the other, in prosperity and adversity, is rightly stressed. This is equally valued by all people, whatever their sexuality.[23]

Finally, we conclude this section with quotes from one speech in particular, which stands out and bears reading in its entirety, as it summarises many of the themes we have developed in the preceding chapters.[24] Lord Deben referred to the debates on the Deceased Wife's Sister Bills, which he pointed out that the House of Lords had 'scuppered' from 1835 until 1907, and recounted the arguments against it: that such unions would be the end of marriage, would encourage incest, might lead to polygamy and had never been contemplated in 2,000 years of Christian history. Once the statute passed in 1907, however, the Church of England changed its Table of Kindred and Affinity, and what had been an abomination became holy matrimony. Change became possible through science:

> Once we understood consanguinity, we distinguished between relationships that were genetically dangerous and those which were simply culturally arguable, and so it is with gay marriage. Once we understand scientifically that some people are solely attracted to their own sex, we realise that homosexual practice is not heterosexuals behaving badly, but gay people behaving naturally … State marriage has diverged from church teaching for more than 150 years; some would even say since Henry VIII rigged the rules to his own advantage, but that would be an embarrassment to some members of this noble house. As a convert Catholic, I have chosen to accept that Christian marriage is about procreation, that it is indissoluble, and that there is no such thing as divorce. Yet, as a parliamentarian, I cannot demand that non-Catholics should accept that definition.

C. S. Lewis would, we believe, agree.

Love and law in the US

Several of the high courts that we have discussed in previous chapters are permitted to give what are called 'advisory opinions'.[25] The

United States Supreme Court is different in this regard. Article III of the US Constitution provides:

> The judicial Power of the United States shall be vested in one supreme Court, and in such inferior Courts as the Congress may from time to time ordain and establish ... The judicial Power shall extend to all Cases, in Law and Equity, arising under this Constitution, the Laws of the United States, and ... to Controversies to which the United States will be a party ...[26]

The requirement that there be a 'case or controversy' limits the authority of the court to concrete disagreements; it cannot pronounce abstractly on the constitutionality of a statute. One aspect of the requirement is that the plaintiff has standing: that is, that he or she has suffered an injury which is causally traceable to conduct by the defendant, and that a favourable decision by the court will redress that injury.[27] Among other things, the doctrine protects the separation of the judiciary from the other branches of government. This refusal to offer advisory opinions dates back to 1793, before Justice John Marshall had asserted the power of judicial review.[28] The doctrine of standing, one of the 'passive virtues' of the court, was developed most fully by Alexander Bickel, who had clerked for Justice Felix Frankfurter.[29]

Although journalists and some political scientists assume that judicial decision-making is *purely* political and that Supreme Court justices line up along party lines like Democratic and Republican members of the US Congress, legal procedure, including questions of standing, can be orthogonal: it can cut in a different direction from social or economic policy. Another part of the 'case or controversy' requirement is that the parties be adverse: two parties cannot agree to bring a friendly suit to test the constitutionality or interpretation of a law; both must have a real stake in the outcome, over and above the decision of the court.

Standing was at issue in both *United States* v. *Windsor*[30] and *Hollingsworth* v. *Perry*,[31] which were decided at the end of the Supreme Court's October 2013 term, on 26 June 2013. In *Windsor* the question was whether Section 3 of the Defense of Marriage Act (DOMA),[32] which bars the US federal government from recognising same-sex marriage, was unconstitutional. In *Perry* the question was whether California's constitutional amendment, adopted by popular referendum in 2008, which defined marriage as between a man and a woman was unconstitutional. Both challengers to these laws prevailed, but they did so in the second one for reasons very different from the first.

The facts

Windsor

Edith ('Edie') Windsor and Thea Spyer met in 1963 in Portofino, a restaurant in Greenwich Village, in New York City. The pair kept dancing until, as Windsor has told journalists, she got a hole in her stocking.[33] They started living together in 1967, when Spyer proposed to Windsor, offering her a brooch rather than a ring in order to head off intrusive comments. In 1977, Spyer was diagnosed with multiple sclerosis. As her health deteriorated, Windsor became her full-time carer. In 2007, Spyer received a terminal prognosis. They immediately flew to Toronto and were married there, returning afterwards to New York, where Spyer died in February 2009.[34]

Spyer left her entire estate to Windsor, who claimed a refund of the $363,053 in federal estate taxes she had paid, based on the exemption for 'property which passes or has passed from the decedent to his [or her] surviving spouse'.[35] When Spyer died, New York state had not enacted a same-sex marriage law, but it had decided to recognise valid same-sex marriages solemnised in other jurisdictions. However, in 1996, by passing Section 3 of DOMA, Congress had amended the Dictionary Act, which gives definitions for federal statutes, to limit marriage to opposite-sex couples.[36] Windsor's attempt failed because of this definition, and she brought suit to recover the taxes in the United States district court (the federal trial court) in New York, based on a claim that the definition was unconstitutional. Both that court and the Second Circuit Court of Appeals agreed that the federal statute limiting marriage to opposite-sex couples violated Windsor's right to equal protection of the laws.

While the suit was pending, the US Department of Justice announced that it would no longer defend the definition of marriage as laid down by the Dictionary Act. Instead, the Bipartisan

Legal Advisory Group (BLAG), five members of the leadership of the US House of Representatives (three of whom were Republicans), was allowed to defend the law through the House Office of General Counsel as an interested party. Although the Department of Justice refused to defend the law, it nevertheless continued to enforce it, and it did not comply with the lower courts' orders to refund the tax. Instead it continued to cooperate in BLAG's appeals to higher courts.

Windsor's lawyer in the Supreme Court was Roberta Kaplan, a New York attorney who specialises in commercial litigation and who is herself in a same-sex marriage. Watching from the sidelines during oral argument, however, was Mary Bonauto, an attorney from Portland, Maine, who had been one of the early architects of the litigation on same-sex marriage, had represented the plaintiffs in the case that legalised same-sex marriage in Massachusetts, and had won a parallel case challenging DOMA in the First Circuit Court of Appeals.[37]

Perry

The facts in the *Perry* case, or rather series of related cases, are more complex, but we have already outlined them briefly in Chapter 2, when we discussed quick reversals in marriage policy.[38] In November 2000, the voters of California adopted Proposition 22 through the state's initiative process. Entitled the California Defense of Marriage Act, Proposition 22 amended the state's Family Code by adding the following language: 'Only marriage between a man and a woman is valid or recognized in California.' In spite of this act, in February 2004 the mayor of San Francisco instructed county officials to issue marriage licences to same-sex couples. The following month, the California Supreme Court ordered San Francisco to stop issuing such licences and later nullified marriages performed under them.

Shortly thereafter, San Francisco and various other parties filed state court actions challenging or defending California's exclusion of same-sex couples from marriage under the state constitution. These actions were consolidated in San Francisco Superior Court; the presiding judge determined that, as a matter of law, California's bar against marriage by same-sex couples violated the equal-protection guarantee of Article I, section 7 of the California constitution. The court of appeal reversed, and the California Supreme Court granted review. In May 2008, the California Supreme Court invalidated Proposition 22 and held that all California counties were required to issue marriage licences to same-sex couples. From 17 June 2008 until the passage of Proposition 8 in November of that year, San Francisco and other California counties issued approximately 18,000 marriage licences to same-sex couples.

Opponents of same-sex marriage in California, who had thus seen a voter-initiated law (Proposition 22) held unconstitutional under the state constitution, then used the initiative process to reinstate a rule that marriage was only between one man and one woman, but this time inserting it into the constitution of California, in the hope that it could not be reversed by the state courts. The result, with the same wording as Proposition 22, became known as Proposition 8. Backed by a coalition of conservative Christians, including the Roman Catholic and Mormon churches, Proposition 8 was carried in the November 2008 election by 52 per cent to 48.

After the November 2008 election, opponents of Proposition 8 challenged the initiative through an original writ of mandate in the California Supreme Court as violating the rules for amending the California constitution and on other grounds; the California Supreme Court upheld Proposition 8 against those challenges in a case called *Strauss* v. *Horton*.[39] Almost certainly without knowing it, the California courts were following the example laid down by Edward VI and Charles II, regularising a temporary change in the law of marriage. *Strauss* left undisturbed the 18,000 marriages of same-sex couples performed in the four and a half months between *In re Marriage Cases*, in which the California Supreme Court required marriage licences to be issued to same-sex couples, and the passage of Proposition 8. After Proposition 8 passed, no same-sex couple was permitted to marry in California until the Supreme Court's recent decision.

As *Strauss* v. *Horton* closed off all remedies in the California courts, the plaintiffs in *Perry* decided to sue in federal court. The challengers there were two couples who wished to marry but who had been denied marriage licences because they were same sex: Kristen Perry and Sandra Stier, and Paul Katami and Jeffrey Zarillo. They sued the governor of California, at the time Arnold Schwarzenegger, and various state officials on the grounds that Proposition 8 violated their rights under the Fourteenth Amendment's due-process and equal-protection clauses.

This was the first occasion in which gay-marriage advocates had sued in a federal, as opposed to a state, court. It was a controversial move, even among supporters of same-sex marriage. Both the upside and the downside stakes were higher than in state courts. A ruling by the US Supreme Court (where all sides expected that the case would end up) could require all fifty-one jurisdictions of the USA to institute same-sex-marriage. Or it could withhold support in all of them. Or anything in between. For some years the Supreme Court has contained four consistently conservative justices (currently Chief Justice Roberts and Justices Scalia, Alito and Thomas), four consistently liberal justices (currently Justices Kagan, Sotomayor, Breyer and Ginsburg) and the expected swing voter, Justice Kennedy.

Perry and her co-plaintiffs secured a remarkable legal team led by two of the most prominent advocates in the US federal courts: David Boies and Theodore (Ted) Olson. Boies, a liberal, and Olson, a conservative, were celebrated as lead counsel for the opposite sides in *Bush* v. *Gore*, the 2000 judgment which had awarded the 2000 US presidential election to George W. Bush by virtue of stopping recounts in Florida. Olson may be a political conservative but he is a social liberal.[40] None of the state officials named as defendants was willing to defend the state's actions, so the courts allowed the citizen group who had promoted Proposition 8 to defend it in the federal district court, where the California officials remained as parties. The district court found for the plaintiffs on all counts. The proponents of Proposition 8 appealed, the state having declined to, and the state officials failed to appear in court in the subsequent appeals.[41] The federal appeals court asked the California Supreme Court to rule on whether, under California law, initiative proponents had legal standing to pursue appeals in the event that the State of California declined to. The California court agreed that they did. On that basis, the appeal court went ahead, and affirmed the district court's ruling, but on narrower grounds: namely, that it was unconstitutional under the US constitution for a state to grant a right to a class of citizens (here, same-sex marriage) but then to take it away without a legally compelling reason.[42] The proponents appealed again, to the US

Supreme Court. It held oral hearings on both *Perry* and *Windsor* in March 2013.

The decisions

Windsor

In *Windsor*, the court decided by five votes to four that Section 3 of DOMA was unconstitutional. The ruling was written by Justice Kennedy, who was joined by the four liberals. It reflects both Kennedy's concern about federalism ('marriage is a state matter, where the federal government has no constitutional power to intervene') and the liberals' concerns about federal violations of equal protection under the law ('Windsor was treated less favourably than the widow of a man, for no defensible reason'). The majority judgment stated:

> When the State [of New York] used its historic and essential authority to define the marital relation in this way [i.e. to include same-sex marriages], its role and its power in making the decision enhanced the recognition, dignity, and protection of the class [married same-sex couples] in their own community. DOMA, because of its reach and extent, departs from this history and tradition of reliance on state law to define marriage. Discriminations of an unusual character especially suggest careful consideration to determine whether they are obnoxious to the constitutional provision . . . For same-sex couples who wished to be married, the State acted to give their lawful conduct a lawful status. This status is a far-reaching legal acknowledgment of the intimate relationship between two people, a relationship deemed by the State worthy of dignity in the community equal with all other marriages. It reflects both the community's considered perspective on the historical roots of the institution of marriage and its evolving understanding of the meaning of equality . . . DOMA seeks to injure the very class New York seeks to protect. By doing so it violates basic due process and equal protection principles applicable to the Federal Government . . . DOMA's unusual deviation from the usual tradition of recognizing and accepting state definitions of marriage here operates to deprive same-sex couples of the benefits and

responsibilities that come with the federal recognition of their marriages. This is strong evidence of a law having the purpose and effect of disapproval of that class. The avowed purpose and practical effect of the law here in question are to impose a disadvantage, a separate status, and so a stigma upon all who enter into same-sex marriages made lawful by the unquestioned authority of the States.[43]

Kennedy offers evidence of the types of disadvantages (and perverse advantages) afforded to same-sex couples who marry under state law but whose marriages are not recognised by federal law. The federal definition prevents them from obtaining spousal health-care benefits and from filing tax returns jointly. It even prevents same-sex couples from being buried together in veterans' cemeteries.[44] It also fails to oblige one spouse to support another, which affects a student's ability to obtain loans (favourably for the student), and to impose the same ethics rules on spouses of federal employees that opposite-sex couples must observe. Finally it harms children: 'It humiliates tens of thousands of children [by making] it even more difficult for the children to understand the integrity and closeness of their own family and its concord with other families in their community and daily lives.'[45]

There were three dissents: one by Chief Justice Roberts, which argued that the case reaffirmed the states' power to define marriage as they wished, a rampaging one by Justice Scalia and a quieter but possibly more profound one from Justice Alito. Justice Scalia began by claiming that the Supreme Court had no jurisdiction over the case because BLAG lacked standing[46] and continued seamlessly into explaining why its decision (that it should not have had the power to take) was wrong. Principally, he argued that the majority's statement that their decision applied only to same-sex couples married in states which allowed them to do so was untenable. A judgment that DOMA violated equal protection, he thundered, risked being used against every state that still had a statutory or constitutional ban on same-sex marriage.[47] He questioned the good faith of the majority:

When the Court declared a constitutional right to homosexual sodomy, we were assured that the case had nothing, nothing at all to do with 'whether the government must give formal recognition to any relationship that homosexual persons seek to enter' ... Now we are told that DOMA is invalid because it 'demeans the couple, whose moral and sexual choices the Constitution protects' ... It takes real cheek for today's majority to assure us, as it is going out the door, that a constitutional requirement to give formal recognition to same-sex marriage is not at issue here ... I promise you this: The only thing that will 'confine' the Court's holding is its sense of what it can get away with.[48]

Justice Alito said that at stake were two rival conceptions of marriage:

Windsor and the United States are really seeking to have the Court resolve a debate between two competing views of marriage. The first and older view, which I will call the 'traditional' or 'conjugal' view, sees marriage as an intrinsically opposite-sex institution ... there is no doubt that, throughout human history and across many cultures, marriage has been viewed as an exclusively opposite-sex institution and as one inextricably linked to procreation and biological kinship.

The other, newer view is what I will call the 'consent based' vision of marriage, a vision that primarily defines marriage as the solemnization of mutual commitment – marked by strong emotional attachment and sexual attraction – between two persons.[49]

Justice Alito clearly associates the 'conjugal' view of marriage with the new natural law (NNL) school, reviewed in Chapter 5, as he quotes extensively from their publications in footnotes as well as the text of his dissent.[50] However, rather than adopting such a view, he argues that it is for the legislature, not the courts, to decide which view is right:

The Constitution does not codify either of these views of marriage ... The silence of the Constitution on this question should be enough to end the matter as far as the judiciary is concerned ... I would not presume to enshrine either vision of marriage in our constitutional jurisprudence.[51]

Underlying all of these disputes was a quite serious disagreement about standing. Justice Kennedy argued (and all four liberal justices agreed) that BLAG had standing, because Congress's leadership had a sufficient interest in defending the law and that in the absence of a defence on appeal, every individual case involving a deprivation of benefits under Section 3 of DOMA would have had to be litigated: 'Rights and privileges of hundreds of thousands of persons would be adversely affected, pending a case in which all prudential concerns about justiciability are absent.'[52] The conservatives, however, split on the issue of standing. Justice Scalia, joined by Chief Justice Roberts and Justice Thomas, believed that the court lacked standing, because the two parties, Windsor (the plaintiff) and the US government (the defendant), were happy with the result invalidating Section 3 in the district court. Once the district court entered its judgment, it became a 'friendly suit'. When the US decided not to defend DOMA, it lost its right to appeal, and BLAG was not a sufficiently interested party to be able to do so instead. The fourth 'conservative', Justice Alito, disagreed and would have agreed that BLAG had standing but reversed, finding that Congress had the power to pass DOMA. These kinds of argument became even more important in the other same-sex marriage case decided that day.

Perry

In *Perry* no justice decided (or even made any statements about) whether Proposition 8 was constitutional. Justice Roberts wrote for the majority of the court, which included liberal Justices Kagan, Ginsburg and Breyer and conservative Justice Scalia. He held that the proponents of Proposition 8 had lacked standing from the time of the appeal, when the state defendants failed either to appeal or to appear. The dissent was by Justice Kennedy, joined by conservative Justices Thomas and Alito and liberal Justice Sotomayor. Standing was orthogonal in this case: it divided conservatives from liberals along non-ideological, procedural lines.

As Table 6.2 shows, Kennedy must at least have been uncomfortable voting against Proposition 8 outright (possibly because he knew that the district court's judgment would go into effect anyway). But he managed to divide the conservatives, gaining two votes from Thomas and Alito, while losing all the liberals except Sotomayor. We

Table 6.2 Justices' votes on constitutionality and standing in
US v. *Windsor* and *Hollingsworth* v. *Perry*

US v. *Windsor*		
	Standing	*No standing*
Unconstitutional	Breyer, Ginsburg, Kagan, Kennedy, Sotomayor	
Constitutional	Alito	Roberts, Scalia, Thomas

Hollingsworth v. *Perry*		
	Standing	*No standing*
Unconstitutional	Sotomayor	Breyer, Ginsburg, Kagan
Constitutional	Alito, Kennedy, Thomas	Roberts, Scalia

assume the justices' positions on the constitutionality of Proposition 8 based both upon their conduct at oral argument and their votes in *Windsor*. It was the justices' votes that forced both Roberts and Kennedy to evade the main issue in the case: Roberts could not have had his majority without the liberals, but they would not have joined an opinion that made any comment about the substance of the case (which they almost undoubtedly disagreed with him about). The decision is consistent with what Jeffrey Toobin has called Roberts's theory of judging: achieving more unanimity and writing narrower opinions – judicial minimalism.[53]

The substance of the arguments between the two sides is somewhat technical, but they are really about the nature of democracy. Roberts focused on the Proposition 8 proponents' lack of accountability. Although they were supposed to act on behalf of the people of California, they were unelected, unappointed and subject to no control from anyone other than themselves.[54] Kennedy, on the other hand, concentrated on the importance of initiatives and referenda in California's political culture. The entire point of initiatives and referenda is to bypass the institutions of government, which in the past Californians had found to be unsatisfactory for making certain kinds of policy. By allowing those same institutions to nullify a referendum by refusing to defend it in court (and not appointing anyone to do so on their behalf), the court undermined the entire process.[55] Finally, and equally importantly, Kennedy returned to his federalist arguments, emphasising the fact that the state of California (and its courts) should be allowed to determine who may act on its behalf, and the Supreme Court should defer to that determination.[56]

More important than these procedural points for our purposes is the practical outcome of the case. In an important sense, the plaintiffs in *Perry* lost: they were challenging the wrong party, and their case was thrown out of court without a decision about the constitutionality of Proposition 8. Why, then, was the court of appeals' stay, delaying the effect of its decision, lifted so quickly so that same-sex marriages began taking place on Friday 28 June 2013? Some commentators predicted that this could only happen after twenty-five days had passed (normally, twenty-five days are allowed to a losing party to petition for a rehearing before the lower court must comply with the Supreme Court's decision).[57] Others thought that the only two same-sex couples to be married would be Perry–Stier and Katami–Zarillo. One argument is that since the parties lacked standing in the court of appeal, the court had lacked power to enter the stay in the first place.[58] More cynically, the judges in the Ninth Circuit Court of Appeal in California may have been engaging in provocative behaviour in response to the Supreme Court's reversal of their court's decision.[59] But once the stay was lifted, the judgment of the district court, where the California defendants had appeared and the same-sex couples had won, came into effect.

The federal district court judgement by US District Chief Judge Vaughn Walker, which has now become binding on the state, was sweeping, reflecting what had been a very one-sided trial.[60] The plaintiffs submitted expert testimony from leading specialists on the history of marriage and of gays and lesbians in the USA, on the economic consequences of encouraging or restricting gay and lesbian equality, and on the social psychology of marriage, including the effects of parental marriage on the mental well-being of children.[61] The proponents of Proposition 8 produced only two so-called expert witnesses, the remainder having withdrawn before the trial, since, according to counsel, they 'were extremely concerned about their personal safety, and did not want to appear with any recording of any sort whatsoever' (although the possibility of televising the trial had been squashed by the date of that statement).[62] The court found that one of the witnesses had had only limited relevant expertise, and that the other had none at all.[63]

Judge Walker made eighty findings of fact. The material ones, and our summary of the judge's conclusions, are shown in Table 6.3.

How weighty are these findings? On the one hand, the findings of a US district court do not bind other courts, and these findings do not discuss some claims made in other courts (such as Justice Alito's claim that the traditional definition of marriage is conjugal). On the other hand, the vacation of the narrower Appeal Court judgment and the refusal of the Supreme Court to reach the merits of the case leave Judge Walker's findings unchallenged (except perhaps by a nasty footnote in Justice Alito's dissent in *Windsor*).[64] There will be other cases. In some of them, the opponents of same-sex marriage will produce more credible witnesses and pursue the case differently. But Judge Walker's findings of fact are solidly based in the relevant social science and a sophisticated understanding of social statistics and experimental design. They may be hard to budge, they are relevant to the debate in jurisdictions outside the USA, and they are likely to be analysed at length in the literature, just as *Goodridge* v. *Department of Public Health*, legalising same-sex marriage in Massachusetts, has been since 2004.[65]

Before ending this description of these two cases, it seems worthwhile to make a point about social science. Social science has been used in the US Supreme Court since Louis D. Brandeis filed his so-called Brandeis brief in *Muller* v. *Oregon*, arguing in support of an Oregon law limiting the number of hours women could work.[66] Perhaps most famously, the Supreme Court relied heavily on social science evidence in *Brown* v. *Board of Education* when it found that segregation has a tendency to retard the educational and mental development of African-American children and to deprive them of some of the benefits they would receive in a racially integrated school system.[67]

In both *Windsor* and *Perry* a group of medical and mental health professional associations, including the American Psychological Association, the American Medical Association, the American Academy of Pediatrics and the American Psychiatric Association

Table 6.3 Findings of fact in *Perry* v. *Schwarzenegger*, US District Court for Northern California, August 2010

Question posed by court	Findings nos	Summary of findings
Does any evidence support California's refusal to recognise marriage between two people because of their sex?	19–41	No. Marriage has always been a civil matter. Religious leaders may decide which marriages to recognise but cannot control the law. Marriage has never required the ability of the partners to procreate. Some past restrictions and conditions (e.g. banning interracial marriage, making a wife the legal property of her husband) have changed during the history of California. Marriage brings many benefits to both the state and the couple, but none of those benefits are incapable of being enjoyed by same-sex couples.
Does any evidence show that California has an interest in differentiating between same-sex and opposite-sex unions?	42–56	No. Sexual orientation is a well-defined and stable part of people's identities. Individuals do not choose and cannot change their orientations. 'California has no interest in asking gays and lesbians to change their sexual orientation or in reducing the number of gays and lesbians in California' (Finding 47). Same-sex couples in California are allowed to adopt; 18 per cent of them are raising children. Domestic partnership is not marriage and is not an adequate substitute.
Does the evidence show that Proposition 8 enacted a private moral view without advancing a legitimate government interest?	57–80	Yes. The only effect of Proposition 8 is to stigmatise same-sex couples. 'Children raised by gay or lesbian parents are as likely as children raised by heterosexual parents to be healthy, successful and well-adjusted. The research supporting this conclusion is accepted beyond serious debate in the field of developmental psychology' (Finding 70). Gays and lesbians have long been stigmatised; religious and other beliefs that they are inferior harm them. The Proposition 8 campaign depended on groundless fears that exposing children to gays and lesbians would make them gay.

Source: Perry v. Schwarzenegger, pp. 956–91; our précis of findings in column 3.

filed *amicus* briefs (filed by third-party 'friends of the court' to offer the justices additional information). The briefs traced trends in the scientific literature concerning (a) the stability of same-sex relationships, (b) the importance of marriage in reinforcing those relationships, (c) the non-dependence of children's adjustment upon the gender or sexual orientation of their parents and (d) the fitness of gay and lesbian parents to raise children.[68] In part, that brief responded to what has become known as the Regnerus study, which claimed to show that children with gay and lesbian parents were less well adjusted than other children. These professional associations showed that the methodology underlying the Regnerus study was flawed; indeed, an independent auditor determined that it was so seriously flawed that he called it a 'non-scientific study' and said it should not have been published.[69]

In the face of these problems, another group submitted an *amicus* brief in support of Proposition 8 arguing that any brief submitted by the American Psychiatric Association should be ignored, because that association had eliminated homosexuality from its *Diagnostic and Statistical Manual of Mental Disorders* because of political pressure, not scientific research.[70] They argued:

> This case should be decided on the basis of the law, without reliance on the social science studies and authorities that Respondents and their *amici* will undoubtedly put before the Court. The social and behavioral sciences have a long history of being shaped and driven by politics and ideology.

Another group of social science professors, including Professor Regnerus himself, filed a brief in support of the petitioners in both cases, citing Regnerus's study.[71]

Although Justice Kennedy did not cite the American Psychological Association group's brief, it is consistent with his statement about the children of same-sex couples quoted above. More to the point, however, no justice dissenting from *Windsor* cited the opposing briefs, including Justice Scalia, and their arguments do not rely upon that kind of empirical evidence. The general conclusion to be drawn here, which is also supported by Judge Walker's findings about experts in the district court, is that social science can offer helpful data that is useful in making decisions like the ones before these courts, but at the same time social scientists, like scientists generally, have a professional responsibility to monitor their colleagues to maintain the integrity of their disciplines.

Love and law: an analysis

The Ginsburg proviso

The Supreme Court's reluctance to discuss the merits of the case in *Perry* has many precedents. Some of its most famous judgments have involved, at least on the surface, a declaration that it has no power to intervene.[72] Justice Ruth Bader Ginsburg, one of the liberal members of the current court, has warned her colleagues against overreach, specifically against getting too far ahead of public opinion. She has several times stated that the *Roe* v. *Wade* ruling of 1973 went too far when it required abortion to be permitted in all fifty states, rather than making a judgment restricted to the Texas circumstances in the case. In her view, *Roe* halted an advance of public opinion towards acceptance of abortion rights and turned abortion into a party-political football: almost every Republican office seeker is against it and the great majority of Democratic office seekers are in favour of it.[73] The Ginsburg proviso may have led the court to make its restricted judgment in *Perry*: on the face of it, as in 1803 in *Marbury* v. *Madison*, declaring that it had no power to do more than it did. A court ruling that prohibiting same-sex marriage violated equal protection might have had the same effect as the sweeping judgment in *Roe*. This position has been developed more fully by Michael J. Klarman.[74]

However, the evidence on the Ginsburg proviso is mixed. There is a striking counterexample, also about marriage. In 1967, a unanimous Supreme Court handed down its judgment in *Loving* v. *Virginia*.[75] As we explained in Chapter 4, Richard and Mildred Loving, who were of different races, married in Washington, DC. After returning to their home in Virginia, they were convicted under that state's law against miscegenation, and sentenced to a jail term which would be suspended on condition that they left Virginia. The unanimous reversal of that ruling has long been seen as one of the key decisions of the

Civil Rights era. Towards the end of her life, the surviving spouse of that marriage, Mildred Loving, said:

> I believe all Americans, no matter their race, no matter their sex, no matter their sexual orientation, should have that same freedom to marry. Government has no business imposing some people's religious beliefs over others. Especially if it denies people's civil rights. I am still not a political person, but I am proud that Richard's and my name is on a court case that can help reinforce the love, the commitment, the fairness and the family that so many people, black or white, young or old, gay or straight, seek in life. I support the freedom to marry for all. That's what *Loving*, and loving, are all about.[76]

Some people might therefore have expected *Loving* to have been cited extensively in *Windsor* and *Perry*. It was not: just twice in *Windsor*, and not at all in *Perry*. This is eloquent evidence in favour of the justices' having taken note of the Ginsburg proviso. But they may have been too cautious. For more than fifty years Gallup has been asking Americans: 'Do you approve or disapprove of marriage between blacks and whites?' In 1968, the year after the Supreme Court's decision in *Loving*, only 20 per cent of respondents approved of it; 73 per cent disapproved. *Loving* did not freeze that share. Majority approval of mixed-race marriages came in 1991, and by 2007, the proportions were 77 per cent in favour and 17 per cent against.[77] In *Loving*, the court was ahead of public opinion, which has caught up with it. In *Roe*, if Ginsburg is right, the court chilled it. In *Perry* and *Windsor*, it was slightly behind, according to the numbers in Table I.2. It may have been prudent for the court to have avoided another sweeping judgment like *Roe*. But, if it had made a judgement as sweeping as *Loving*, it might still have survived. Same-sex marriage might have arrived nationwide, and the world might not have come to an end.

There is also a point of political theory to be made here, however. Our colleague Jeremy Waldron has argued forcefully that in a society like the United States or the United Kingdom, with good working democratic institutions and citizens who take rights seriously, the legislature, not the courts, is the best place to make policy, as legislatures are more accountable. They are elected, and they argue about policy without using technicalities like standing.[78] This point was brought out rather eloquently by Justice Scalia in *Windsor*:

> Few public controversies [like the one over same-sex marriage] touch an institution so central to the lives of so many, and few inspire such attendant passion by good people on all sides. Few public controversies will ever demonstrate so vividly the beauty of what our Framers gave us, a gift the Court pawns today to buy its stolen moment in the spotlight: a system of government that permits us to rule *ourselves*.[79]

Waldron points specifically to the debates about abortion when the Medical Termination of Pregnancy Bill was being considered by the UK parliament in 1966. The MPs 'debated the questions passionately, but also thoroughly and honorably, with attention to the rights, principles, and issues on both sides'.[80] He believes that that was a better way to decide the question than having a supreme court rule in a case such as *Roe v. Wade*.

We suspect that many readers of this book in the UK will be sceptical, as Waldron is, about the legitimacy of a court like the Supreme Court that can invalidate a statute enacted by the legislature, as DOMA was. Those in the US who disagree with *Windsor* may feel the same way. Both groups should recall important facts about one another's political systems. British readers who are sceptical of judicial review should recall that their position is frequently supported by Scalia and others like him: it's best for the legislature to decide. And it is important for readers in the US to bear in mind that the judiciary has far more power there than in many other countries, including the UK. The decision about which institution, the courts or the legislature, should make the final determination should not depend upon whether one agrees with a particular policy outcome. We take no position on the normative question of which system is better; there are good arguments both ways. But it is worth asking these kinds of systematic questions: who decides?

Simply put, 'the state' may take different forms. In some jurisdictions, the legislature is sovereign, or almost so. In England and Wales, the formal constitutional doctrine is that Parliament is sovereign and can make any law it pleases. The Scottish Parliament is not sovereign: although marriage is a devolved matter, it is legally (if not politically) conceivable that the UK parliament could nullify the act of the Scottish Parliament allowing same-sex marriage that is being prepared as we write. In other jurisdictions, the legislature is not sovereign because a constitution limits what it may or may not do. Ireland, Canada, South Africa and the USA are all cases in point, which we have discussed in earlier chapters. In Ireland, same-sex marriage cannot be approved without a change in the Irish constitution, as was recommended by the Constitutional Convention in 2013. In the other three jurisdictions, the courts have ruled on the constitutionality of marriage law. In both Canada and South Africa, the supreme constitutional court held that marriage laws that forbade same-sex couples to marry contravened the constitution.

A telling observation from Douglas Laycock and Thomas C. Berg draws inferences from this point that relate to the same-sex marriage debate. Speaking of the ten US jurisdictions that permitted same-sex marriage at the time of writing their article, they say:

> All six jurisdictions that enacted same-sex civil marriage legislatively also enacted religious liberty protections for religious organizations that do not recognize same-sex marriages. Pending bills for same-sex civil marriage in Hawaii, Illinois, and Rhode Island all contain religious liberty protections. In the four states that recognized same-sex marriage judicially, by constitutional interpretation, the situation is very different. There is reasonably robust statutory protection, like that enacted in most of the states that enacted same-sex marriage by legislation, only in Connecticut.[81]

The reason is obvious. For a bill to pass a legislature in which there is bound to be opposition reflecting the proportion (usually substantial) of the people who have religious objections, a bargaining process takes place. Proponents of legal change offer concessions to their opponents in order to make, or increase, a winning coalition. Judges face no such obligation. Courts are inherently counter-majoritarian bodies, above all when determining human rights cases, including the right to marry.

Final remarks

If the projections in Table I.2 and similar data for other democracies are correct, then within twenty years of this book's appearance marriage between two people of the same sex will be no more controversial than marriage of a man and his deceased wife's sister. If that is to happen, however, at least three things are essential, things that have all been running themes of this book.

The first is that freedom of religion and belief must be rigorously respected. Freedom of religion and belief means, of course, that the consciences of those who do and those who do not wish to marry any given couple according to the rites of their religion must be equally respected. For that reason, we reject both absolutisms, which we have discussed at many points. As currently applied to same-sex marriages,[82] we reject the absolutism that says 'Nobody may change the definition of marriage'. It follows that we do not accept the argument of the NNL scholars that a same-sex marriage is literally impossible because marriage is defined in a way that precludes it. Equally, we reject the absolutism of requiring religious believers to act against their consciences. Exactly where that line is to be drawn is difficult, and we have discussed some of the hard cases already. We have presented some tentative solutions, but we do not expect to have persuaded all our readers.

The second point on which we insist is the distinction between 'public reason' and 'reasonable comprehensive doctrine'. Public reason is a form of argument that may appeal to any citizen, regardless of the hearer's beliefs or lack of them. Reasonable comprehensive doctrines are those which make sense to those who accept the tenets of some belief system. They should be respected and protected, at least up to the point where they would harm others. But they do not qualify as arguments in the public square. That is why, ultimately, we find NNL entirely unconvincing.

Finally, we are federalists. We believe that different laws suit different places. The USA, Canada, and India are formal federations. Formally, the UK is not, but in fact it is becoming more federal. In some areas, and marriage is one of them, the new British federalism involves (re)discovering some very old distinctions. Marriage law in Scotland differed from that in England in 1707, and it has continued to differ, despite the efforts of Lord Hardwicke in 1753. We think that Gretna marriages are a sign of the health, not the sickness, of the federal UK. In *Windsor* Justice Kennedy made our point for us:

> The dynamics of state government in the federal system are to allow the formation of consensus respecting the way the members of a discrete community treat each other in their daily contact and constant interaction with each other . . . This status [same-sex marriage] is a far-reaching legal acknowledgment of the intimate relationship between two people, a relationship deemed by the State worthy of dignity in the community equal with all other marriages. It reflects both the community's considered perspective on the historical roots of the institution of marriage and its evolving understanding of the meaning of equality.[83]

But mature federalism requires a mature 'full faith and credit' regime. As we explained in Chapter 4, the 'full faith and credit' clause of the US constitution (Article IV, section 1) has only selectively been held to apply to marriage law. But every jurisdiction in a federal country needs to have some comity with every other jurisdiction, in the area of marriage law just as elsewhere. Only with such comity will the loose ends be satisfactorily tied up. What happens when a Scottish same-sex married couple move to Northern Ireland, or a New York couple to Texas? As Justice Scalia says in his dissent in *Windsor*, these are large questions. But solving them is not beyond the wit of man.

Notes

1. (2d Cir. 2012) 699 F. 3d 169, 188.
2. Michael Klarman, *From the Closet to the Altar: Courts, Backlash, and the Struggle for Same-sex Marriage* (New York: Oxford University Press, 2013), p. 196.
3. Jackie Calmes and Peter Baker, 'Obama says same-sex marriage should be legal', *New York Times*, 9 May 2012, http://www.nytimes.com/2012/05/10/us/politics/obama-says-same-sex-marriage-should-be-legal.html (last accessed 6 July 2013).
4. Scottish Parliament, Marriage and Civil Partnership (Scotland) Bill, available online, together with Explanatory Notes, Policy Memorandum, and Delegated Powers Memorandum, at http://www.

scottish.parliament.uk/parliamentarybusiness/Bills/64983.aspx (last accessed 6 July 2013).

5. 'Registration of Civil Partnerships, Same-Sex Marriage: Consultation Analysis', Scottish Government website, http://www.scotland.gov.uk/ Publications/2012/07/5671; HM Government, *Equal Marriage: The Government's Response*, December 2012, available online at https://www.gov.uk/government/uploads/system/uploads/attachment_data/file/133262/consultation-response_1_.pdf (both last accessed 6 July 2013).

6. For example, Scots law recognises the crime of 'reset', receiving stolen goods, but a defence is available to a wife who receives stolen goods from her husband. Under the proposed bill, this defence would not be available to a woman in a same-sex marriage. Marriage and Civil Partnership (Scotland) Bill, Explanatory Notes, para. 33.

7. The membership of Parliament is described in detail on its website (http://www.parliament.uk/mps-lords-and-offices/), as is the process for approving legislation (http://www.parliament.uk/about/how/laws/; both websites last accessed 6 July 2013).

8. George V considered withholding royal assent to the act that gave Ireland home rule in 1914: see Iain McLean, *What's Wrong with the British Constitution?* (Oxford: Oxford University Press, 2010), p. 113.

9. 'Statement from the Convenor of the Lords Spiritual on the Marriage (Same Sex Couples) Bill', Church of England website, 5 June 2013, http://churchofengland.org/media-centre/news/2013/06/statement-from-the-convenor-of-the-lords-spiritual-on-the-marriage-(same-sex-couples)-bill.aspx (last accessed 6 July 2013).

10. This special provision was necessary because changes to the Church of England's doctrine, worship and discipline must be approved by Parliament and because both churches arguably have a common-law duty to marry those who live in their parishes. See for example Nicholas Roberts, 'The Historical Background to the Marriage (Wales) Act 2010', *Ecclesiastical Law Review* 13(1) (2011), pp. 39–56.

11. An amendment was pressed, unsuccessfully, in the House of Lords to allow existing registrars to opt out of participating in same-sex civil marriages. Hansard, HL Deb, 8 July 2013, vol. 747, cols 39–62.

12. See for example Sir Tony Baldry (Second Church Estates Commissioner), Hansard, HC Deb, 5 February 2013, vol. 558, col. 145. Their position is supported by an opinion by the eminent civil rights attorney Aidan O'Neill QC, selections of which have been published (see http://c4m.org.uk/downloads/legalopinionsummary.pdf; last accessed 6 July 2013). The government has responded: see https://www.gov.uk/government/uploads/system/uploads/attachment_data/file/

86499/RESPONSE_TO_AIDAN_O_NEILL_QCs_LEGAL_OPINION. pdf (last accessed 6 July 2013).

13. Hansard, HC Deb, 5 February 2013, vol. 558, cols 160–1.
14. Ibid., col. 172. Timms admitted that Docherty was correct.
15. Ibid., col. 145.
16. Ibid., col. 161.
17. Ibid., cols 144 (Sir Tony Baldry), 147 (Nadine Dorries, Con., Mid Bedfordshire). Even some supporters of the bill, seemingly not realising exactly what the problem is, asked that adultery be included in order to ensure sexual fidelity in same-sex marriage (ibid., col. 178 (Helen Goodman, Lab., Bishop Auckland)).
18. Ibid., col. 165.
19. Hansard, HL Deb, 3 June 2013, vol. 745, col. 953.
20. Richard Chapman, 'The Lords Spiritual and Civil Partnerships Legislation', http://www.churchofengland.org/media/1472983/cptimeline.doc (last accessed 6 July 2013); see also Hansard, HL Deb, 24 June 2004, vol. 662, col. 1391. Only after the House of Commons had rejected the amendment did eight bishops vote against it while two supported it (Hansard, HL Deb, 17 November 2004, vol. 666, col. 1484). Even taking the second vote into account, a total seven bishops voted for the wrecking amendment and eight voted against it (the Bishop of Peterborough voted both ways at different times). Any 'majority' is a thin and unstable one, at best.
21. Hansard, HL Deb, 3 June 2013, vol. 745, col. 963.
22. Ibid., col. 995.
23. Hansard, HL Deb, 3 June 2013, vol. 745, col. 969.
24. Ibid., cols 1026–8.
25. For example the Supreme Court of Canada, discussed in Chapter 4.
26. US Constitution, Article III, §§ 1–2.
27. See for example *Lujan v. Defenders of Wildlife* (1992) 504 US 555 (wildlife conservation group lacks standing to challenge regulations issued by the departments of commerce and the interior); *Fairchild v. Hughes* (1922) 258 US 126 (Brandeis J); *Muskrat v. United States* (1911) 219 US 346.
28. Thomas Jefferson, then Secretary of State, wrote to John Jay, Chief Justice of the Supreme Court, in the context of the wars breaking out in Europe: 'The war . . . produces frequent transactions within our ports and limits, on which questions arise . . . [which] depend for their solution upon the construction of our treaties, of the laws of nature and of nations . . . The president therefore would be much relieved if he found himself free to refer questions of this description to the opinions of the judges of the Supreme Court . . .' Jay responded that the 'lines of separation drawn by the Constitution between the three departments of the

government . . . being in certain respects checks upon each other, and our being judges of a court in the last resort, are considerations which afford strong arguments against the propriety of our extra-judicially deciding the questions alluded to'. (Letter from Thomas Jefferson to John Jay dated 18 July 1793, letter from John Jay to George Washington dated 8 August 1793, Henry P. Johnston (ed.), *The Correspondence and Public Papers of John Jay* (New York: G. P. Putnam's Sons, 1890–3), vol. 3, pp. 486–9.

29. Alexander M. Bickel, *The Least Dangerous Branch: The Supreme Court at the Bar of Politics* (Indianapolis: Bobbs-Merrill, 1962).

30. (US 2013) No. 12-307, 2013 WL 3196928. Citations to *Windsor* and *Perry*, below, are to the slip opinions, available at http://www.supremecourt. gov/opinions/12pdf/12-307_6j37.pdf and http://www.supremecourt. gov/opinions/12pdf/12-144_8oko.pdf respectively (last accessed 7 July 2013).

31. (US 2013) No. 12-144, 2013 WL 3196927.

32. 110 Stat. 2419.

33. For example Adam Gabbatt, 'Edith Windsor and Thea Spyer: "A love affair that just kept on and on and on"', *Guardian*, 26 June 2013, http: //www.guardian.co.uk/world/2013/jun/26/edith-windsor-thea-spyer-do ma (last accessed 7 July 2013).

34. Ibid.; Susan Muska and Greta Olofsdottir, *Edie & Thea: A Very Long Engagement* (Bless Bless/Breaking Glass, 2009), trailer available at http://youtu.be/lL83Yl4-9Vc, (last accessed 27.06.2013).

35. *Perry v. Windsor*, slip op., p. 3.

36. 1 USC § 7 ('In determining the meaning of any Act of Congress, or of any ruling, regulation, or interpretation of the various administrative bureaus and agencies of the United States, the word "marriage" means only a legal union between one man and one woman as husband and wife, and the word "spouse" refers only to a person of the opposite sex who is a husband or a wife.')

37. Sheryl Gay Stolberg, 'In fight for marriage rights, "she's our Thurgood Marshall"', *New York Times*, 27 March 2013, http://www.nytimes. com/2013/03/28/us/maine-lawyer-credited-in-fight-for-gay-marriage. html (last accessed 7 July 2013); *Gill v. Office of Personnel Management* (1st Cir. 2012) 682 F. 3d 1. *Gill* was before the court when it decided to take *Windsor*, but Justice Elena Kagan had admitted discussing *Gill* with President Obama, and she would have had to recuse herself had the justices granted *certiorari* in *Gill* rather than *Windsor*.

38. *Perry v. Brown* (9th Cir. 2012) 671 F. 3d 1052; *Perry v. Schwarzenegger* (9th Cir. 2010) 704 F.Supp. 2d 921; see also *Strauss v. Horton* (CA 2009) 46 Cal. 4th 364, 207 P. 3d 48; *In re Marriage Cases* (CA 2008) 43 Cal. 4th 757, 183 P. 3d 384.

39. (CA 2009) 207 P. 3d 408.
40. Theodore B. Olson, 'The conservative case for gay marriage: why same-sex marriage is an American value', *Newsweek*, 8 January 2010, http://www.thedailybeast.com/newsweek/2010/01/08/the-conservative-case-for-gay-marriage.html (last accessed 7 July 2013).
41. In his dissent in *Windsor*, Justice Scalia points out: 'One could spend many fruitless afternoons ransacking our library for any other petitioner's brief [like the United States' in *Windsor*] seeking an affirmance of the judgment against it.' *Windsor*, slip op., Scalia J dissenting, p. 5. The California officials did not adopt this approach and were entirely absent from the appeals process, which is one explanation for the difference in the outcomes of the two cases.
42. The court relied heavily upon *Romer* v. *Evans* (1996) 517 US 620, in which Justice Kennedy, writing for the court, held that the state of Colorado could not take away non-discrimination rights that LGBT people had been granted by local communities' statutes.
43. *Windsor*, slip op., pp. 18–19 (internal quotes and citations omitted), 20–1.
44. Ibid., p. 23.
45. Ibid.
46. *Windsor*, slip op., Scalia J dissenting, pp. 1–14. In this part of the opinion only, he was joined by Chief Justice Roberts; Justice Thomas joined the entire opinion.
47. Ibid., pp. 15–26. For analysis of this opinion see Larry Tribe, 'DOMA, Prop 8, and Justice Scalia's Intemperate Dissent', SCOTUSblog website, http://www.scotusblog.com/2013/06/doma-prop-8-and-justice-scalias-intemperate-dissent (last accessed 7 July 2013).
48. *Windsor*, slip op., Scalia J dissenting, p. 22.
49. *Windsor*, slip op., Alito J dissenting, pp. 13–14.
50. Ibid., p. 9 n. 6, p. 13.
51. Ibid., pp. 14–15.
52. *Windsor*, slip op., p. 11.
53. Jeffrey Toobin, *The Nine: Inside the Secret World of the Supreme Court* (New York: Anchor, 2008), p. 384. A third component is to decide more cases.
54. *Perry*, slip op., pp. 15–16.
55. *Perry*, slip op., Kennedy J dissenting, pp. 6–8.
56. Ibid., p. 3.
57. Rules 44, 45, Rules of the Supreme Court of the United States (effective 16 February 2010).
58. For more analysis of these points, see Tom Goldstein, 'Emergency Stay of California Same-Sex Marriages Sought' *SCOTUSblog*, 19 June 2013 available at http://www.scotusblog.com/2013/06/emergency-

stay-of-california-same-sex-marriages-sought/ (last accessed 5 July 2013). The proponents appealed the order lifting the stay to the Supreme Court; appeals of that kind are dealt with summarily by a Justice assigned to the circuit, which was in this case Justice Kennedy, who summarily denied the appeal.

59. Some slight evidence for this position exists in the fact that the court published its one-sentence order lifting the stay in the official reports (http://cdn.ca9.uscourts.gov/datastore/general/2013/06/28/Doc ument(44).pdf (last accessed 7 July 2013)).

60. *Perry v. Schwarzenegger* (ND CA 2010) 704 F.Supp. 2d 921.

61. Ibid., pp. 938–44.

62. Ibid., p. 944.

63. Ibid., pp. 946–52.

64. After reciting some of Walker's findings of fact and describing the position taken by a group of law professors towards them in an *amicus* (friend of the court) brief, Alito said: 'Only an arrogant legal culture that has lost all appreciation of its own limitations could take such a suggestion [by the law professors] seriously.' *Windsor*, slip op., Alito J dissenting, pp. 14–15 n. 7.

65. See, for example, Linda C. McClain, *The Place of Families: Fostering Capacity, Equality, and Responsibility* (Cambridge, MA: Harvard University Press, 2006), ch. 5; Klarman, *From the Closet to the Altar*, pp. 178–80.

66. (1908) 208 US 412. The entire brief is available online at http://www. law.louisville.edu/library/collections/brandeis/node/235 (last accessed 7 July 2013).

67 *Brown v. Board of Education* (1954) 347 US 483, 494, n. 11.

68. Brief of the American Psychological Association et al. in *Perry* and *Windsor*. All briefs in the two cases are available online at http://www. americanbar.org/publications/preview_home/alphabetical.html (last accessed 7 July 2013).

69. Darren E. Sherkat, 'The Editorial Process and Politicized Scholarship: Monday Morning Editorial Quarterbacking and a Call for Scientific Vigilance', *Social Science Research* 41(6) (2012), p. 1346. In addition, some reports argue that the study was funded specifically to provide evidence for the critics of same-sex marriage in *Windsor* and *Perry*. Sofia Resnick, 'UT Releases Docs Related to Controversial Parenting Study' *The American Independent*, 1 February 2013, available online at http://americanindependent.com/218658/ut-releases-docs-related-to-controversial-parenting-study (last accessed 4 July 2013).

70. Brief of Leon R. Kass, Harvey C. Mansfield and the Institute for Marriage and Public Policy as *Amici Curiae* in Support of Petitioners.

71. *Amici Curiae* Brief of Social Science Professors in Support of

Hollingsworth and Bipartisan Legal Advisory Group Addressing the Merits and Supporting Reversal.

72. Including the most famous of all, *Marbury* v. *Madison* (1803) 5 US 137.

73. See for example Meredith Heagney, 'Justice Ruth Bader Ginsburg offers critique of *Roe* v. *Wade* during law school visit', University of Chicago Law School website, 15 May 2013, http://www.law.uchicago.edu/news/justice-ruth-bader-ginsburg-offers-critique-roe-v-wade-during-law-school-visit (last accessed 8 July 2013): '"My criticism of Roe is that it seemed to have stopped the momentum on the side of change," Ginsburg said. She would've preferred that abortion rights be secured more gradually, in a process that included state legislatures and the courts, she added. Ginsburg also was troubled that the focus on *Roe* was on a right to privacy, rather than women's rights.' See also Andrew Koppelman, 'Antonin Scalia's gay marriage mystery', *Salon* website, available at http://www.salon.com/2013/07/15/scalias_gay_marriage_mystery/ (last accessed 16 September 2013).

74. Klarman, *From the Closet to the Altar*.

75. 388 US 1 (1967).

76. Mildred Loving, 'Loving for All', available at http://www.freedomtomarry.org/page/-/files/pdfs/mildred_loving-statement.pdf (last accessed 8 July 2013).

77. Joseph Carroll, 'Most Americans approve of interracial marriages', Gallup website, 16 August 2007, http://www.gallup.com/poll/28417/most-americans-approve-interracial-marriages.aspx (last accessed 8 July 2013).

78. Jeremy Waldron, 'The Core of the Case against Judicial Review', *Yale Law Journal* 115 (2006), pp. 1346–1406.

79. *Windsor*, slip op., Scalia J dissenting, p. 24 (emphasis in original).

80. Waldron, 'The Core of the Case against Judicial Review', p. 1384.

81. Douglas Laycock and Thomas C. Berg, 'Protecting Same-sex Marriage and Religious Liberty', *Virginia Law Review Online* 99(1) (2013), http://www.virginialawreview.org/content/pdfs/99/Online/LaycockBerg.pdf (last accessed 8 July 2013). In a telling sign of how fast things are moving, their paper, which is not yet in hard-copy form, is already out of date. But as we discussed in Chapter 5, in New York, which is one of the most recent to approve same-sex marriage legislatively, the religious protections are robust, which reinforces their point.

82. But equally, if we had been writing in 1907, we would have said 'to marriages with a deceased wife's sister'.

83. *Windsor*, slip op., pp. 19–20.

Bibliography

Books, book chapters and journal articles

Abbate, Lindsay L., 'What God Has Joined "Let" Man Put Asunder: Ireland's Struggle between Canon and Common Law Relating to Divorce', *Emory International Law Review* 16(2) (2002), pp. 583–637.

Abrams, Kerry, 'Polygamy, Prostitution, and the Federalization of Immigration Law', *Columbia Law Review* 105(3) (2005), pp. 641–716.

Ahmad, Khurshid, *Family Life in Islam* (Leicester: Islamic Foundation, 1974).

Al-Hibri, Azizah Y. and Raja' M. El Habti, 'Islam', in Don S. Browning, M. Christian Green and John Witte Jr (eds), *Sex, Marriage and the Family in World Religions* (New York: Columbia University Press, 2006).

Anderson, Melissa Cully and Bruce E. Cain, 'The Warren Court and Redistricting', in H. N. Scheiber (ed.), *Earl Warren and the Warren Court: The Legacy in Foreign and American Law* (Berkeley, CA: Lexington, 2007).

Anderson, Nancy F., 'The "Marriage with a Deceased Wife's Sister Bill" Controversy: Incest Anxiety and the Defense of Family Purity in Victorian England', *Journal of British Studies* 21(2) (1982), pp. 67–86.

Anderson, Olive, 'The Incidence of Civil Marriage in Victorian England and Wales', *Past & Present* 69 (1975).

Anderson, Virginia DeJohn, 'Migrants and Motives: Religion and the Settlement of New England, 1630–1640', *New England Quarterly* 58(3) (1985), pp. 339–83.

Aristotle, *Nicomachean Ethics*, tr. Martin Ostwald (Indianapolis: Liberal Arts Press, 1962).

Aristotle, *Politics*, tr. Ernest Barker (Oxford: Oxford University Press, 1977).

Arshad, Raffia, *Islamic Family Law* (London: Sweet & Maxwell, 2010).

Ashby, Abby and Audrey Jones, *The Shrigley Abduction: A Tale of Anguish, Deceit and Violation of the Domestic Hearth* (Stroud: Sutton, 2003).

Bailey, Martha, 'Regulation of Cohabitation and Marriage in Canada', *Law and Policy* 26(1) (2004), pp. 153–75.

Baker, J. H., *An Introduction to English Legal History*, 2nd ed. (London: Butterworths, 1979).

Ball, Barbara et al. (eds), *The Encyclopedia of Jewish Life and Thought* (Jerusalem: Carta, c. 1996).

Bamforth, Nicholas, *Sexuality, Morals & Justice: A Theory of Lesbian & Gay Rights Law* (London: Cassell, 1997).

Bamforth, Nicholas and David A. J. Richards, *Patriarchal Religion, Sexuality and Gender: A Critique of the New Natural Law* (Cambridge: Cambridge University Press, 2008).

Bannet, E. Tavor, 'The Marriage Act of 1753: "A Most Cruel Law for the Fair Sex"', *Eighteenth Century Studies* 30(3) (1997).

Bari, Muhammad Abdul, *Marriage and Family Building in Islam* (London: Ta-Ha, 2007).

Barker, Nicola, 'Ambiguous Symbolisms: Recognising Customary Marriage and Same-sex Marriage in South Africa' *International Journal of Law in Context* 7(4) (2011) pp. 447–66.

Bennett, Bruce S., '*Banister* v. *Thompson* and Afterwards: The Church of England and the Deceased Wife's Sister's Marriage Act', *Journal of Ecclesiastical History* 49(4) (1998), pp. 668–82.

Berger, Iris, *South Africa in World History* (Oxford: Oxford University Press, 2009).

Bickel, Alexander M., *The Least Dangerous Branch: The Supreme Court at the Bar of Politics* (Indianapolis: Bobbs-Merrill, 1962).

Blackstone, William, *Commentaries on the Laws of England* (Chicago: University of Chicago Press, [1765] 1979).

Blumstein, Philip and Pepper Schwartz, *American Couples: Money, Work, Sex* (New York: Morrow, 1983).

The Book of Common Prayer (London: Everyman's Library, [1662] 1999).

Bossy, John, 'The Counter-Reformation and the People of Catholic Europe', *Past & Present* 47(1) (1970), pp. 51–70.

Brake, Elizabeth, *Minimizing Marriage: Marriage, Morality and the Law* (New York: Oxford University Press, 2012).

Bray, Gerald (ed.), *Documents of the English Reformation* (Cambridge: James Clarke, 1994).

Bromley, P. M. and Hugh K. Bevan (eds), *Butterworth's Family Law Service* (London: Butterworths, 1983).

Brontë, Charlotte, *Jane Eyre* (Auckland: Floating Press, [1847] 2008).

Brown, R. L., 'The Rise and Fall of the Fleet Marriages', in R. B. Outhwaite (ed.), *Marriage and Society: Studies in the Social History of Marriage* (London: Europa, 1981), pp. 117–36.

Brown, Stewart J., *The National Churches of England, Ireland, and Scotland, 1801–46* (Oxford: Oxford University Press, 2001).

Brownstein, Alan, 'Gays, Jews and Other Strangers in a Strange Land: The Case for Reciprocal Accommodation of Religious Liberty and the Right of Same-sex Couples to Marry', *University of San Francisco Law Review* 45 (2010), pp. 389–436.

Bibliography

Burke, W. P., *Irish Priests in the Penal Times (1660–1760)* (Shannon: Irish University Press, [1914] 1969).

Burleigh, J. H. S., *A Church History of Scotland* (London: Oxford University Press, 1960).

Bushman, Claudia L. and Richard L. Bushman, *Building the Kingdom: A History of the Mormons in America* (New York: Oxford University Press, 2001).

Calvin, Jean, *Institutes of the Christian Religion*, in *Works and Correspondence*, ed. J. T. McNeill (London: SCM Press, 1960).

Capp, Bernard, 'Bigamous Marriage in Early Modern England', *Historical Journal* 52(3) (2009), pp. 537–56.

Carlson, Eric Josef, *Marriage and the English Reformation* (Oxford: Blackwell, 1994).

Catholic University of America, *New Catholic Encyclopedia* (New York: McGraw-Hill, 1967).

Chadwick, Owen, *The Victorian Church* (London: Adam & Charles Black, 1966).

Chambers, Robert (ed.), *The Life and Works of Robert Burns* (Edinburgh: W. & R. Chambers, 1856)

Chambers, Robert (ed.), *The Scottish Songs* (Edinburgh: William Tait, 1829).

Chandler, Matthew, 'Moral Mandate or Personal Preference? Possible Avenues for Accommodation of Civil Servants Morally Opposed to Facilitating Same-sex Marriage', *Brigham Young University Law Review* 2011(5) (2011), pp. 1625–68.

Cobbett, William (ed.), *Cobbett's Parliamentary History* (London: T. C. Hansard, 1813).

Collins, Wilkie, *No Name* (Auckland: Floating Press, [1862] 2009).

Corvino, John and Maggie Gallagher, *Debating Same-sex Marriage* (New York: Oxford University Press, 2012).

Cott, Nancy F., *Public Vows: A History of Marriage and the Nation* (Cambridge, MA: Harvard University Press, 2000).

Cunningham, Allan, *The Works of Robert Burns with His Life* (London: James Cochrane, 1834).

Curra, John, *The Relativity of Deviance*, 2nd ed. (Thousand Oaks, CA: Pine Forge Press, 2011).

Dawkins, Richard, *The God Delusion* (London: Black Swan, 2007).

Dempsey, Brian, 'Making the Gretna Blacksmith Redundant: Who Worried, Who Spoke, Who Was Heard on the Abolition of Irregular Marriage in Scotland?', *Journal of Legal History* 30(1) (2009), pp. 23–52.

Dempsey, Brian, 'The Marriage (Scotland) Bill 1755', in Hector L. MacQueen (ed.), *Miscellany Six* (Edinburgh: Stair Society, 2009).

Dillon, Kathleen M., 'Divorce and Remarriage as Human Rights: The Irish Constitution and the European Convention on Human Rights at Odds in *Johnston v. Ireland*', *Cornell International Law Journal* 22(1) (1989), pp. 63–90.

Dodson, John (ed.), *A Report of the Judgment Delivered in the Consistorial Court of London . . . in the Cause of Dalrymple the Wife against Dalrymple the Husband* (London: Butterworth, 1811).

Durston, Christopher, *The Family in the English Revolution* (Oxford: Basil Blackwell, 1989).

El Menyawi, Hassan, 'Same-sex Marriage in Islamic Law', *Wake Forest Journal of Law & Policy* 2(2) (2012), pp. 375–530.

Elon, Menachem et al., *Jewish Law* (New York: Matthew Bender, 1999).

Euler, Carrie, 'Heinrich Bullinger, Marriage and the English Reformation: *The Christen state of Matrimonye* in England, 1540–53' *Sixteenth Century Journal* 34(2) (2003), 367–93.

Feldblum, Chai, 'Moral Conflict and Conflicting Liberties', in Douglas Laycock, Anthony R. Picarello Jr and Robin Fretwell Wilson (eds), *Same-sex Marriage and Religious Liberty: Emerging Conflicts* (Lanham, MD: Rowman & Littlefield, 2008).

Feldman, Noah, *Divided by God: America's Church–State Problem – and What We Should Do about It* (New York: Farrar, Straus & Giroux, 2005).

Fineman, Martha Albertson, *The Autonomy Myth: A Theory of Dependency* (New York: New Press, 2004).

Finnis, John, 'Law, Morality and "Sexual orientation"', *Notre Dame Law Review* 69(5) (1994), pp. 1049–76.

Fischer, David Hackett, *Albion's Seed: Four British Folkways in America* (New York: Oxford University Press, 1989).

Foner, Eric, *Reconstruction: America's Unfinished Revolution, 1863–1877* (New York: Harper & Row, 1988).

Fox, George, *A Collection of Select and Christian Epistles* (London: T. Sowle, 1698).

Fuller, Lon L., *The Morality of Law*, rev. ed. (New Haven, CT: Yale University Press, 1969).

Fuller, Lon L., 'Positivism and Fidelity to Law: A Reply to Professor Hart', *Harvard Law Review* 71(4) (1958), pp. 630–72.

Gardiner, Samuel Rawson (ed.), *The Constitutional Documents of the Puritan Revolution, 1625–1660*, 3rd ed. (Oxford: Clarendon Press, 1979).

George, Robert P. and Jean Bethke Elshtain, *The Meaning of Marriage: Family, State, Market, and Morals* (Dallas: Spence, 2006).

Gillis, John R., *For Better, for Worse: British Marriages, 1600 to the Present* (New York: Oxford University Press, 1985).

Girgis, Sherif, Ryan T. Anderson and Robert P. George, *What Is Marriage? Man and Woman – a Defense* (New York: Encounter, 2012).

Green, Leslie, 'Sex-neutral marriage' *Current Legal Problems* 64 (2011), pp. 1–21.

Guy, John, *Queen of Scots: The True Life of Mary Stuart* (Boston: Houghton Mifflin, 2005).

Hamburger, Philip, *Separation of Church and State* (Cambridge, MA: Harvard University Press, 2002).

Hammerton, A. James, 'Victorian Marriage and the Law of Matrimonial Cruelty', *Victorian Studies* 32(2) (1990), pp. 269–92.

Hart, H. L. A., 'Positivism and the Separation of Law and Morals', *Harvard Law Review* 71(4) (1958), pp. 593–629.

Hegel, G. W. F., *Philosophy of Right*, tr. T. M. Knox (Oxford: Clarendon Press, 1942).

Hobbes, Thomas, *Leviathan*, ed. C. B. Macpherson (Harmondsworth: Penguin, [1651] 1968).

Hoffman, Stephanie B., 'Behind Closed Doors: Impotence Trials and the Trans-historical Right to Marital Privacy', *Boston University Law Review* 89(5) (2009), pp. 1725–52.

Hogg, James, *The Jacobite Relics of Scotland* (Edinburgh: William Blackwood, 1819).

Hogg, Peter W., *Constitutional Law of Canada*, 4th ed. (Toronto: Carswell, 1997).

Holmes, Oliver Wendell Jr, 'The Path of the Law', *Harvard Law Review* 10(8) (1897), 457–78.

Hooker, Richard, *Of the Laws of Ecclesiastical Polity*, ed. John Keble (Indianapolis: Liberty Fund, [1594–73] 1888).

Horle, C. W., *The Quakers and the English Legal System, 1660–1688* (Philadelphia: University of Pennsylvania Press, 1988).

Hoyt, J. K., *Hoyt's New Cyclopedia of Practical Quotations* (New York and London: Funk & Wagnall, 1922).

Hume, David, 'Of Polygamy and Divorces', in *Essays, Moral, Political and Literary*, ed. Eugene F. Miller (Indianapolis: Liberty Fund, [1777] 1985), pp. 181–90.

Isaacson, Eric Alan, 'Are Same-sex Marriages Really a Threat to Religious Liberty?', *Stanford Journal of Civil Rights and Civil Liberties* 8(1) (2012), pp. 123–54.

Jacobs, Margaret D., 'The Eastmans and the Luhans: Interracial Marriage between White Women and Native American Men, 1875–1935', *Frontiers: A Journal of Women's Studies* 23(3) (2002), pp. 29–54.

Jacobson, Cardell K. and Lara Burton (eds), *Mormon Polygamy in the United States: Historical, Cultural, and Legal Issues* (New York: Oxford University Press, 2011).

James, Christine P., 'Céad míle fáilte? Ireland Welcomes Divorce: The 1995 Irish Divorce Referendum and the Family (Divorce) Act of 1996', *Duke Journal of Comparative & International Law* 8(1) (1997), pp. 175–228.

Jefferson, Thomas, *Writings*, ed. Merrill D. Peterson (New York: Literary Classics of the United States, 1984).

Johnston, Henry P. (ed.), .), *The Correspondence and Public Papers of John Jay* (New York: G. P. Putnam's Sons, 1890–3).

Kahana, Kopel, *The Theory of Marriage in Jewish Law* (Leiden: E. J. Brill, 1966).

Kant, Immanuel, *Metaphysics of Morals*, tr. Mary Gregor (Cambridge: Cambridge University Press, 1996).

Kelly, James, 'The Abduction of Women of Fortune in Eighteenth-century Ireland', *Eighteenth-century Ireland* 9 (1994), pp. 7–43.

Kirk, James (ed.), *The Second Book of Discipline* (Edinburgh: Saint Andrew Press, 1980).

Klarman, Michael, *From the Closet to the Altar: Courts, Backlash, and the Struggle for Same-sex Marriage* (New York: Oxford University Press, 2013).

Koppelman, Andrew, *Same Sex, Different States: When Same-sex Marriages Cross State Lines* (New Haven, CT: Yale University Press, 2006).

Lacey, Nicola, 'Philosophy, Political Morality and History: Explaining the Enduring Resonance of the Hart–Fuller Debate', *New York University Law Review* 83(4) (2008), pp. 1059–87.

Langford, Paul, *A Polite and Commercial People: England, 1727–1783* (Oxford: Oxford University Press, 1989).

Laycock, Douglas, 'Afterword', in Douglas Laycock, Anthony R. Picarello Jr and Robin Fretwell Wilson (eds), *Same-Sex Marriage and Religious Liberty: Emerging Conflicts* (Lanham, MD: Rowman & Littlefield Publishers, Inc. 2008).

Laycock, Douglas and Thomas C. Berg, 'Protecting Same-sex Marriage and Religious Liberty', *Virginia Law Review Online* 99(1) (2013), http://www.virginialawreview.org/content/pdfs/99/Online/LaycockBerg.pdf (last accessed 14 May 2013).

Lee, Patrick and Robert P. George, *Body–Self Dualism in Contemporary Ethics and Politics* (Cambridge: Cambridge University Press, 2008).

Lehmann, Helmut T. (ed.), *Luther's Works* (Philadelphia: Fortress Press, 1967).

Lehmberg, Stanford E., *The Later Parliaments of Henry VIII, 1536–1547* (Cambridge: Cambridge University Press, 1977).

Lemmings, David, 'Marriage and Law in the Eighteenth Century: Hardwicke's Marriage Act of 1753', *Historical Journal* 39(2) (1996), pp. 339–60.

Leneman, L. and R. Mitchison, 'Clandestine Marriages in the Scottish Cities, 1660–1780', *Journal of Social History* 26(4) (1993), pp. 845–61.

Lewis, C. S., *Mere Christianity*, rev. ed. (London: HarperCollins, 2001).

Lupu, Ira C. and Robert W. Tuttle, 'Same-sex Equality and Religious Freedom', *Northwestern Journal of Law & Social Policy* 5(2) (2010), pp. 274–306.

McBride, Ian, *Eighteenth-century Ireland: The Isle of Slaves* (Dublin: Gill & Macmillan, 2009).

McClain, Linda, *The Place of Families: Fostering Capacity, Equality and Responsibility* (Cambridge, MA: Harvard University Press, 2006).

MacCulloch, Diarmaid, *A History of Christianity: The First Three Thousand Years* (London: Allen Lane, 2009).

MacCulloch, Diarmaid, *Thomas Cranmer: A Life* (New Haven, CT: Yale University Press, 1996).

Machin, G. I. T., *Politics and the Churches in Great Britain, 1832 to 1868* (Oxford: Clarendon Press, 1977).

McLean, Iain, *Adam Smith, Radical and Egalitarian: An Interpretation for the Twenty-first Century* (Edinburgh: Edinburgh University Press, 2006).

McLean, Iain, *What's Wrong with the British Constitution?* (Oxford: Oxford University Press, 2010).

McLean, Iain and Alistair McMillan, *State of the Union: Unionism and the Alternatives in the United Kingdom since 1707* (Oxford: Oxford University Press, 2005).

McLean, Iain and Scot Peterson, 'Adam Smith at the Constitutional Convention', *Loyola Law Review* 56(1) (2010), pp. 95–133.

McLean, Iain and Scot Peterson, 'Secularity and Secularism in the United Kingdom: On the Way to the First Amendment', *Brigham Young University Law Review* 2011(3) (2011), pp. 637–56.

Madison, James, *Writings*, ed. Jack N. Rakove (New York: Library of America, 1999).

Madsen, Carol Cornwall, '"At Their Peril": Utah law and the Case of Plural Wives, 1850–1900', in John S. McCormick and John R. Sillito (eds), *A World We Thought We Knew: Readings in Utah History* (Salt Lake City: University of Utah Press, 1995), pp. 68–84.

Malik, Maleiha, *Minority Legal Orders in the UK: Minorities, Pluralism and the Law* (London: British Academy, 2012).

Mantz, Ruth Elvish and J. Middleton Murry, *The Life of Katherine Mansfield* (London: Constable, 1933).

Marshall, James Scott, 'Irregular Marriage in Scotland as Reflected in the Kirk Session Records', *Scottish Church History Records* 37 (1972), pp. 10–25.

Matthew, H. C. G., *Gladstone, 1875–1898* (Oxford: Clarendon Press, 1995).

Matthews, J. Scott, 'The Political Foundations of Support for Same-sex Marriage in Canada', *Canadian Journal of Political Science* 38(4) (2005), pp. 841–66.

Melvill, James, *The Autobiography and Diary of James Melvill, with a Continuation of the Diary*, ed. R. Pitcairn (Edinburgh: Wodrow Society, 1842).

Milligan, Edward H., *Quaker Marriage* (Kendal: Quaker Tapestry Booklets, 1994).

Milton, John, *The Doctrine & Discipline of Divorce* (London, c. 1643).

Mitchison, Rosalind, *Lordship to Patronage: Scotland, 1603–1745* (Edinburgh: Edinburgh University Press, 1983).

Nasir, Jamal J., *The Islamic Law of Personal Status*, 3rd ed. (The Hague: Kluwer Law International, 2002).

NeJaime, Douglas, 'Marriage Inequality: Same-sex Relationships, Religious

Exemptions, and the Production of Sexual Orientation Discrimination', *California Law Review* 100(5) (2012), pp. 1169–1238.

Nicholson-Crotty, Sean, 'Reassessing Madison's Diversity Hypothesis: The Case of Same-sex Marriage', *Journal of Politics* 68(4) (2006), pp. 922–30.

Noonan, John T. Jr, *A Church that Can and Cannot Change: The Development of Catholic Moral Teaching* (Notre Dame, IN: University of Notre Dame Press, 2005).

Noonan, John T. Jr, 'Marriage in the Middle Ages: Power to Choose', *Viator* 4 (1973), pp. 419–34.

Outhwaite, R. B., *Clandestine Marriage in England, 1500–1850* (London: Hambledon Press, 1995).

Parker, Stephen, *Informal Marriage, Cohabitation and the Law, 1750–1989* (Basingstoke: Macmillan, 1990).

Pascoe, Peggy, 'Miscegenation Law, Court Cases, and Ideologies of 'Race' in Twentieth-century America', *Journal of American History* 83(1) (1996), pp. 44–69.

Pascoe, Peggy, *What Comes Naturally: Miscegenation Law and the Making of Race in America* (New York: Oxford University Press, 2009).

Plato, *Symposium*, tr. M. C. Howatson (Cambridge: Cambridge University Press, 2008).

Poll, R. D., '"Buchanan's Blunder": the Utah War, 1857–1858', *Military Affairs* 25(3) (1961), pp. 121–31.

Posel, Deborah, *The Making of Apartheid, 1948–1961: Conflict and Compromise* (Oxford: Clarendon Press, 1991).

Posel, Deborah, 'State, Power and Gender: Conflict over the Registration of African Customary Marriages in South Africa, c. 1910–1970', *Journal of Historical Sociology* 8(3) (1995), pp. 223–56.

Posner, Richard, *Sex and Reason* (Cambridge, MA: Harvard University Press, 1992).

Powell, T. R., 'And Repent at Leisure: An Inquiry into the Unhappy Lot of Those Whom Nevada Hath Joined Together And North Carolina Hath Put Asunder', *Harvard Law Review* 58 (1945), pp. 930–1017.

Probert, Rebecca, *The Changing Legal Regulation of Cohabitation: From Fornicators to Family, 1600–2010* (Cambridge: Cambridge University Press, 2012).

Probert, Rebecca, *Marriage Law and Practice in the Long Eighteenth Century: A Reassessment* (Cambridge: Cambridge University Press, 2009).

Rawls, John, *A Brief Inquiry into the Meaning of Sin and Faith*, ed. Thomas Nagel (Cambridge, MA: Harvard University Press, 2009).

Rawls, John, 'The Idea of Public Reason Revisited', *University of Chicago Law Review* 64(3) (1997), pp. 765–807.

Rawls, John, *Political Liberalism* (New York: Columbia University Press, 1993).

Rawls, John, *A Theory of Justice*, rev. ed. (Oxford: Oxford University Press, 1999).

Riley, Glenda, *Divorce: An American Tradition* (New York: Oxford University Press, 1991).

Roberts, Nicholas, 'The Historical Background to the Marriage (Wales) Act 2010', *Ecclesiastical Law Review* 13(1) (2011), pp. 39–56.

Robinson, Mairi (ed. in chief), *Concise Scots Dictionary* (Edinburgh: Scottish National Dictionary Association, 1985).

Rodger of Earlsferry, Lord, *The Courts, the Church and the Constitution: Aspects of the Disruption of 1843* (Edinburgh: Edinburgh University Press, 2008).

Russell, Bertrand, *Marriage and Morals* (London: Routledge, [1929] 2009).

Rutt, John Towill (ed.), *Diary of Thomas Burton, Esq.* (London: Henry Colburn, 1828).

Savage, Gail L., 'The Operation of the 1857 Divorce Act, 1860–1910: A Research Note', *Journal of Social History* 16(4) (1983), pp. 103–10.

See, Scott W., *The History of Canada* (Westport, CT: Greenwood Press, 2001).

Shanley, Mary Lyndon, '"One Must Ride Behind": Married Women's Rights and the Divorce Act of 1857', *Victorian Studies* 25(3) (1982), pp. 355–76.

Shelford, L., *A Practical Treatise of the Law of Marriage and Divorce and Registration* (London: S. Sweet, 1841).

Sherif-Trask, Bahira, 'Muslim Families in the United States', in Marilyn Coleman and Lawrence H. Ganong (eds), *Handbook of Contemporary Families: Considering the Past, Contemplating the Future* (Thousand Oaks, CA: Sage, 2004).

Sherkat, Darren E., 'The Editorial Process and Politicized Scholarship: Monday Morning Editorial Quarterbacking and a Call for Scientific Vigilance', *Social Science Research* 41(6) (2012), pp. 1346–9.

Smith, Adam, *An Inquiry into the Nature and Causes of the Wealth of Nations* (Indianapolis: Liberty Classics, [1776] 1981).

Smith, Adam, *Lectures on Jurisprudence* (Oxford: Clarendon Press, 1978).

Snell, James G. and Cynthia Comacchio Abeele, 'Regulating Nuptiality: Restricting Access to Marriage in Twentieth-century English-speaking Canada', *Canadian Historical Review* 69(4) (1988), pp. 466–89.

Stone, Lawrence, *The Family, Sex and Marriage in England, 1500–1800* (London: Weidenfeld & Nicolson, 1977).

Stone, Lawrence, *Road to Divorce: England, 1530–1987*, new ed. (Oxford University Press, 1992).

Sullivan, Andrew, *Virtually Normal: An Argument about Homosexuality* (London: Picador, 1995).

Symonds, Deborah A., 'Death, Birth and Marriage in Early Modern Scotland', in Elizabeth Foyster and Christopher A. Whatley (eds), *A History of Everyday Life in Scotland, 1600–1800* (Edinburgh: Edinburgh University Press, 2010).

Taylor, Verta, Katrina Kimport, Nella Van Dyke and Ellen Ann Andersen, 'Culture and Mobilization: Tactical Repertoires, Same-sex Weddings, and the Impact on Gay Activism', *American Sociological Review* 74(6) (2009), pp. 865–90.

Thayer, James Steel, 'The Berdache of the Northern Plains: A Socioreligious Perspective', *Journal of Anthropological Research* 36(3) (1980), pp. 287–93.

Tobin, Brian, 'Gay Marriage – A Bridge Too Far?', *Irish Student Law Review* 15 (2007), pp. 175–96.

Toobin, Jeffrey, *The Nine: Inside the Secret World of the Supreme Court* (New York: Anchor, 2008).

Trollope, Anthony, *Barchester Towers* (Oxford University Press, [1857] 2008).

Trollope, Anthony, *The Eustace Diamonds* (Auckland NZ: Floating Press, [1971] 2010).

Underkuffler, Laura S., 'Odious Discrimination and the Religious Exemption Question', *Cardozo Law Review* 32(5) (2011), pp. 2069–91.

van Kirk, Sylvia, 'From "Marrying-in" to "Marrying-out": Changing Patterns of Aboriginal/Non-Aboriginal Marriage in Colonial Canada', *Frontiers: A Journal of Women Studies* 23(3) (2002), pp. 1–11.

Wagner, Peter, 'The Pornographer in the Courtroom: Trial Reports about Cases of Sexual Crimes and Delinquencies as a Genre of Eighteenth-century Erotica', in Paul-Gabriel Boucé (ed.), *Sexuality in Eighteenth-Century Britain* (Manchester University Press, 1982).

Waldron, Jeremy, 'The Core of the Case against Judicial Review', *Yale Law Journal* 115 (2006), pp. 1346–406.

Walker, D. M., *A Legal History of Scotland* (Edinburgh: W. Green/T. & T. Clark, 1988–).

Warner, Michael, *The Trouble with Normal: Sex, Politics, and the Ethics of Queer Life*, new ed. (Cambridge, MA: Harvard University Press, 2000).

White, G. Edward, *Earl Warren: A Public Life* (New York: Oxford University Press, 1982).

Wilson, A. N., *C. S. Lewis: A Biography* (London: Collins, 1990).

Wilson, Robin Fretwell, 'The Calculus of Accommodation: Contraception, Abortion, Same-sex Marriage, and Other Clashes between Religion and the State', *Boston College Law Review* 53(4) (2012), pp. 1417–513.

Wilson, Robin Fretwell, 'Insubstantial Burdens: The Case for Government Employee Exemptions to Same-sex marriage laws', *Northwestern Journal of Law & Social Policy* 5(2) (2010), pp. 318–68.

Wilson, Robin Fretwell, 'The Perils of Privatized Marriage', in Joel A. Nichols (ed.), *Marriage and Divorce in a Multicultural Context: Multi-tiered Marriage and the Boundaries of Civil Law and Religion* (New York: Cambridge University Press, 2012).

Witte, John Jr, *From Sacrament to Contract: Marriage, Religion, and Law in the Western Tradition* (Louisville, KY: Westminster John Knox Press, 1997).

Wormald, Jenny, *Court, Kirk and Community: Scotland, 1470–1625* (London: Edward Arnold, 1981).

Zagarri, Rosemarie, 'Morals, Manners, and the Republican Mother', *American Quarterly* 44(2) (1992), pp. 192–215.

Zwingli, Huldrych, *Selected Works*, ed. Samuel Macauley Jackson (Philadelphia: University of Pennsylvania, 1901).

Government publications

'Constitutional Convention: Government Proposals', Merrion Street (Irish Government News Service) website, 28 February 2012, http://www.merrion street.ie/index.php/2012/02/constitutional-convention-government-proposa ls-28-february-2012/ (last accessed 13 May 2013).

Jackson, G. W., *Marriages at Gretna, 1975–2000* (Edinburgh: General Register Office for Scotland, 2001), http://www.gro-scotland.gov.uk/files/op4-gretna. pdf (last accessed 7 May 2013).

Office of National Statistics, 'Religion in England and Wales 2011', 11 December 2012, http://www.ons.gov.uk/ons/dcp171776_290510.pdf (last accessed 9 May 2013).

Registrar General, *Eighth Annual Report*, P.P. (1847–48), vol. 25, p. 28 (967).

Report of the Departmental Committee Appointed to Enquire into the Law of Scotland Relating to the Constitution of Marriage (1937), Cmd 5354.

News articles

'75% support same-sex marriage: poll', *Irish Times*, 28 January 2013, http:// www.irishtimes.com/news/75-support-same-sex-marriage-poll-1.1072147 (last accessed 13 May 2013).

Bingham, John, 'Coalition "faffing around with gay marriage"', *Daily Telegraph*, 29 March 2013, http://www.telegraph.co.uk/news/politics/9962095/coalition-faffing-around-with-gay-marriage.html (last accessed 5 August 2013).

Calmes, Jackie and Peter Baker, ', 'Obama says same-sex marriage should be legal', *New York Times*, 9 May 2012, http://www.nytimes.com/2012/05/10/us/politics/obama-says-same-sex-marriage-should-be-legal.html (last accessed 6 July 2013).

Gabbatt, Adam, 'Edith Windsor and Thea Spyer: "A love affair that just kept on and on and on"', *Guardian*, 26 June 2013, http://www.guardian.co.uk/world/2013/jun/26/edith-windsor-thea-spyer-doma (last accessed 7 July 2013).

Grossman, Anna Jane, 'Vows: Chris Barley and Marc Kushner', *New York Times*, 13 April 2012, http://www.nytimes.com/2012/04/15/fashion/weddings/chris-barley-and-marc-kushner-vows.html (last accessed 7 May 2013).

Hammell, Lee, 'Diocesan retreat in Whitinsville sold for $800K', *Worcester*

Telegram & Gazette (Worcester, MA), 18 October 2012, http://www.telegram.com/article/20121018/NEWS/110189860 (last accessed 14 May 2013).

McDonald, Henry, 'Ireland to hold gay marriage referendum', *The Guardian*, 14 April 2013, http://www.guardian.co.uk/world/2013/apr/14/ireland-hold-gay-marriage-referendum (last accessed 13 May 2013).

Murray, Gary V., 'Diocese sued for sex bias', *Worcester Telegram & Gazette* (Worcester, MA), 11 September 2012, http://www.telegram.com/article/20120911/NEWS/109119835/1246 (last accessed 14 May 2013).

Olson, Theodore B., 'The conservative case for gay marriage: why same-sex marriage is an American value', *Newsweek*, 8 January 2010, http://www.thedailybeast.com/newsweek/2010/01/08/the-conservative-case-for-gay-marriage.html (last accessed 7 July 2013).

Reagan, Michael, 'Churches: time to fight back', *Ironton Tribune* (Ironton, OH), 2 April 2013, http://www.irontontribune.com/2013/04/02/churches-time-to-fight-back, last accessed 14 May 2013.

'Russian fundamentalists sue US, want Alaska back' RIA Novosti website, 16 March 2013, http://en.rian.ru/russia/20130316/180055377/Russian-Fundamentalists-Sue-US-Want-Alaska-Back.html (last accessed 13 May 2013).

Stolberg, Sheryl Gay, 'In fight for marriage rights, "she's our Thurgood Marshall"', *New York Times*, 27 March 2013, http://www.nytimes.com/2013/03/28/us/maine-lawyer-credited-in-fight-for-gay-marriage.html (last accessed 7 July 2013)

White, Michael and Sarah Hall, 'Gay marriage bill "wrecked" in Lords', *The Guardian*, 25 June 2004, http://www.guardian.co.uk/politics/2004/jun/25/lords.gayrights (last accessed 8 May 2013).

Other sources

Chapman, Richard, 'The Lords Spiritual and Civil Partnerships Legislation', http://www.churchofengland.org/media/1472983/cptimeline.doc (last accessed 6 July 2013)

Douglas, Gillian, Norman Doe, Sophie Gilliat-Ray, Russell Sandberg and Asma Khan, *Social Cohesion and Religious Law: Marriage, Divorce and Religious Courts* (Cardiff: Cardiff Law School, 2011), http://www.law.cf.ac.uk/clr/research/cohesion (last accessed 8 May 2013).

'Gay Pride is now respectable, and the worse for it', Peter Tatchell website, July 2002, http://www.petertatchell.net/lgbt_rights/queer_theory/gaypride.htm (last accessed 8 May 2013).

Heagney, Meredith, 'Justice Ruth Bader Ginsburg offers critique of *Roe* v. *Wade* during law school visit', University of Chicago Law School website, 15 May 2013, http://www.law.uchicago.edu/news/justice-ruth-bader-ginsburg-offers-critique-roe-v-wade-during-law-school-visit (last accessed 8 July 2013)

Bibliography

Koppelman, Andrew, *Careful with That Gun: Lee, George, Wax, and Geach on Gay Rights and Same-sex Marriage* (Chicago: Northwestern University School of Law, 2010), available online at http://ssrn.com/abstract=1544478 (last accessed 14 May 2013).

Macedo, Stephen, 'The Future of Marriage: Liberal Justice, Love and the Law', paper presented at the Western Political Science Association, 28–30 March 2013, available online at http://wpsa.research.pdx.edu/papers/docs/macedo. docx (last accessed 14 May 2013).

Recognition of Customary Marriages (Cape Town: Women's Legal Centre, 2011), http://www.wlce.co.za/morph_assets/themelets/explorer/relationship %20rights/general/Recognition%20of%20Customary%20Marriages.pdf (last accessed 13 May 2013).

Index

abortion, 209–12
Abraham, biblical patriarch, 7, 21
Acts and Treaty of Union 1706–7, xiv, 35–6, 64–5, 82, 92
adultery, legal definition of, 154–5: in C18 Scotland, 66–8
Alaska, 152
al-Humaydi, Imam, vii
Alito, Samuel, Assoc. Justice, US Supreme Court, 193, 201–2, 203, 206
Anderson, Olive, 104
anti-miscegenation statutes *see Loving v. Virginia*
Appalachia, 68
Argentina, 4
Aristophanes, 15–17, 159–60
Aristotle, 16–18
Austen, Jane, 81

Baldry, Sir Tony, 191–2
Barrington, William, 2nd Viscount, 61
bed-and-breakfast owners and discrimination against same-sex couples, 165–6
Belgium, 4
berdache, 135–6
bigamy, 52–5, 70–1, 172–8
    President Andrew Jackson accused of, 69
Birmingham (as destination for clandestine marriages), 84, 90, 107

Bipartisan Legal Advisory Group (BLAG), US Congress, 197, 203
Blackstone, Sir William, xiii, 1, 80, 88
Boies, David, 199
Boleyn, Anne, 49, 52
Bothwell, James Hepburn, 4th Earl of, 50–1, 69
Bowers v. Hardwick (1986) 478 US 186, 154
Brandeis, Louis, Assoc. Justice, US Supreme Court, 177, 206
Brazil, 4
breach of promise to marry, 61
British Social Attitudes, 4–5
Brougham and Vaux, Henry Brougham, 1st Baron, 66–7, 96, 104, 106
Brown v. Board of Education (1954) 347 US 483, 131, 206
Bull v. Preddy [2012] EWCA Civ 83, 165
Bullinger, Heinrich, 21, 22

California, 3, 56–7, 136, 140, 150, 195–214
Calvin, Jean, 20–1
Cana, wedding at, 20
Canada, xi, 3, 7, 129–35
Canadian Charter of Rights and Freedoms, 130
Charles II, king of England, 56
Charles V, Holy Roman Emperor, 49

Church of England, 2, 14–15, 48–55, 66, 69, 92, 192
  bishops in House of Lords, 190–4
  given regulatory function by 1753 Act, 80–9, 108
  marriage canons, 54
  withdraws campaign against same-sex marriage bill, 2013, 191
Church of Scotland, 2, 20, 35, 51–2, 62–3, 66, 92, 108
  Disruption of (1843), 36
  patronage in, 36, 64–5
  schisms of, eighteenth century, 64–5
Church Patronage (Scotland) Act 1711, 10 Ann. c. 12, 64
civil marriage
  in Canada, 130,
  introduction during English Civil War, 55–7
  reintroduction in England in 1830s, 102–5
Clandestine Marriage Act *see* Marriage Act 1753
clandestine marriage, 70–1; *see also* Eyre, Jane
Clement VII, pope, 49
Cleves, Anne of: allegedly so ugly that she made Henry VIII impotent, 53–4
Colombia, 4
Commonwealth v. *Loving* see *Loving* v. *Virginia*
complementarity, 14–15, 25, 39–40, 158–61
conjugal view of marriage *see* complementarity
Connecticut, 174
consummation, 52–4, 154–5
  irrelevance to validity of marriage, 154–6
contraception, 32
Cott, Nancy, 136
Council of Trent, 17–18, 51, 53, 80, 118

coverture, xiii
Cranmer, Thomas, 49

Dalrymple v. *Dalrymple* (1811) 2 Hag Con 54, 161 ER 665, 60, 93, 178
Darnley, Henry Stuart, Lord, 49–51
De Valera, Eamon, 120
Dear, Geoffrey, Baron, 189–90
Deben, Lord *see* Gummer, John, Baron Deben
Defense of Marriage Act 1996 *see* US v. *Windsor*
Delaware River settlements, 68
Dennis v. *Dennis* [1955] P. 153, 2 WLR 817, 155
divorce, 18
  absence of, in Ireland, 120
  adultery, no longer necessary to cite in England & Wales, 155
  of Henry VIII, 48–9
  Hume on, 30
  in Islam, 26
  in Judaism, 23–4
  in Scotland, 65–8
  in South Africa, 125
  in England & Wales, 105–7
  variability of right to, across US states, 174–7
Docherty, Thomas, 191
Doctrine of the Trinity Act 1813, 53 Geo. 3 c. 160, 98
Doogan & Anor v. *NHS Greater Glasgow and Clyde Health Board* [2012] CS0H 32; *rev'd* [2013] CSIH 36, 172 n.

Edward VI, king of England, 56
Eisenstadt v. *Baird* (1972) 405 US 438, 154
Elizabeth I, queen of England, 50
English Civil War, 35, 54–7
Enlightenment view of marriage, 27–30
equal marriage *see* same-sex marriage
Equality Act 2010, c. 15, 172

Erskine of Carnock, John, 62–3
Erskine, Ebenezer, 92
European Convention on Human
    Rights, 153–4, 157
European Court of Human Rights
    (ECHR), 4, 169
European Union, 4
Eyre, Jane: her interrupted marriage,
    53

federalism, 7, 213–14
Federalist, The (Hamilton, Madison
    and Jay), 38–40
Feldblum, Chai, 167–8, 191
feminist view of marriage, 33–4
Fineman, Martha, 32, 34
Finnis, John, 157
First Amendment (of US
    Constitution), 36–7, 119, 137
Fischer, David Hackett, 68
Fleet marriages, 58, 70–1, 83
Fourteenth Amendment (of US
    Constitution), 141–2
Fox, George, 58
Fox, Henry, 86–7, 161
France, 4
Frankfurter, Felix, Assoc. Justice, US
    Supreme Court, 175, 195
full faith and credit, 173–8
Fuller, Lon L., 157

gender dysphoria *see* transgender
    issues
gender-neutral marriage *see* same-sex
    marriage
Gillis, John R., 95
Ginsburg, Ruth Bader, Assoc. Justice,
    US Supreme Court, 209–12
Gladstone, W. E., 106, 119
God's sillie vassal (description of
    James VI by Andrew Melvill),
    51
Gordon, Johanna, 93
Government of Ireland Bill 1886, 119
Green, Leslie, 154

Greenshields v. *Provost and
    Magistrates of Edinburgh* (1710)
    Colles 427, 1 ER 356, 64
Gresham, Joy Davidman, 41
Gretna Green, xi, 9, 82, 94–7, 107,
    108, 113, 214
Griswold v. *Connecticut* (1965) 381
    US 479, 153–4, 157
Gummer, John, Baron Deben, 194

Halpern v. *Canada (Attorney-
    General)* [2002 ON SCDC]
    CanLII 42749, 131–2
Hardwicke, Philip Yorke, 1st Earl of,
    x–xi, 82–3, 89, 90–2, 94, 161, 214
Harries, Richard, Baron Harries of
    Pentregarth, 193–4
Hart, H. L. A., 157
Hawaii, 4
Hegel, G. W. F., 80
Henry VIII, king of England, x, 48–9,
    52
Herbert, A. P., 106
Hinduism, 27
Hobbes, Thomas, 21–2, 48
Hodson, Francis Lord Charles, Baron
    Hodson, 155
Hollingsworth v. *Perry* (2013) 570 US
    ___, 133 S.Ct. 2652 (formerly
    Perry v. *Schwarzenegger* and
    Perry v. *Brown*), 179, 188,
    195–214
Holmes, Oliver Wendell, Jr, Assoc.
    Justice, US Supreme Court, 12
homosexuality
    alleged consequence of stricter
        regulation of marriage in 1753,
        88, 111
    religious attitudes to *see* names of
        religions and denominations
Hooker, Richard, 37
humanist weddings, 2, 188
Hume, David, 29–30, 34, 162
Hyde v. *Hyde* (1866) LR 1 P & D 130,
    133, 161–2, 182–3

Ireland, xi, 3, 35–6, 117–24
  Constitution 1937, 120, 122, 159
  constitutional convention 2012,
    124, 212
  see also Northern Ireland
Islam, 24–7
  homosexuality in, 26–7
  Muslim marriage practice in
    England, 60

James I of England (VI of Scotland),
  50, 51
Jefferson, Thomas, 137, 216
Judaism, x, xi, 12–13, 23–4, 58–9, 71,
  82, 91
  Liberal, 7, 164
  Reform, 7

Kant, Immanuel, 80
Kaplan, Roberta, 197
Katherine of Aragon, 49–50
Kelly, James, 118
Kennedy, Anthony M., Assoc. Justice,
  US Supreme Court, 199, 200–1,
  203–5, 208, 214
Klarman, Michael, 187

Ladele v. *London Borough of Islington*
  [2009] EWCA Civ 1357; *aff'd*
  as *Eweida & Ors v. UK* [2013]
  ECHR 37, 169, 185
land sales and same-sex marriage,
  166, 172
Latter-Day Saints, Church of Jesus
  Christ of *see* Utah
Lawrence v. *Texas* (2003) 539 US 558,
  153–4
Laycock, Douglas, 212–13; *see*
  also Wilson, Robin
  Fretwell
Leigh, Edward, 191, 192
Lemmings, David, 71
Lewis, C. S., 40–1, 194
Lord Hardwicke's Act *see* Marriage
  Act 1753

Lothian, William Kerr, 4th Marquess
  of, 92
Loving v. *Virginia* (1967) 388 US 1,
  15, 116, 139–42, 209–12
Loving, Mildred (née Jeter), 140–1,
  210
Luther, Martin, 19–20

Macedo, Stephen, 162–3
Madison, James, 38–40, 142, 176
Manners, Lady Laura, 93
Marriage (Same Sex Couples) Bill
  2012–13, xi, 189–94
  Enactment, 190
Marriage (Scotland) Act 1977, c. 15,
  97
Marriage (Scotland) Bill 1755
  (withdrawn after first reading),
  89–92
Marriage Act 1753, 26 Geo. 2 c. 33, x,
  52, 59, 61, 71, 80–9, 108–10, 164
Marriage Act 1836, 6 & 7 Will. 4 c. 85,
  81–2, 108, 161
Marriage Act 1949, 12 & 13 Geo. 6 c.
  76, xi, 104–5
Marriage and Civil Partnership Bill
  (Scotland) 2013, 3, 188, 212
marriage as patriarchy or oppression,
  32–4
marriage
  in colonial USA, 68–9
  with deceased wife's sister, 79,
    104–5, 109, 114–15, 194, 213
  by habit and repute (Scotland),
    62
  history of in UK: from Reformation
    to 1753, 48–78
  minimum ages for, 97
  prevalence of anti-miscegenation
    laws in USA before 1967, 139–41
  since 1753, 79–115
  slaves debarred from, 69, 139
  per verba de futuro, 53
  per verba de futuro com copula
    (Scotland), 62–3, 83, 97

marriage (*cont.*)
  per verba de praesenti, 53, 59–60,
    62–3, 83, 92, 97, 118
Marshall, John, Chief Justice, US
  Supreme Court, 195
Mary Queen of Scots, x, 49–51
Massachusetts, 4, 68, 166
masturbation: not defined as adultery,
  180
Matrimonial Causes Act 1857, 20 &
  21 Vict. c. 85, 105–7, 108
Matrimonial Causes Act 1973, c. 18,
  107, 155
McClain, Linda, 33–4
Melbourne, William Lamb, 2nd
  Viscount, 102
Melvill, Andrew, author of *Second
  Book of Discipline* and haranguer
  of James VI, 51–2
Mennonites, x, 12–13
Mexico, 4
Milton, John, 23
Minister of Home Affairs v. *Fourie*
  [2005] ZACC 19, 116,
  127–8
Mormons (Church of Jesus Christ of
  Latter-Day Saints) *see* Utah

Nevada, 174–5
new natural law theory, xii, 157–61,
  191, 192, 202, 213
New York State, 12–13, 172; *see also*
  US v. *Windsor*
New Zealand, 3
Nonconformist weddings, moves to
  permit in 1830s, 99–102
Noonan, John T. Jr, 19, 79–80
North Dakota, 174
North Leith, kirk session of, 65
Northern Ireland, 3, 177, 188
Nugent, Robert, 61, 85–8

O'Cathain, Detta, Baroness
  O'Cathain, 33
Olson, Theodore (Ted), 199

openness to procreation, said to be
  prerequisite for marriage, 14–15,
    18, 39–40, 160–1
  in Canada, 132
  in Texas, 176–7

Parker, Stephen, 71
Paul, Saint, 19
Peel, Sir Robert, 98–9, 109
Pelham, Henry, 91
Perez v. *Lippold* (1948) 32 Cal. 2d 711,
  198 P.2d 17, 140
Perry, Kristin *see Hollingsworth* v.
  Perry
Perry v. *Schwarzenegger* (ND Cal
  2010) 704 F.Supp.2d 921 *see
  Hollingsworth* v. *Perry*
Perry v. *Brown* (9th Cir 2012) 671
  F.3d 1052 *see Hollingsworth* v.
  Perry
Pew Research Center, 5–6
Phillpotts, Henry, bishop of Exeter,
  101–2
Plato, *Symposium*, 15–16, 159–60
polygamy, 44
  biblical justifications for, 161
  Hume on, 30
  in Islam, 25–6
  in South Africa, 126–7
  in Utah, xii, 173
portability and predictability of
  marriage, 172–8
Posner, Richard, 162
Powell, Thomas Reed, 175, 178
Pride and Prejudice (Austen): Mr
  Collins' dependence on Lady
  Catherine de Bourgh, 81
Probert, Rebecca, 59–61, 70, 83, 88–9
procreation *see* openness to
  procreation, said to be
  prerequisite for marriage
property rights and marriage, 59–62,
  71–2
Proposition 8 (California), 3, 58,
  197–214

Proposition 22 (California), 197
Protestantism *see* Reformation and
    names of individual Protestant
    churches
public reason, x, xii, 37–40, 135,
    159–61, 163, 172–9, 192, 213–14

Quakers, xi, xiv–xv, 7, 40, 58–9, 65,
    68, 71–2, 82, 98–9, 113, 164

R. v. *Lolley* (1835) 1 Russ & Ry 237,
    168 ER 779, 66–7, 107, 172, 175
R. v. *Millis* (1843–4) 10 Cl & Fin 534,
    8 ER 844, 118, 177–8
rationalist view of marriage, 30–2
Rawls, John, x, xii, 37–40, 165
reasonable comprehensive doctrines,
    37–42, 159–61, 168, 171, 177–9,
    213–14
Reference re Same-Sex Marriage [2004
    CanLII] SCC 79; 3 SCR 698,
    133
Reformation, Protestant, x, 19–23,
    48–51
    differences between Scotland and
    England, 71–2
Regnerus, Mark, 208
Representation of the People Act
    [Reform Act] 1832, 2 & 3 Will. 4
    c. 45, 81
religious freedom, and same-sex
    marriage, 164–72
reset, 215
Reynolds v. *United States* (1878) 98
    US (8 Otto.) 145, 137, 140
Rhode Island, 174
Roberts, John, Chief Justice, US
    Supreme Court, 201, 204
Roe v. *Wade* (1973) 410 US 113,
    209–12
Roman Catholicism, 17–19, 34–5,
    79–80, 164–5, 171, 191
    penalties against: in Scottish
    marriage law, 63, 65; in Ireland,
    117–24, 142

Root and Branch Petition, 1640,
    54–5
royal marriages, 48–51
Russell, Bertrand, 30–2, 35
Russell, Lord John, 1st Earl
    (grandfather of Bertrand), 81–2,
    100–2
Ryder, Sir Dudley, 84–5

Sachs, Albie, 116, 127–8, 143, 160
same-sex marriage
    arguments for and against
    legalisation, 153–61, 163–79
    in Canada, 130–5
    in England & Wales, 189–94
    in Ireland, 122–4
    in Scotland, 188, 191
    in South Africa, 127–30
    in the USA, 195–214
Scalia, Antonin, Assoc. Justice, US
    Supreme Court, 201–14
Scotland, xiv, 2, 80, 82
    marriage law in, 89–97
    same-sex marriage in *see* Marriage
    and Civil Partnership Bill
    (Scotland) 2013
    see also Acts and Treaty of Union
    1706–7; Gretna Green
Scottish Enlightenment, 27–30
Scottish Episcopalians Act 1711, 10
    Ann. c. 7, 64
Second Book of Discipline, 63
Shannon, Jim, 192
sharia, 26
Silver, Nate, 6–7
Smith, Adam, 27–9, 88
Solomon, biblical king, 7
South Africa, xi, 3, 124–9, 171–2
South Dakota, 174
Spain, 4
Speyer, Thea *see US* v. *Windsor*
Stair, James Dalrymple, 1st Viscount,
    62
standing doctrine (US Supreme
    Court), 194–5, 203

State v. *Bell* (1872) 66 Tenn.
(7 Baxter) 9, 173
Stone, Laurence, 60, 70, 82–3
Strauss v. *Horton* (CA 2009) 46 Cal.
4th 364, 207 P.3d 48, 198
Submission of the Clergy Act 1533, 25
Hen. 8 c. 19, 193
Sweetapple, Rev. Amos, 70

Tatchell, Peter, 32–3
Terce Act 1503, ASP ii, 252, c. 22,
62, 76
Texas, 176
Timms, Stephen, 191
Tinwald, Charles Erskine, Lord
Justice Clerk, 90–1
transgender issues, xiii–xiv
Traynor, Roger, Assoc. and Chief
Justice, CA Supreme Court,
140

Unitarians, 7, 97–9, 109, 164
Uruguay, 4
US v. *Windsor* (2013) 570 US ___,
133 S.Ct. 2675; (2012) 833
F.Supp.2d 394, xii, 4, 174, 187,
188, 195–214
USA
polygamy in, xi–xii
same-sex marriage in, 3, 135–42
separation of church and state,
36–7
Supreme Court of, 4, 15,
195–214
see also names of states and names
of cases
Utah, xi–xii, 135, 136–7, 142, 161–2,
174

Veritatis Splendor encyclical, 19
Vermont, 4, 174, 178
Virginia, 68, 140–2

Wade v. *Scruton* (1837) 4 Cl & Fin
378, 7 ER 145, 95
Wakefield, Edward Gibbon, 95,
108
Waldron, Jeremy, 210–11
Wales, 36
Walker, Vaughn, US District Judge,
205–9
Warnken, Todd, 178
Warren, Earl, Chief Justice, US
Supreme Court, 143
Warrender v. *Warrender* (1835) 2 Cl
& Fin 488, 6 ER 1239, 67
Welby, Justin, Archibishop of
Canterbury, 193
wedding photography and same-sex
marriage, 165, 170
Westminster Confession of Faith
(1647), 65–6
Williams v. *North Carolina* (1942)
317 US 287; (1945) 325 US 226,
174–5
Wilson, Robin Fretwell, 169–70
Windsor, Edith *see US* v. *Windsor*
Wynne, Sir William, 92

Yelverton v. *Yelverton* (1859) 1 Sw &
Tr 574, 164 ER 866, 119
Young, Brigham, 137

*Zappone and Gilligan v. Revenue
Commissioners* [2006] IEHC
404, 122
Zwingli, Huldrych, 22